THE CLAPBACK

Elijah Lawal is a PR manager at Google and is passionate about helping underrepresented people grow their careers in creative industries. He was a finalist of the Penguin WriteNow scheme.

This is his first book.

THE CLAPBACK

YOUR GUIDE TO
CALLING OUT RACIST STEREOTYPES

ELIJAH LAWAL

HODDER

First published in Great Britain in 2019 by Hodder & Stoughton
An Hachette UK company

This paperback edition published in 2020

1

A CIP catalogue record for this title is
available from the British Library

Paperback ISBN 9781529380811

Typeset in Fournier MT by Palimpsest Book Production Limited,
Falkirk, Stirlingshire
Printed and bound in Great Britain by Clays Ltd, Elcograf S.p.A.

Hodder & Stoughton policy is to use papers that are natural, renewable
and recyclable products and made from wood grown in sustainable
forests. The logging and manufacturing processes are expected to
conform to the environmental regulations of the country of origin.

Hodder & Stoughton Ltd
Carmelite House
50 Victoria Embankment
London EC4Y 0DZ

www.hodder.co.uk

To three very special women:

My mum, who made sacrifices so I wouldn't have to.

My best friend, Aysha, who's always
been there for me — even when I was super weird.

Alison, the first person to call me a writer and mean it.

CONTENTS

INTRODUCTION

Clapback: [*noun/verb*] Responding to a (often ignorant) notion with a withering comeback; with the aim of **shutting it down.**

Hello. My name is Elijah and thanks for buying my book. If you are simply reading this in the bookshop and considering buying it, you should totally do it – all the cool kids are reading it and you don't wanna be left out.

I have a confession: I've always wanted to be a writer, but I never expected my first book to be about race. In truth, when I first started fantasising about getting published, I was writing a story about a boy who ran away from home to be the President of Panama – I was ten.

Even though I'm black, writing about race simply wasn't a priority for me, because, well . . . I'm privileged as fuck. Sure, I'm black – but I'm a man, which makes life significantly easier for me. I am well educated and middle class, and I work for one of the largest, most profitable companies in the world, for God's sake. So even though I have suffered discrimination in my life, my personal experiences really weren't going to inspire a cultural and racial revelation.

In addition to that, pretty much any study you read today will tell you that this is the best time to be alive. There are fewer wars, significantly higher life expectancy rates, and we have the eighth wonder of the modern world that is Netflix. This also rings true statistically for civil rights; in the past few years alone, black people have seen strong movements such as Black Lives Matter, increased representation in movies such as *Black Panther* and *Girls Trip*, and a black president of the most powerful country in the world.

However, for black people and minorities in general, progress always seems to be a case of 'one step forward, two steps back'. Because for every Black Lives Matter movement, there's an All Lives Matter or Blue Lives Matter movement. For every movie with a predominant minority cast, a white person gets cast in a high-profile role meant for a person of colour (Scarlett Johansson's role in *Ghost in a Shell*, for example), and immediately after America elected its first black president, they elected a president who referred to white nationalists as 'very fine people' and told four congresswomen of colour to 'go back to where they came from'.

This lack of consistent progress in racial awareness has caused an inevitable social and cultural divide between the majority (by and large white, wealthy and men) and the unrepresented minority (often people of colour, less well-off, and women) – and momentum is most definitely on the side of the majority; particularly those who are prejudiced against the minority. It's bad enough that institutionally, people of colour have always been at a disadvantage, but we are starting to see the majority become more vocal in their rhetoric, and often this is used to justify their prejudice or racism.

This negative rhetoric about people of colour is especially painful for me as a black man, because black people have always had to fight back against harmful stereotypes such as: our community is fraught and synonymous with poverty and crime (see 'black on black crime'), that we are less British than our white neighbours (see the Windrush scandal), or that we are less qualified for the same opportunities that are afforded to white people in our education or professional lives (see . . . well, any professional or educational institution).

Make no mistake, these prejudicial statements or stereotypes are not simply casual knee-slapping jokes, they help perpetuate a system used to discriminate, prevent progress, and inflict hurt. By and large, stereotypes are not created by the communities they are about, rather they are an outsider's view of how that community is perceived, in the mistaken belief that we can know things about people based on what we know about their group.

For example, there is the stereotype that black people are naturally gifted runners, but black people don't automatically expect themselves to excel at sprinting. In the same way that there is a stereotype that Germans are efficient; but no German manager would ever give negative feedback to an employee, by saying: 'Now come on, Helmut, you have to do better. We are German; we're supposed to be efficient.'

My personal motivation for starting to document my research into stereotypes started when a mate of mine asked me about the Black Lives Matter movement on a night out. 'I get that black lives do matter, but shouldn't it be "All Lives Matter"? Doesn't #BLM elevate black lives above all others?' Now, this person was a mate and one I considered as 'woke', so it occurred to me that he had never experienced a negative interaction with the police, like I and most black people have.

I was way too drunk at this point, so I put it as simply as I could: 'Well, mate, imagine if someone you loved had terminal cancer and you threw a rally trying to raise money for them. And I interrupted that rally because I had irritable bowel syndrome and started yelling, "All Diseases Matter!" How would you feel about that?'

A similar retort to this question was given by the US comedian Michael Che in his comedy special, *Michael Che Matters*, where he said,

'Imagine if I turned up at a 9/11 remembrance ceremony with a T-shirt that said, "All Buildings Matter".' I know these seem like ludicrous examples; of course, no one is going to turn up at a cancer rally with a T-shirt saying 'All Diseases Matter'; but therein lies the turning point of the argument. If you appreciate how ludicrous and hurtful it is that one would do that, then it brings you closer to understanding how black people feel at the 'All Lives Matter' movement.

Being able to articulate an argument about race and stereotypes in the right context – either with the right metaphors or with an appropriate historical context – is key if we are aiming to change hearts and minds and create advocates for racial awareness. For instance, we'll have a far easier time getting someone to stop making offensive jokes about black people's perceived love for chicken, when we can explain that the origin of that stereotype was a movie that glorifies the . . . . . . sorry, no spoilers, you've got to read the whole book!

And so, the need for this book. I want us to be empowered to respond to negative stereotypes about the black community with authority, with facts, and with established research – and most importantly, shut them down once and for all. In short, I want to give you . . . a clapback. I want to arm you with knowledge – credible knowledge – to discuss, argue, and advocate for the black community. Now this'll be no mean feat: it's not easy to change the mind of someone who believes in negative stereotypes, or believes them to be only jokes, particularly one who has had a privileged life and sees the progressive movement towards equality as nothing more than political correctness.

This is because these people have been ingrained in this stereotype since birth and have learnt to accept what they have seen, heard, been taught, or wrongly understood to be true. This is so very important to understand, because we are never going to change hearts and minds by simply saying something is racist; we must explain why it's racist and the circumstances by which it became so.

For instance, it's easy to explain police brutality and support the Black Lives Matter movement. But very rarely are we equipped to explain the history of police brutality against black people, the problem of systematic racism in law enforcement, and the injustices against the black community at large. But (particularly in this nationalistic climate) we no longer have the luxury of not getting this right.

We can't afford to counter racist and stereotypical prejudices with flimsy arguments. No longer can we simply be satisfied with the retort of, 'You can't say that, because it's racist.' And no longer can we sit idly by when the narrative of 'we're all too PC today' becomes prevalent. So, it's becoming increasingly important to present the other side of the narrative, and have this discussion based on facts.

Another reason why I never envisioned writing about race is because it's exhausting. It's tiring to always have to push back against the notion that we are lesser; to constantly have to justify our existence, our entitlement to basic civil rights, and the need for equality.

As the American novelist, Toni Morrison, said: 'The function, the very serious function of racism is distraction. It keeps you explaining, over and over again, your reason for being. Somebody says you have no language and you spend twenty years proving that you do. Somebody says your head isn't shaped properly, so you have scientists working on the fact that it is . . . There will always be one more thing.'

And yet, we must. We, the disenfranchised, must bear the burden of teacher, not only because it is our truth to tell, but because mainstream sources such as the media, publishing, and the current education system . . . don't. I spent several history classes learning about the Second World War and the atrocities the Nazis committed, but not a word about the crimes of the British Empire. I was taught that the concentration camps in Auschwitz were an example of one of the most heinous things human beings have done to another, but nothing of the Mau Mau concentration camps run by the British Empire in Kenya – a good five years *after* the liberation of the Auschwitz camps.

So, it's not surprising that fifty-nine per cent of British respondents to a YouGov Survey believe that the British Empire is more something to be proud of rather than ashamed of, and that thirty-four per cent of British people say they would like it if Britain still had an empire. Because to them, the Empire was a force for good; spreading Western values and Christianity to the savage natives. Whereas we know the truth; it was brutal imperialism to establish power for the British and was based on nothing other than racial superiority.

It will come as no surprise that a lot of these stereotypes have their origins in slavery. In reviewing this book, a lot of people have said, 'Are you not angry? You need to be angrier,' but this book is not about blame, or 'oh, aren't white people terrible for all the stereotypes and slavery' – as a matter of fact, I also address stereotypes that black people have about each other (see displeasure at interracial dating).

To quote the late James Baldwin, 'I'm not interested in anybody's guilt. Guilt is a luxury that we can no longer afford. I know you didn't do it, and I didn't do it either, but I am responsible for it because I am a man and a citizen of this country and you are responsible for it, for the very same reason. *Anyone who is trying to be conscious must begin to dismiss the vocabulary which we've used so long to cover it up, to lie about the way things are.'*

So this book is firstly about laying bare the origins of stereotypes, because once a stereotype becomes mainstream, we forget how and why it was formed in the first place; and secondly, about removing the covers from the narratives that have been used to discriminate against black people for so long. But it is also about empowerment; for the black community, it is about knowing our truth and being able to defend that truth intelligently. For allies in other communities, it is about helping you be a better mouthpiece for us, and specifically for those allies who are white, it is about helping us reach across the lines to people we can't.

Clapping back on negative narratives cannot be the sole responsibility of minorities, or people of colour; it lies on the shoulders of all allies and those who want to stand up for the rights of the underrepresented, but don't feel knowledgeable enough to challenge and dispel the stereotypes perpetuated by people who look and sound like them. This is a huge challenge for allies – to be in solidarity with people of colour, but to physically and historically represent those that are so often against us.

I feel this same challenge as a man who is a feminist. I remain staunch in my fight for gender equality, but I know that every day, I benefit from being a man and from institutions that still favour men. I will never know what it's like to be a woman, and so I try to educate myself in the challenges that women face, and how I can adequately push back on negative stereotypes and rhetoric in order to further the cause. The same must also be done by our allies in the white majority and we should help them to get there. This is why I have included personal stories in this book (much to my family's dismay) – to help allies outside of the black community understand how stereotypes can be harmful.

For black people, systematic racism and prejudice have been our reality since the day we were born, so it's familiar territory, but we can't forget our allies who have not had the same experiences as we have. We must help them speak truth to power and defend us – despite not having the first-hand knowledge that we have. It's just as important for our allies to speak with authority and credibility as it is for us – if nothing other than to empower them to talk about black prejudice without resorting to the dreaded statement, 'I'm not racist, most of my friends are black.'

I really hope you love this book and get as much from it as I did in writing it. We are at a tipping point in our society; there's a fulcrum that is constantly moving – on one side, the rise of nationalism and at the other, increasingly progressive movements towards civil rights and equality. We simply can't afford to let nationalism win. There is too much at stake and we have fought too damn hard to slide back now.

So let *The Clapback* be your guide, your ammunition, your drive to have more intelligent and informed conversations about race and culture. Let's show the flaws in stereotypical beliefs. Let's demonstrate why our culture is not what they believe it to be. Let's show them a vibrant, progressive culture that has thrived and continues to do so, even under the most oppressive of circumstances.

IDENTITY
EXCUSE ME, WHERE ARE YOU FROM . . . ORIGINALLY?

Stereotype/negative narrative: The notion that we can't be British, that we have to reveal our ethnicity to strangers, and the accompanying assumptions when we reveal that ethnicity.

Pop quiz:
How long have there been black people in Britain?
Since the beginning of time
Third century AD
Since the 1600s

For anyone who isn't white, there's a question that leaves us perplexed as to how to answer. It's 3 a.m., you've been dancing (well, flailing wildly) at the club, had a few tequila shots and your post-clubbing kebab, got into an argument with a stranger over whether football will ever come home within our lifetime, thrown up your post-clubbing kebab, and now you're catching an overly priced taxi to your overly priced flat. Suddenly, after asking how your night went, the taxi driver drops the most innocuous and yet tricky question of all time. The 'where are you from?' question.

You might as well have asked me how to defuse a thermonuclear device. What does that question even mean: Where was I born? Where did I grow up? Where do I live now? Where are my parents from? What ethnicity do I identify with? Where did I spend the most years of my life?

In the end, it's not as simple as choosing House Stark in a *Game of Thrones* Buzzfeed quiz. Especially when your answer is 'London' and the taxi driver decides to further complicate the question:

> ***Overly nosy and enthusiastic taxi driver***: 'No, where are you from *originally?*'
> ***Drunk and extremely tired me***: 'What do you mean originally? Mate, I grew up in South London. Oh, you mean, where were my parents from before they came here? Oh right. Nigeria.'
> ***Taxi driver who, worryingly, has now turned around to look at me instead of concentrating on the road***: 'Nigeria, eh? That's the country with all the oil, right? Yeah, my brother's uncle's mother's cousin's nephew went there once, and he said that it's a great place. It's pretty corrupt though, right? And full of Boko Haram, yeah?'
> ***Me***: '. . . . . .' *Eyes rolled firmly back in my head (although to be fair, that's probably because of the tequila shots).*

Of course, the 'where are you from . . . originally' question is an innocent one; in fact, it's what makes being in a taxi more interesting. You're stuck with a stranger in the early hours of the morning, and so it's the taxi driver's attempt to kill the silence, get to know his passenger, and possibly get a tip instead of spending the rest of the journey pretending the other person doesn't exist. And you may be thinking: well, he means no offence and you know what he's getting at, so why don't you just give him the answer he's looking for, so you can get back to concentrating on not throwing up in the back of the taxi?

But, it's not as simple as that.

I'm black. One hundred per cent. By that, I mean I have a black mother and a black father – both are Nigerian. Pretty clear cut, right? But I was born in England and I have a British passport not a Nigerian one, which makes me British. So, am I Nigerian or am I British or am I both? I've lived most of my life in England, so does that make me English? I lived in Ireland for a couple of years, so what impact does that have given Brexit? Does that make me (*gasp*) European?

In truth, the answer to this question is never definitive because given job opportunities abroad, freedom of travel, and interracial marriages, we are very rarely just one thing. We're all a lovely pick 'n' mix of different cultures, nationalities and colours. I remember the first time I found out that the birth name of the actor, Charlie Sheen, is Carlos Irwin Estévez, which explains why his brother is called Emilio Estevez. His grandparents were Irish and Spanish. But he is an American citizen and doesn't look as if he has a drop of Hispanic in him. So, which of these nationalities should he identify with? Some? All? Or can he simply choose one and stick with it?

For people of colour, the defensiveness to the question of 'where are you from' comes from the underlying assumptions or stereotypes after we reveal our ethnicity. We are unique individuals, but when asked this, it's as if someone is trying to fit us into a delineated box of clichés and assumptions they have about people from that area or country. Everyone wants to ask me about oil or Boko Haram, or 419 advance-fee email scams, as soon as I reveal my ethnicity, which is incredibly condescending.

Nigeria is one of the most culturally diverse countries in Africa, with over five hundred ethnic groups; it has a healthy GDP of $405.1 billion, and is believed to be one of few economies set to become among the biggest in the world – and yet, all I get asked about is an antiquated method used to defraud luddites online. What's worse is that it often evolves from condescending to downright insulting.

For example, I once had a census analyst in Ireland compliment me on how good my English is, despite explaining to him that English is my first language. Another example: at a 2018 event in France called *La Nuit des Idées* (The Night of Ideas), the Nigerian award-winning author, Chimamanda Ngozi Adichie, was asked during an interview if there were any bookshops in Nigeria.

When Adichie responded that it reflected poorly on France that the journalist would ask her that, her response was: 'We speak very little about Nigeria in France, certainly not enough, and when we do it's about Boko Haram and the problems of violence and security.' Understandably, that was incredibly insulting and frustrating. It is not up to people of Nigerian heritage to educate others about Nigeria: pick up a book, for Christ's sake.*

While the question of where I'm from is frustrating, my main resistance to being asked this question comes from the fact that it is such a personal one – and from a stranger no less! What's next: is he going to ask me if I'm circumcised? Or if my parents are divorced? Often, people are so eager to confirm their assumptions about where I'm from that this question comes even before asking what my name is.

BLACK PEOPLE ARE CONSTANTLY HAVING TO PROVE THEY ARE BRITISH

Have you ever filled in a census form? Infuriating, isn't it? The premise of the question 'where are you from' is fundamentally flawed in a census, because it is not so cut and dried to identify with the ethnic group options offered in the said form – unless you identify as White British, then you have it easy. You see, the whole point of providing ethnic information to the government is to provide data; and data is

* Preferably from one of the many bookshops in Nigeria.

useless unless it's accurate. But in the current classification of ethnicity in the UK census forms, there is such a broad range of sub-categories for ethnicities that it skews the accuracy.

For instance, you can be White British, White Irish or 'other'. You can be Black African, Black Caribbean or 'other'. In the 'other' ethnic group category, you can be either Arab or well . . . basically another 'other'. What if you're of Guyanan or Sri Lankan heritage and don't feel like being classified as an 'other'? I decided to go straight to the source with my existential crisis and rang up the Office of National Statistics.

Me: 'Hi there, I have a question about the census form.'
Nice white lady from the ONS:* 'Of course, dear, how can I help?'†
Me: 'Well, it just doesn't seem like there are a lot of options in the form. It can be kind of confusing and a little bit insulting. Like what if I'm Sri Lankan, do I just tick "Other Asian" and be lumped in with the rest of the brown people in Asia?'
Nice white lady from the ONS: 'Well, you could be Japanese. Japan is in Asia and I don't think the Japanese are brown, dear.'
Me: 'Erm . . . sure, OK. But what if I'm Sri Lankan?'
Nice white lady from the ONS: 'Are you Sri Lankan?'
Me: 'No! That's not the point.'
Nice white lady from the ONS: 'So . . . you're not Japanese or Sri Lankan?'
Me: 'No, I'm English. Actually, British. Well, also Nigerian. I guess I'm both. I'm black. It's all rather complicated.'
Nice white lady from the ONS: 'Ah, I see. Well, where are you from . . . originally?'
Me: 'Arghhhhh!!'

While this might seem like a perfectly innocuous interaction with the lovely ONS lady, it's actually very important to know what your ethnic and

---

* See, it's that type of stereotyping that we need to stamp out. There was no way for me to know that she was white.
† Way too helpful. Yep, definitely white.

citizen status is. For example, in 2017, the Home Office tried to deport Cynsha Best, a thirty-one-year-old woman born in Hammersmith, who had lived in London all her life. Her grandparents are British, her dad is British, all four of her siblings are British and her two sons are British.

However, she was summoned to the Home Office, detained for seven hours, and told that not only was she not a British citizen, but she had no right to stay in the country and would have to leave. This was because of a ridiculous immigration exemption from 1983, which states that even if you are born in the UK, you are not automatically British if your parents are not British at the time of your birth. So Cynsha faced deportation from her home in England to Barbados, a country she knows nothing about.

What makes this story even more ironic is that this was a situation born of colonialism – Cynsha's grandparents moved to the UK from Barbados in 1956. And because at that time Barbados was still a colony of the UK, it meant that they were considered as British citizens. And this is a similar story to thousands of British families in the UK today, emigrating from Africa and the Caribbean to the UK under a resettlement scheme, ensuring that their descendants are British citizens.

Most of these people are known as the 'Windrush generation' after the ship, the *Empire Windrush*, which brought many Caribbean people to Britain in 1948 – more on them in Chapter Eleven. But the very idea that the Home Office thought it appropriate to deport a resident, born in the UK, is indicative of the false idea that a British citizen has to fit a specific race, language, culture or heritage – and why this stereotype is harmful.

It killed me to read about this, because the black immigrants who allowed us to become citizens by birth gave everything to this country. They fought and died in our wars, helped rebuild the country afterwards, and endured unbelievable discrimination – and for their children and descendants to not even be allowed to enjoy the benefits from the fruits of their labour is wrong by all accounts. Anyone who can't see that is simply blind to our nation's history and the contribution of black immigrants.

THE PROBLEM OF BEING IDENTIFIED BY RACE

Race is often one of the main qualifiers used to identify where you are from, in other words, there will be an underlying assumption that you are British if you are white and have a British accent, but you will still get asked where you are from if you are black and have a British accent.

But what is this thing called race anyway? Most academics don't believe race to be anything other than a social and political construct. The historian, Barbara J. Fields, explained in her presentation on PBS, *Race: The Power of an Illusion*, that race was simply a way of distinguishing people, in order to justify treating some people better than others. For example, during the transatlantic slave trade, if 'white people' were a separate category of human, i.e. better, then it became a lot easier to defend enslaving people who were not white.

We saw something similar during the Nazi regime; for Hitler to justify ostracising and enslaving Jews, he had to argue that the Aryan race was superior. We can see evidence of this in the propaganda of the time, with the Nazis distributing posters showing Aryans as effectively 'supermen', and Jews and Gypsies as frail and weak. The hilarious irony is that there were relatively so few physiological differences between Germans and white Jews that one of the children used in Nazi propaganda posts as the 'perfect Aryan' child — Hessy Taft — was later discovered to be Jewish!

Another problem with identifying individuals by one race or ethnicity is that race is not a permanent concept — it's ever-changing. For example, Mexicans were considered 'white' until a census in 1930 deemed them to be Hispanic. And while we are at it, the term 'Latino' would be more accurate in describing Mexicans, given that it is used to refer to anyone of Latin-American origin or ancestry – Mexico being already populated by indigenous people before the arrival of and colonisation by the Spanish – while 'Hispanic' is a narrower term that refers only to people whose ancestors came from Spain.

In fact, it was only in the year 2000 when the American government decided that Americans could be more than one race and added other options to their census forms. In truth, most of the Europeans that immigrated to America in the early 1900s, such as the Greeks and the Irish, weren't considered as white at that time due to their low-income status and poor education. The American author, James Silk Buckingham, referred to the Irish as: 'drunken, dirty, indolent, and riotous, so as to be the objects of dislike and fear to all in whose neighbourhood they congregate in large numbers.' And it wasn't until the Irish assimilated into the American mainstream, with jobs in the police force and fire department,* that they were considered white.

Also, during apartheid in South Africa, Chinese people living there were considered black, because of their low income and social status – even though they clearly were not black. So, a huge problem that the government of any country faces is that it is hard for citizens to consistently identify as of one race or ethnicity. The ongoing political and cultural disputes in Russia and Ukraine, or Taiwan and China – countries which grew out of each other – is testament to how geography, heritage, and looks are no indication as to which ethnicity someone can identify with.

Even as far back as the 1800s, the issue of race or 'where you are from' was not easily defined. In the American legal case of Plessy v. Ferguson in 1896, one of the major rulings that established the Jim Crow laws enforcing racial segregation in the Southern USA, even the Supreme Court didn't want to wade into the difficult waters of who could identify as black.

Homer Plessy, a thirty-year-old shoemaker in New Orleans, had bought a first-class ticket on the East Louisiana local train in the 'whites

---

* Not to mention the influence of the long-reaching arm of the Irish Catholic Church.

only' car. When questioned if he was 'coloured', he replied in the affirmative and was asked to leave for the 'coloured car'. What was particularly interesting in this case was the fact that he didn't even look like he was black – in fact, he was only one-eighth black.* In the resulting Supreme Court ruling, the Associate Justice, Henry Billings Brown, explained that it was just too damned hard to come up with a universally acceptable definition of who was black, noting: 'There is a difference of opinion in the different States, some holding that any visible admixture of black blood stamps the person as belonging to the coloured race . . . others that it depends upon the preponderance of blood; and still others that the predominance of white blood must only be in the proportion of three-fourths.'†

Disregarding the circumstances of the case, there is certainly logic to that train of thought – most people classify themselves as other than their physical attributes would suggest. We see how this would have become a problem for law enforcement during the Jim Crow era, as looking black was essentially the only criteria for being segregated.

Let's use former President Barack Obama as an example. He is of mixed race; his mother is a white American and his father, black from Kenya. So even though he is half white and half black, he is considered black. This could certainly be because of his complexion, as research from the Pew Center on social and demographic trends, *Multiracial in America*, shows that overall, biracial adults who are of white-and-black mixed race, have more in common and feel more accepted by black people than they do white. By contrast, biracial adults who are white and Asian tend to have stronger ties to whites than they do to Asians. But by virtue of his heritage, Obama has as much right to be considered white as he does black.

So, is complexion the true determining factor of where one is from; or is it heritage? Many Brazilians applying to go to university would argue in favour of heritage. In 2016, the Brazilian federal government implemented a scheme ensuring that federal institutions have a quota of places for black, mixed-race and Amerindian students. As such, they have seen

---

* Lord knows how the hell you work that out.
† Seriously, how are you working this out?

an uptake in applications from students who have white complexions, but black heritage, in order to secure their place at the universities.

However, this remains subjective, as the administrative lawyer, Luiz Paulo Viveiros de Castro notes in a 2016 article in *O DIA* magazine: 'A person can self-declare whatever they want . . . but it has to be a matter of common sense, because all Brazilians could be considered black' – due to their African and Amerindian heritage. We have even seen instances of white people trying to take advantage of opportunities created for the advancement of black people and other minorities.

In 2018, Ralph Taylor, who presents as white and had always believed himself to be white, applied to be recognised as a minority business owner after taking a home DNA ancestry test and found out he was ninety-per-cent Caucasian, six-per-cent indigenous American and four-per-cent sub-Saharan African. Because Washington State had an initiative to help minority business owners to secure lucrative business contracts, he felt his four per cent entitled him to benefit. After his application was (rightfully) denied, he decided to sue the state of Washington.*

What people like Taylor don't seem to understand is that black and minority businesses need a helping hand because of the systemic discrimination they've faced based on what they look and sound like, as well as 'where they are from, originally' and not because of their non-visible DNA. The sheer nerve of Taylor looking to benefit from something set aside for minorities tells you a lot about the idea of white privilege.†

For members of the black community, this whole concept of distinguishing and accepting people based on where they are from 'originally' (i.e. born or their ethnicity) as opposed to where they identify, can have a severe negative social impact. Again, let's use President Obama as an example – one of the most high-profile African-Americans in recent times.

Even though he has released his birth certificate to the press, proving that he was born in Hawaii, not to mention the fact that the US Constitution calls for a president to be a natural born citizen; in

---

* The Caucasitu!

† Meanwhile, I can't even walk past the Home Office without people in there looking at me funny.

2015, when he was still in office, eighty per cent of Americans still believed Obama was born outside of the United States. A further twenty-nine per cent of Americans thought he was Muslim, including forty-three per cent of Republicans.

If this is the scrutiny that the president of the most powerful nation in the world (with his army of PR teams, advisors and political strategists) faces, imagine how terrible this must be for a blue-collar, African-American worker from Brooklyn.

This fundamental assumption of genuine citizens being perceived to be from another country was one of the bases of support during Donald Trump's presidential campaign. Analysis of data from the 2016 American National Election Study showed that, 'Those who express more resentment toward African Americans, those who think the word "violent" describes Muslims well, and those who believe President Obama is a Muslim, have much more positive attitudes of Trump.'

This misconception around accuracy of religion or ethnicity (particularly when it comes to politics) is not always due to malicious intent; it's simply a case of inherent bias – what people want to be true often influences what they believe to be true.

Another problem with categorising people into those 'not from here' is that it is often inflated – we hugely overestimate the number of minorities; one report showed that Americans thought thirty-three per cent of their population is black, when it is just over twelve per cent.

Unfortunately, this misrepresentation of who constitutes a minority or nowadays, a Muslim, is not only an American misunderstanding; a survey from Buzzfeed News online and Ipsos Mori revealed that British respondents thought the Muslim population of the UK was more than three times bigger than it really is, estimating it at fifteen per cent, when it's actually under five per cent. So, they thought that one in seven Brits identify as Muslim, whereas in reality, it's one in twenty. In fact, the average estimate for the Muslim population was almost twice the UK's entire ethnic minority population of eight per cent (according to the 2011 UK census).

As the survey revealed, this is not only a UK or American problem either. The research was replicated in other countries in Europe and the trend was consistent; most European respondents routinely thought the Muslim population was at least ten percentage points higher than it really was, even in countries where Muslims make up less than one per cent of the population.

BLACK VS. AFRICAN AMERICAN

Surely, colour or long-forgotten ancestry cannot be the only denominators of what makes you black? But let us consider the adjective – black. How descriptive is it? What about the term 'African American' (made popular in the 1980s to give Americans of African descent an equivalent of German American, Italian American, and so on), which is used synonymously with the term 'black', referring to a generalisation of black people in America?

But what if you are American, but of Caribbean heritage? Then surely being referred to as African American could be considered as offensive as calling a Scottish person Welsh. Perhaps that's why in the UK census form, you are offered the choice of being 'Black African' or 'Black Caribbean'; but what if you want to identify as 'Black British', as so many first-generation (first person of a minority group born outside of their country of heritage or ethnicity) black people in England do?

The Bloomberg style guide (as its name implies) offers some guidance here, noting: 'We say that someone is black rather than African American. Ethnic descriptions used in hyphenation with "American" are best reserved for immigrants or first-generation Americans.' But it's not always as simple as using whichever term you prefer; there are connotations to each term. For instance, a study in the *Journal of Experimental Social Psychology* found that 'black' people are viewed more negatively than 'African Americans', because of a perceived difference in socioeconomic status and competence.

The reality is that most people aren't even clear as to when to refer to people as 'black' or not. For instance, I was at my New Zealand friend's engagement party and his father had said to him, 'I really like your African-American friend,' even though he knew for a fact that I was British. He just didn't know how to describe me, because while it's perfectly okay to describe someone as 'black' in the UK, it seemed to be culturally unacceptable in New Zealand. For clarity, I once asked my mother if I was black, or Black-British. She just kissed her teeth and said: 'You are *Nigerian*!'*

There is understandably some reticence from white people in referring to black people as black. After all, the denotation of colour was invented by white people to distinguish between the two races. But rest assured, I don't know of any black person in the UK that is offended by being referred to as black; while it might not have been a distinction that we gave ourselves, we take pride in the fact that we are black – always. Although it is hilarious to watch people trip over themselves trying to describe you to someone else without saying the word black:

A: 'You should meet my friend, Elijah.'

B: 'Of course. Which one's Elijah?'

A: (*points to our group of friends*): 'The tall guy.'

B: 'They're all tall.'

A: 'He's wearing glasses.'

B: 'At least three of them are wearing glasses.'

A: 'Oh, come on, don't make me say it. The . . . not-white one.'

Me: 'Hey guys, it's a Vampire Weekend concert, I'm the only black person here. You can just say the black guy.'

For the record, it is perfectly ok to call someone who is comfortable with being called black, black. We don't find it offensive, if anything, it is a label of pride. But, if colour is not a determinant of whether you are black or not, then what? The acclaimed actor, Denzel Washington, would suggest it is culture. Denzel directed the 2016 movie, *Fences*, about a black family trying to get by in 1950s Pittsburgh – which was an adaptation of the Pulitzer Prize-winning play of the

* Nigerian mothers make the worst adjudicators.

same name by August Wilson. In 1990, Wilson penned an essay making it clear that he'd only allow a black director to bring the play to life on the big screen.

In a press interview about the movie with Sirius XM radio, Denzel comments on Wilson's essay, noting: 'It's not [about] colour, it's culture. Steven Spielberg did *Schindler's List*. Martin Scorsese did *Goodfellas*, right? Steven Spielberg could direct *Goodfellas*. Martin Scorsese probably could have done a good job with *Schindler's List*. But there are cultural differences. I know, you know, we all know what it is when a hot comb hits your head on a Sunday morning, what it smells like. That's a cultural difference, not just colour difference.'

And as he made the reference to the 'hot comb', all the black cast members laughed – because that was something they could relate to as members of the black community: black parents using a hot comb to tame the unruly Afro hair that we are blessed and equally cursed with.

Another cultural anecdote that's common within the black community is 'the nod'. It would not have escaped your notice that when two black people who don't know each other meet, bump into, or simply pass by each other, they give a subtle nod. This means a lot of different things to a lot of different people within the black community – mere politeness, a recognition of someone who looks like you, or simply an acknowledgement that we as a people still exist, so far from our ancestral home. But at its essence, it doesn't matter. There's no rhyme or reason to it. It's something that we all do, because it's something we've always done as a community.

OK, SO WHO'S ACTUALLY FROM HERE . . . ORIGINALLY?

Because of its history, England is one of the most ethnically ambiguous countries. So, how many people within England can claim to be one-hundred-per-cent English, i.e. Anglo-Saxon? In fact, very few. Technically, to be a true native of Great Britain, you'd need to be Irish and Scottish (from the Celts), Italian (from the Romans), Belgian (from the Belgae), French (from the Gauls and the Normans) and German (from the Suebis).

As a Londoner, what I find most interesting about this issue is the fact that London is one of the cities where it is most ridiculous to ask 'where are you from?' due its dense ethnic population – and this diversity goes back thousands of years. Even as far back as AD 50, London had a diverse population. Examination by the Museum of London of four skeletons found from that period showed that only one of them was born in Britain; the others came from North Africa and possibly Eastern Europe. Additionally, in historian David Olusoga's renowned TV series, *Black and British: A Forgotten History*, he reveals that black people have been in England (via the Cumbrian village of Burgh by Sands) since the third century AD, when a unit of North-African Roman soldiers were garrisoned in a fort there.

Interestingly, black people were also present in Tudor times – even prevalent in the royal courts of Henry VII, Henry VIII, Elizabeth I, and James I. The most compelling argument for 'here' being a legitimate response to 'where are you from originally' comes from recent research from scientists at the Natural History Museum, who proved that the earliest Brits were black-skinned, with dark curly hair!* This was based on the genetic sequencing and facial reconstruction techniques on the DNA of the 'Cheddar Man', the oldest complete skeleton ever found in the UK. So, scientific and anthropological research supports the notion that black people can claim to be from here . . . originally.

However, the number of people who believe that in order to be English, you need to present as white, has reduced in recent years. Research from the Centre of English Identity and Politics revealed that just over 10% of people believe that ethnicity is a determining factor in being English. Interestingly, the biggest change (from 35% to 16%) has been from over-65s, which simply goes to show that even the attitudes of older generations can be susceptible to change.

The concept of needing to know someone's identity, or to a more simplified extent, where they are from, is not a recent thing. As far back as Biblical times, a lot of emphasis was placed on whether you

* That's right, we've been rocking afros since before the 1970s.

were a Jew or Gentile, and if you were a Jew, which of the twelve tribes of Israel you were from. In those times, even simple pronunciation of words was enough to distinguish where you came from.

In a war between two tribes, the Ephraimites and Gileadites, the latter used a simple 'where are you from?' method to identify their Ephraimite enemies. They asked them to pronounce the word 'Shibboleth', but because of the accent of the region, the Ephraimites could not pronounce the 'Sh' sound, so instead they said 'Sibboleth'. They were then easily identified and killed – according to the book of Judges in the Bible, 42,000 Ephraimites were caught and killed by this method. The fact that the two tribes were so alike that the only way to tell one from the other was the pronunciation of one word, should probably have tipped them off that they shouldn't be fighting in the first place, but hey, they played by different rules back then.

War is one of the situations where it matters most where you're from. However, in the throes of war, emotions run high and it's very easy to forget the distinction between one region and another; and this misunderstanding can often lead to discrimination of citizens not fighting in the war. After the towers fell on September 11 and the war commenced in Afghanistan, there was distinct animosity toward people from the Middle-Eastern regions – at demonstrations in the United States against Muslims entering and living in the country, you could see some picket signs and sandwich boards from protesters with the phrases 'dirty Arabs' and 'fucking Arabs'.

Unsurprising behaviour, given the death toll in the 9/11 attack, but something very important was missed in those protests: people from Afghanistan aren't Arabs. They're Afghans. In fact, many people in Afghanistan don't even speak Arabic. Their official languages are Dari, Poshto, and Uzbek. Thinking people from Afghanistan speak Arabic, because it's a predominantly Islamic country, is like thinking everyone in Ireland speaks Latin because it's a predominantly Catholic country.

DO WE EVEN KNOW WHERE WE ARE FROM?

Shocking revelations can occur when we cling too tightly to our identity in connection with race and ethnicity, and we discover something different. One instance of note was in 2012, when a Hungarian far-right politician with strong ties to anti-Semitism discovered that he was actually Jewish. Csanad Szegedi was the deputy leader of a radical nationalist Jobbik party in Hungary, who blamed Jewish people for what he perceived as the ills of Hungarian society. In fact, Szegedi co-founded the Hungarian Guard – a paramilitary formation that marched in uniform through Roma neighbourhoods.

Upon realising his heritage, he has now become a devout Orthodox Jew, and has visited Israel, and the concentration camp at Auschwitz which his own grandmother survived. This shows the dynamic and fluid nature of what we consider as 'where we are from', or even 'who we are'.

The reality is that we are very rarely the entirety of what we think we are anyway. According to a research paper, *The Genetic Ancestry of African Americans, Latinos, and European Americans across the United States*, around six million Americans who describe themselves as white, have some African ancestry going back no further than seven generations. By contrast, the research also shows that the average self-described African-American has about twenty-four-per-cent European ancestry, indicating that descriptors like 'black' and 'white' mean a lot less from a biological or hereditary standpoint than they do from a cultural one.

Consider the case of Lacey Schwartz, who upon acceptance to Georgetown University was enrolled in the black student association, despite identifying as white. Schwartz had grown up in a Jewish household in Woodstock, New York, and had assumed her light dark skin was from her Sicilian grandfather, and had thus always identified as being white. It was only after confronting her mother, it was revealed that Schwartz's biological father was a black man. She has since made a documentary on her journey, titled *Little White Lie*, to reconcile her newly discovered identity and understand why this was kept a secret in the first place.

An extension of this point is that no one chooses to be a particular race. You are born into the family you have, and there isn't anything you can do to change that. Sure, Hitler hated blacks and Jews and considered the Aryan race to be superior, but he himself had no more control over being white than he had over controlling the weather. This decision is mostly down to the parents, in other words, if you're white and you choose to have a baby with a white person, your offspring will be white.

However, this is not one-hundred-per-cent guaranteed – the children of Alyson and Errol Kelly are a great example in proving that skin colour is not an effective differentiator of race or ethnic origin. In 1993, the couple had twin boys, but with a difference – one of them was white and the other was black! And that wasn't the only difference between the twins. In an interview, the twins revealed that one of them is gay and the other is straight, one is academic and the other can't stand school, one is gregarious and the other is the shy, retiring type.

The point here is that genetics is one giant throw of the dice, which is nigh impossible to predict. Our advancement in human genetics continues to challenge the notion of having a definitive answer to race or indeed, where one is from, because it is open to manipulation.

For instance, in 2002, a deaf, lesbian couple, Candace A. McCullough and Sharon M. Duchesneau, set out to have a deaf child by intentionally looking for a deaf sperm donor. To them being deaf is as part of their genetic make-up as being white or women or gay. The fact that the technology exists, which could result in a child's appearance being fundamentally different from its parents and that of their ethnicity, throws a wrench in using skin colour or physical traits to determine where you are from.

A CASE OF THE BIZARRE

But can we choose what race to belong to? The infamous story of Rachel Dolezal seems to suggest so. Dolezal was an American civil rights activist and former president of the National Association for the Advancement of Colored People (NAACP) in Washington, who identified as black. This was until June of 2015, when her parents voiced confusion as to why their daughter was posing as black, as they were both white. In fact, Rachel's parents told media outlets that their heritage is Czech, Swedish, and German – possibly some Native American.

Rachel also allegedly claimed that her sons were black, going as far as posting pictures of her with two black kids on social media. It later transpired that they were her adopted brothers. Finally, Rachel admitted that she was born white, but 'identified as black'. Since then, she's changed her name to Nkechi Diallo – to better represent her belief in being black. Naturally, this has received a lot of negative criticism, particularly among the black community, who have described this as cultural appropriation.

Taking a much larger view, it obviously shouldn't matter which race she identifies with; there is no question whatsoever around the positive work she has done with the NAACP, and if we are to take the position that race is simply a social construct, should this matter? The flip side of that position is that Rachel herself made race an issue to take advantage of.

As referenced by her father in an interview: 'She's a very talented woman doing work she believes in. Why can't she do that as a Caucasian woman, which she clearly is?' And this is where a lot of that criticism from the black community comes from – the ability for Rachel Dolezal to pick and choose her ethnicity, according to how the situation suits her.

For instance, since the controversy, she has written a book, *In Full Colour: Finding My Place in a Black and White World*, but has chosen to publish it under her birth name instead of her 'black name'. Given the fact that publishing is not well known for the success of diverse or black and minority ethnic authors, it leads me to believe she is fully aware that she is white and the accompanying advantages of being white.

What Rachel clearly doesn't understand is that being black isn't something you can dress up in and use to your advantage, and then discard when it becomes difficult. Being black is not a choice; it's a birthright. Blackness to her is something she can dress up in and then remove as she pleases, like a garment.

Having said that, it does sound absurd that something as insignif-icant as our skin colour can make such a huge difference in our lives. I am black because of a pigment called melanin. That isn't to say that all black people have melanin and white people don't. Melanin is present in all humans. It's in our hair, our eyes, ears, and even our brains. Black people just have more of it and for good reason.

It's been scientifically proven that life began in Africa, but around 100,000 years ago, people started to migrate out and occupy the rest of the world. Those that remained in Africa evolved to have dark skin for protection against the harsh ultraviolet radiation from the sun, and those that migrated to the northern latitudes evolved pale skin, the better to produce vitamin D from softer sunlight.

It's funny isn't it; the fact that the colour of our skin, which deter-mines so much about us and how we are treated, boils down to nothing more than simply being a consequence of ultraviolet light. Human DNA does not differ across nationalities, population or race. So, as a black man of African descent, I am essentially composed of the same stuff as a white, European man. And that is the stuff of the stars . . . literally.

It's been proven by astronomers at the Sloan Digital Sky Survey in New Mexico, who used the APOGEE (Apache Point Observatory Galactic Evolution Experiment) spectrograph to show the abundance of 'CHNOPS' elements (carbon, hydrogen, nitrogen, oxygen, phosphorous, and sulphur aka the building blocks of life on earth) across the galaxy.

So, regardless of good manners, we must always challenge the basis of that question, 'Where are you *really* from?' If only for the fact that the question is a false binary, because it insinuates that the answer can't be 'here'. Black people have as much right to be British as any other race — if not by virtue of us being born here, then certainly for our contributions to this country. And really, we have the absolute right to get offended if someone questions our identity. We are so much more complicated than the simple question of 'where are you from?'

To truly answer that question, one should have a level of intimacy and friendship that is beyond polite conversation. And if it is simply polite conversation that you are after, what does it matter if someone who looks like they are of Asian or African heritage says they are from Camden, instead of China or Kenya? Or fuck it, do we just say exactly what the driver expects to hear – even if it's only so you can pass out in peace in the back seat of your Uber.

Answer to pop quiz: Black people have reportedly been in England since the third century AD, when a unit of North-African Roman soldiers were garrisoned in a fort in Burgh by Sands.

SPORT
BUT . . . BLACK GUYS CAN'T SWIM

Stereotype/negative narrative: Black people can't swim, but are good at certain sports such as running, thereby funnelling us into specific sports and denying us opportunities in others.

Pop quiz:

*In what year's Olympics did a black person
first win a medal for swimming?*

Rio 2016

Atlanta 1996

Montreal 1976

14-year-old me to my aunt, with whom I was living at the time: 'It's winter, so we're going to start playing water polo instead of rugby for sports at school. I need you to sign this permission slip saying I know how to swim.'

My aunt: 'What's water polo?'

14-year-old me: 'It's essentially handball in a swimming pool.'

My aunt: 'Hmmm, that sounds dangerous. Can you even swim?'

14-year-old me: 'Of course I can swim. I go to the leisure centre every Saturday.'

My aunt: 'I thought you were at the library every Saturday?'

14-year-old me: 'Yes . . . well I go to the library after the leisure centre.'*

My aunt: 'Are you sure you know how to swim?'

14-year-old me [exasperated]: 'Yes, I know how to swim! I wouldn't want to play a sport with "water" in the name if I didn't know how to swim.'

My aunt [claps me round the head]: 'Don't sass me, boy! If I sign this piece of paper and you end up drowning, do you know how much trouble I'll be in? I've never been in trouble in this country and I'm not going to start now, just because you've got it into your moo-moo head that you can swim. And then when you drown, I'm going to have to pay for your funeral because it was my fault.† No way, boy! No water polo for you. You can sit and read your book while everyone else is swimming.'

At the time, I couldn't for the life of me understand why my aunt had this aversion to me swimming. At first, I put it down to Nigerians not wanting their name or signature on any official form or document.‡ But it wasn't until I was cruelly informed by my classmates (after taunting me and calling me gay for reading, instead of stripping down to my trunks and playing in the pool with a group of other

---

* Nope. Playing PlayStation or watching WWE at my friend's house.
† Note: Money *always* trumps relatives to Nigerians.
‡ She still doesn't even have an Oyster card to this day.

half-naked boys)* that it was just as well, because black people can't swim anyway.

When it comes to sport, there are two main stereotypes that most people believe about black people: that we are better at running than other races, and terrible at swimming. At first sight, this is a hard one to challenge, given there is such a small number of black swimmers and a relatively high number of black people dominating sprinting and long-distance running. However, once you investigate this notion without the lens of stereotyping, you can start to see how ridiculous it is. And not only ridiculous, but harmful. Perpetuating the stereotype that black people are only good at certain sports is something that has been readily adopted into the cultural zeitgeist, thereby isolating us to those sports and limiting our opportunities in other areas.

WILD THEORIES HAVE PERPETUATED THESE STEREO-TYPES

For the purposes of being objective, let's look at swimming statistics from the past couple of years – because they certainly seem to suggest that (most) black people can't swim. A 2010 study by the University of Memphis and US Swimming, America's governing body of competitive swimming, found that around seventy per cent of black children couldn't swim – compared to forty per cent of white and fifty-eight per cent of Hispanic children who couldn't swim.

If you look at the statistics around drowning as well, they paint a similar picture. Research from the Center for Disease Control and Prevention on drowning revealed that at every age, black children are the victims of drowning far more than white children. Among young people age five to nineteen, black children drown in pools at a rate 5.5 times that of white children. When all age groups are combined, the ratio is 3.2 to one.

---

* Because they spent their time swimming instead of reading, they didn't get the irony. Suckers!

It is not only the statistics, over the years, there have been wild theories and speculations that there is something about the physiology of black people that prevent us from being good swimmers. And a lot of these theories rely on the history of slavery as an example. For instance, it has been hypothesised by experts such as Agnes Davis, president and CEO of the minority-owned swimming company called 'swim swim swim I SAY', that slavery had an impact on black people's attitudes and consequently, fear of the water.

The most popular trade route for sending slaves from Africa to Europe and America was, via the Atlantic Ocean, commonly known then as the 'Middle Passage'. For these slaves, it was theorised that this was the first time they were on a large body of water, which would be unsettling in and of itself. Add to this the fact that they and their families were robbed of their freedom, and would be made to work perilously for the rest of their lives, and you can start to understand why there would be a deep-rooted fear of the water.

The journey from Africa to Europe took as long as twelve weeks; that's three months at sea, with as many as five hundred slaves in a small cage, with no access to hygiene or proper nutrition. And when any of the slaves fell ill, rebellious, or if the slavers simply felt like it, or thought they could profit, they were simply tossed overboard.

For example, in 1781, more than 130 African slaves aboard the British slave ship, *Zong*, were tossed overboard in what is now referred to as the Zong Massacre. The ship's captain had missed a docking in Jamaica and got lost, so when the crew were running out of water, the slavers threw the slaves overboard and tried to cash in on their insurance for the loss of the slaves.

If you think the story could not possibly get more revolting, when the insurers refused to pay for the loss of the slaves, they were taken to court in the case of Gregson v. Gilbert, where it was ruled that in some circumstances, the deliberate killing of slaves was legal and that insurers could be required to pay for the slaves' deaths.

Even if a slave could swim, his master would go to great lengths to make it impossible to keep this skill alive, because if a slave could swim, it meant another avenue for escape from servitude. And so, it is possible that an inherent fear of the water was born and then passed on to future generations. Aside from this being a culture lesson handed down, it has been hypothesised that it could also have been inherited via genetics. Researchers at the Emory University School of Medicine in Atlanta showed that when mice are taught to fear an odour, both their offspring and the next generation are born fearing it − proving that memories and phobias can be passed down to later generations through genetic switches.

This was further proven by research from Rachel Yehuda, professor of psychiatry and neuroscience at the Icahn School of Medicine at Mount Sinai. She revealed that when people experience trauma, it changes their genes in a very specific way, which is then passed down the genetic line to their children, who also inherit the genes affected by trauma. Given this research, it's not so unreasonable then to conclude that this fear was passed through generations and could have an impact on attitudes towards swimming in today's generation of black people.

Other theories supporting the stereotype include a journal published in 1969, *The Negro and Learning to Swim: The Buoyancy Problem Related to Reported Biological Difference*, which claimed that black people had difficulty learning how to swim, because of longer limbs and denser bones. Another theory was presented by Frank Braun, president of the South African National Olympics Committee, saying, 'The African is not suited to swimming. The water closes their pores, so they cannot get rid of carbon dioxide and they tire quickly.'

This is also a stereotype being reinforced by the media reports, hence becoming ingrained in our collective consciousness. A study titled *A Level Playing Field? Media Constructions of Athletics, Genetics, and Race*, examined news media coverage implying that particular races (mostly black) succeeded at sports due to genetic differences, and measured how often this narrative showed up in journalism. The study looked at around 24,000 English-language newspaper articles across the globe from 2003–2014 and found that nearly fifty-five per cent of these media narratives perpetuated the belief that black people excel at running because of genetic differences. Following the 2012 Olympics, nearly one-third of the news articles that discussed race, genetics and athletics implied that black runners are fastest, because they descend from testosterone-heavy ancestors who survived the brutal conditions of the slave era.

DON'T BELIEVE THE HYPE

While these all feel like perfectly reasonable theories, upon closer scrutiny, they simply don't hold water.* For example, while the theory that the fear of water could be passed through generations has merit, it is not conclusive enough to make it fact. What it does is create a logical fallacy, which dictates that because something can be done (i.e. the transfer of fear through generations), that means it will always be done.

Yes, the perilous journey of the sea could have caused an inherent fear of the water for African Americans, but that wasn't the only dangerous situation in that scenario. The slaves were held in chains and were beaten regularly with whips, but that doesn't mean black people have an inherent fear of chains and whips. The slaves were made to pick cotton for long hours of the day, but black people don't freak out when we see Egyptian cotton bed linen in IKEA. Also, this doesn't explain the black people who are of African heritage and can't swim, but their parents weren't slaves or were born into slavery, as opposed to being shipped over from Africa.

As to the other theory that black people have denser bones and longer limbs, which negatively impacts swimming ability. This is true – black people do tend to have denser bones – but is it significant enough to determine swimming ability between races? Matt Bridge, senior lecturer in Coaching & Sports Science at the University of Birmingham, estimates in an article for swimming without stress, that the difference in skeletal mass between black people and white is just

---

* Bad pun, I know but writing is very lonely work, so I have to keep myself amused somehow!

300 grams (or 0.3 kg), which is not enough to affect the buoyancy and swimming ability of an entire race.

In 2011, Pauline Potter, the then Guinness World Record holder for being the world's heaviest woman, went swimming between three and five times a week – and she was white! So this pokes serious holes in the bone density theory. With regards to limb length, Michael Phelps, the world's most decorated Olympian in swimming, is 6 feet 4 inches (193 cm) and he manages just fine. Cullen Jones, an American competition swimmer and Olympic gold medallist, is 6 feet 5 inches (1.96 m) and his long limbs don't seem to hold him back.

As for Mr Braun's notion that black people can't swim because the water closes our pores, a paper published in the *Journal of Cosmetic Science*, titled 'Ethnic skin types: are there differences in skin structure and function?', shows that black people tend to have the largest pores out of all the races. So, if anything, black people's pores would be least likely to be blocked, or blocked at a lower rate than other races.

That aside, it's a huge misconception that humans breathe through our skin. We don't. The skin, as part of the integumentary system, is not responsible for getting rid of carbon dioxide; our respiratory system is. So, it comes as no surprise that Mr Braun's paper has largely been discredited by the scientific community.

THE TRUTH? BLACK PEOPLE WERE FORCIBLY PREVENTED FROM SWIMMING

So, if it is not down to physiology, what can account for the large percentage of black people that can't swim? Well, it's worth looking at the history of swimming as a leisure activity over the years, where we can see that due to social and economic forces, black people were prevented from swimming. There were two main periods in time in the twentieth century when swimming became popularised. The first was the 1920s–1940s, which was the first time that swimming took off as a recreational activity for the family.

Unfortunately for black people, this was also one of the most heightened periods of racial segregation, so the public pools were open to white people only. And even when black people attempted to resist the segregation and gain access to the public pools, they were met with assault and litigation. A common legal trick that worked particularly well was for the city government to lease the pool to a private company to operate; because although the government couldn't legally segregate, a private company could enforce segregation rules. This meant that access to public pools for black people was not an option.

When the Fairground Swimming Pool in St Louis was desegregated in 1949, five thousand white people rioted and indiscriminately beat any black person remotely near the pool. In 1964, a hotel owner poured muriatic acid into the whites-only swimming pool at his Monson Motor Lodge, after several young black men jumped into the pool to swim. There were even instances of white people going to extraordinary lengths to ensure that black people didn't have access to the pool – in 1942, Montgomery, West Virginia, closed its only municipal swimming pool

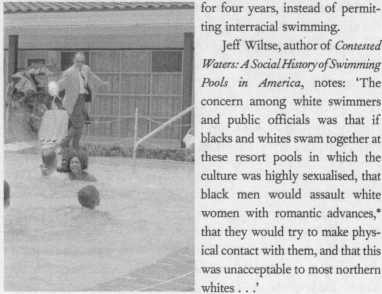

for four years, instead of permitting interracial swimming.

Jeff Wiltse, author of *Contested Waters: A Social History of Swimming Pools in America*, notes: 'The concern among white swimmers and public officials was that if blacks and whites swam together at these resort pools in which the culture was highly sexualised, that black men would assault white women with romantic advances,* that they would try to make physical contact with them, and that this was unacceptable to most northern whites . . .'

---

* Black people may be shit swimmers, but we have mad game with the ladies.

If you're thinking, yes, that's horrible, but that's all in the past now, in July 2018, a white man in the US called the police on a black mother and child for using a neighbourhood swimming pool, as he did not believe they could be wealthy enough to live in the area.

In that same month, a woman from Carolina verbally assaulted two black boys playing in the pool, shoving one of them, claiming they 'didn't belong'. Through these examples, we can clearly see that black people were systematically excluded from swimming, which in turn has a knock-on effect. If my grandfather didn't learn to swim, he never taught my parents – making it unlikely that they would know how to swim – meaning they wouldn't have been able to teach me.

The other period when swimming was at its height of popularity was from the late 1940s going into the 1960s. The post-Second World War economic expansion meant that there was more disposable income for most white families, allowing them to engage in more leisure activities. Unfortunately, this didn't extend to most of the other ethnicities at that time, as the economic divide was still huge between whites and blacks. Simply put, black families couldn't afford a pool of their own, or even had the disposable income to buy swimming equipment or swimming lessons.

There is evidence of this social disparity even today: according to the Urban Institute, which looks at social and economic policy research, white families are about six times wealthier than black families. So, it is not unreasonable to conclude that black families are more likely to use their income on the necessities such as living expenses, food, bills and education, rather than luxury items like swimming gear or lessons.*

Despite this wealth of evidence explaining why swimming is not prevalent in black communities, the strongest evidence to help fight this stereotype is the fact that black people *can swim*. Even as far back as before slavery, black people were known as strong swimmers. According to Professor Phillips and Dr Osmond in their paper, 'The Bloke with a Stroke', historically, black people were good swimmers and it was Westerners who were less likely to know how to swim.

---

* Or as in the case of my family, funeral arrangements.

Supporting this theory is an 1879 pamphlet by US Navy colonel Theodorus Bailey Myers, noting (about white American sailors): 'The great majority of people cannot swim, and strange as it may seem to you, there are many who follow the sea as a profession who cannot swim a stroke.'

Also, here's a quote from a paper entitled, 'Enslaved swimmers and divers in the Atlantic World': 'West Africans, Native Americans and Asians used a variety of freestyle, a stronger and swifter style that enabled them to incorporate swimming into many daily activities, including diving, fishing and surfing.' The author also believes that slave owners encouraged their black slaves in swimming and diving to fish and retrieve pearls.

So, challenge anyone who insinuates that black people cannot swim. It's a terrible stereotype with origins in segregation. Black people can swim, and swim well – for example, Alice Dearing is one of Great Britain's top female swimmers, aiming to be the first black woman to compete for Team GB at the Olympics. And in the most recent 2016 Olympics, an African-American, Simone Manuel, won a swimming gold medal. And as far back as 1976, Enith Brigitha of the Netherlands picked up two bronze medals in the Montreal Olympics for swimming, becoming the first black Olympic swimming medallist, while the first black swimmer to win an Olympic swimming gold medal was Anthony Nesty, from Suriname, at the Seoul Olympics in 1988.

BLACK PEOPLE ARE GREAT AT RUNNING . . . RIGHT?

Another stereotype that is directed towards black people is that we are pretty good runners. At first sight, this might not be offensive, given it is a positive, but there is a lot of harm that can be done by making this the prevailing trope when it comes to athletics and black people. Aside from the unrealistic expectations placed on black people because of it, there is a tendency to funnel black people towards this sport and so we miss out on the joys of others.

For instance, I've always been a pretty good runner. In my

secondary school, I used to enter sprinting competitions, and in all races, I've never come behind third position. As much as stereotypes might have made me believe, it wasn't down to the fact that I am black. I'm good at running, essentially because I practised – and when I say practised, I mean growing up, I used to play football every day and spent a worrying amount of time playing tag and kiss chase.*

But when I was in school, there was the expectation from my (white) teachers that I would be good at long-distance running – which I was terrible at. Still am, in fact. Any sort of physical activity that requires me to move faster than normal for extended periods of time is something my mind can't comprehend, and my body physically can't do.† But still, I was encouraged to participate in long-distance running. I mean, I know why my parents expected me to be good at long-distance running; they expect me to be good at everything.‡ But why on earth did my white teachers expect me to be good at long-distance running? I suspect it might have something to do with the fact that pretty much every marathon or long-distance winner in major sports tournaments is black.§

The London 2012 Summer Olympic Games provided a good opportunity to re-examine the science behind sports. This is because it was the first games in Olympic history where amputees were able to compete in games for 'able-bodied' athletes. As such, there is a plethora of information out there on the body and the advantages that certain races or people have over others.

We know from scientific study that muscles have two types of fibres: fast-twitch (adapted for jumping and sprinting) and slow-twitch (adapted for endurance). An experiment run by geneticist and exercise physiologist Claude Bouchard, at Laval University in Quebec City, showed that West Africans, by a ratio of approximately two to one, had more of the larger fast-twitch fibres – and whites on average have

---

* Adorable game when you are a kid; kinda pervy when you're an adult.
† Read: Won't do.
‡ After a school talent show where my friend played the violin beautifully, my father once asked me why I don't play the violin. This man never paid for a violin lesson. Or come to think of it, a violin.
§ Yeah, Kenyans. I'm looking at you.

a higher percentage of slow-twitch fibres. This would explain why black people are better at sprinting and basketball, wouldn't it?

Well, not entirely. Statistically, black Africans have won the most long-distance running games, of which endurance is key, but white people have more slow-twitch muscles. So, there is an obvious discrepancy and much like with swimming, the theories that are put forward to explain this are often racist.

For example, after Jesse Owens's record-breaking performances at the 1936 Olympics, the then US United States Olympic team's sprint coach, Dean Cromwell wrote in his book, 'The Negro excels. It was not long ago that his ability to sprint and jump was a life-and-death matter to him in the jungle.* His muscles are pliable, and his easy-going disposition is a valuable aid to the mental and physical relaxation that a runner and jumper must have.' Here we see how something that is initially viewed as a positive stereotype has its roots in racism.

Christopher McDougall's novel, *Born to Run*, profiles the runners of the Tarahumara tribe, who live in the high Sierra Madre mountains and canyons in north-western Mexico, and references their incredible ability for endurance running. He argues that humans developed the ability for endurance or persistence running to hunt and literally run-down prey – allowing us to survive. More so, early hunters would pick the hottest times of the year to carry out this style of hunting.

So it is easy to theorise that in the low plains of Africa, descendants of these hunters would naturally evolve to be better long-distance runners compared to people from other more temperate climates. Kenya is a more popular region often used as an example from an environmental perspective, in that it has been theorised that Kenyans are great at distance running. A theory supported by the fact that as of 2017, Kenya has won an astonishing seventy-four medals at the Olympic Games in races of 800 metres and above since 1968.

Upon further inspection, though, it turns out that the individuals that

---

* Jesse Owens grew up in, and started racing competitively in Cleveland, Ohio, not the jungle, you racist bottom-feeder.

usually win these medals are from the Nandi Hills in the former Rift Valley Province of Kenya. So, this reveals that it's not that black people or even Kenyans are particularly good at distance running, but people from the Nandi Hills. To put this into context, the combined nations of other African countries such as Sierra Leone, Nigeria, Côte d'Ivoire, Mali, Senegal, Angola, Congo and so on, have yet to win a marathon medal at the Olympics. Not a gold medal, mind – any medal at all.

A supporting theory as to why the people from the Nandi Hills are such good runners is because of the low oxygen environment in their high-altitude region. High altitude air contains less oxygen than sea-level and low altitude air, so the body is forced to compensate by increasing red blood cell production, which in turn increases the body's capacity for transporting oxygen to your muscles and other tissues. Sounds like kosher science, right?

But if that were the case, why aren't the Nepalese the most proficient long-distance runners? After all, Mount Everest is the highest point from sea level. And the farthest point from the Earth's centre is the summit of Chimborazo, in Ecuador, but Ecuadorians have won only two medals in all Olympic Games – and it was for the Men's 20 kilometres walk.

BIOLOGY ENABLES, CULTURE FORBIDS

Despite the research, it's hard to deny that black people do seem to be better at certain sports. If you were an alien and you had to select a team of earthlings for boxing, running, American football, basketball, or wrestling matches, chances are that your team would be comprised of mostly black people. And this isn't even hard to imagine – Warner Bros already did this for us with the movie, *Space Jam*. It's no surprise that the aliens chose to steal the skills of black basketball players:* Charles Barkley, Patrick Ewing, Larry Johnson, and Muggsy Bogues.

---

* I mean, sure they also took the skills of Shawn Bradley, who's white – but the dude's 7ft 6in! Who wouldn't pick him?

So yes, black people do tend to dominate certain sports. But what is most interesting is that the performance gap between black people and white people appears to be the widest when expensive equipment or facilities are required. Think about all the sports where you typically see a lack of black people participating, or any sort of diversity. Sports such as cycling, equestrian, and sailing are extremely expensive.

The cost of an Olympic cycling bike can range between £15,000 and £20,000 and you'd need access to training facilities. For equestrian sports, you'll need a sports horse, with a price tag from £20,000 to the millions, not to mention the cost of maintaining, feeding and keeping the horse in stables. Olympic sailboards usually start from about £1,195 upwards.

As I pointed out earlier, given the lower amounts of income that most black people are likely to earn, they cannot afford facilities such as swimming pools. But to be a good runner, well . . . you need only your two God-given feet. After all, the first black African to win an Olympic gold was Abebe Bikila of Ethiopia, in the marathon in Rome in 1960. He ran the race barefoot. And it is a hell of a lot cheaper to

buy a basketball and shoot hoops in your neighbourhood, than it is to buy golf clubs and a membership to the local club.

It would be foolish not to acknowledge the interconnection between the impact of our environment and our upbringing, the age-old 'nature vs. nurture' debate. From a nature perspective, there was no biological or evolutionary imperative for white people to learn how to swim better or faster compared to black people – certainly no more than there was for a black person to be a faster runner. As Yuval Noah Harari notes in his critically acclaimed book, *Sapiens*: 'Biology enables, culture forbids'.

So, on the nurture or cultural front, perhaps swimming was simply not something most black people were brought up seeing as important. The aforementioned research from the USA Swimming Foundation and the University of Memphis showed that if a parent does not know how to swim, there is only a thirteen-per-cent chance that a child in that household will learn how to swim – and this is across all ages. If parents believe wholeheartedly that black people can't swim or aren't concerned about it, there's very little chance they'll encourage their children to do it. And because black people can swim, doesn't mean we always have to.

A question we must ask is: Is it that black people *can't* swim, or is it that they *don't care* about swimming? I love swimming but I am always conscious of the chlorine, which is prevalent in swimming pools, because it dries up my black skin and is absolute murder on my hair; I imagine this to be even worse for black females, who spend a lot of money diversifying their hairstyles between weaves and natural hair. So, it is understandable why swimming may not be black people's favourite pastime.

What's offensive about this stereotype is that it's perpetuated by ignorance and refusing to think wider than people's initial beliefs. It is oh, so damaging to make such assumptions based on race and link it to biology. While the stereotype that black people are good at sports complements our physical abilities, it often comes hand in hand with undermining our intellectual abilities – because if it is okay to think that black people aren't able to swim because of biological factors attributed to our race, how long before we start saying black people aren't as smart, or can't become CEOs, or are more likely to carry diseases because of our 'biological factors'?

Making wild generalisations about race based on biology is a harmful and slippery slope that can lead to real cases of racism. As pointed out in the first chapter, race is an artificial social construct, any theories to the contrary are questionable, and thus far unsubstantiated. And because black people win the most races in running sports, doesn't mean there is a specific biological reason why. After all, China has been the most successful nation in Olympic table tennis tournaments, winning fifty-three medals overall and since 1992, have won at least one medal in every event, but no one seems to suggest they naturally evolved to be great table tennis players.

Answer to pop quiz: Enith Brigitha was the first black Olympic swimming medallist, winning two bronze medals in the 1976 Montreal Olympics.

POLICE
IS IT CUZ I'M BLACK? PART I

Stereotype/negative narrative: That when we call out excessive action or brutality by law enforcement, we are playing the race card, and that complaints from the black communities that they are unfairly targeted and mistreated by the police are unfounded.

Pop quiz:

*How many more times are black Britons likely
to be stopped and searched than white Britons?*

40

2.5

6.6

One of the more confusing ideas for a black child to wrap their head around is the notion that the police could be a dangerous force to us. The police? No way, man. Their job is literally to serve and protect.* They're not a danger to anyone but the bad guys . . . right? I mean, have you ever watched a police procedural show on TV? Those guys are always awesome. I don't even want to know anyone who didn't like *Inspector Morse*, or didn't bow down to the superior detective skills of the cops on *NYPD Blue*. *CSI*? Come on. They were crime scene investigators . . . who also solved crime!† That's doubling down on the awesomeness. But sure as day, every black kid experiences what I like to call their moment of clarity, when they start to understand that there are serious problems with institutional racism in the police force. My first experience went a little something like this:

> **14-year-old me, walking home in a tracksuit and hoodie after a run,‡ when approached by two police constables.**
> **Policeman 1**: 'Afternoon, sir, where are you coming from?'
> **Me**: 'I just went for a run and now I'm heading back home.'
> **Police 2**: 'And where is home?'
> **Me, still naively thinking this is a standard conversation**: 'Just off Bates Crescent in Streatham.'
> **Police 2**: 'I see. And where have you been?'
> **Me**: 'It's just as I said, I went for run.'
> **Police 2**: 'Yes, but where did you run to?'
> **Me**: 'Just laps around the park.'
> **Police 1**: 'The park, huh? They sometimes sell drugs in that park. You don't have any drugs on you, do you?'
> **Me, mortified at the very idea of having anything to do with drugs:**§ 'No, not at all. I just went for a run.'

---

* Actually, that's the motto of most US police forces. The motto for the London Metropolitan Police is: 'Total Policing'. Yawn.
† As well as all being disturbingly good looking.
‡ You can tell this was back in my teenage years because nowadays I wouldn't be caught dead wearing a tracksuit. Or running for that matter.
§ When I was at university, I had a decidedly different attitude.

Police 1: 'So you don't mind if I search you?'
Me: 'No, but I really haven't done anything.'
Police 2: 'Well, let's see.'

While you might think that this is a perfectly innocuous police interaction with a citizen, there are two things which made that situation
even worse. While the police were searching me, there was a group
of white kids about my age in the park, looking on and yelling at me,
calling me a criminal.

The other thing was that after the officers had finished searching
me and found nothing, the white kids started yelling at the officers,
calling them 'wankers'. The police officers just yelled at them to clear
out and went back on their beat. Now, at the time I didn't think anything
of it, and it wasn't until I got older and went on to study law, that I
realised not only was the search a breach of the Police and Criminal

Look at this adorable face. No way this kid is up to anything untoward . . . back then.

Evidence Act, but I was targeted specifically because of my race – the white kids who had also been in the park and were actively insulting the police officers were dismissed without a thought.

The saddest part of this whole story was not merely that I had been singled out because of how I look or how I was dressed, but that I felt betrayed by an institution that I used to admire completely. This is the notion that we need to start understanding: that no matter how positively portrayed in the media, the police force is not this perfect objective institution that only seeks to arrest bad guys. There are serious problems with institutional racism in the police force that largely affect black communities and people of colour.

This lack of awareness of the flaws of the police as an institution is harmful to our communities, because if you are not black, you are less likely to scrutinise the actions of the police when it comes to black people, and thereby more likely to believe the narrative that black communities are always at fault when it comes to stop and searches, and even worse, arrests.

A DIFFERENT KIND OF STOP AND SEARCH FOR BLACK PEOPLE

The Police and Criminal Evidence Act 1984, along with its accompanying codes of practice, set out the powers of the police to stop crimes, while protecting the rights and freedoms of the public. The second part of the sentence is just as important as the first; there needs to be a balance between the powers of the police to stop crime, but also to protect the rights of the public. In the case of black people and other minorities, the balance is undoubtedly skewed in favour of preventing crime over our rights. So, let's examine my seemingly innocuous interaction in light of the guidelines in the Act.

Code A of the Act states that: 'Powers to stop and search must be used fairly, responsibly, with respect for people being searched and without unlawful discrimination.' It also states that there must be reasonable grounds for the stop and search: 'Firstly, the officer must have formed a genuine suspicion in their own mind that they will find the object for which the search power being exercised allows them to search, and the suspicion that the object will be found must be reasonable.'

In my scenario, the police officers wholly failed that test on all grounds. I was simply walking back home without bothering anyone when I was stopped, so there were no reasonable grounds to have stopped me. Also, the fact that I had gone for a run in a vicinity where drugs could possibly have been sold is not enough reasonable suspicion to search an individual, particularly if there was nothing to rouse suspicion in the first instance. In fact, they didn't suspect me of having drugs till I mentioned I had gone running in the park, so they would not have had any grounds to stop me in the first place, as the Act states: 'There is no power to stop or detain a person in order to find grounds for a search.'

Not to mention that for police officers to search you under that Act, they need to provide their name, police station, reason for searching you, what they expect to find, and why they are legally allowed to search you – none of which they provided. And even if it can be argued that they had done everything according to the law, there is no way to justify stopping and searching a black teenager who had done nothing, while blatantly ignoring a group of white teenagers who were actively insulting the officers.

I remember discussing this encounter with my cousin, who was older, and it was then I had the conversation that many black parents have with their children. The warning that the police are not always on our side, that we could be arrested or even hurt in a police inter-action, so we should be polite and do everything to extricate ourselves from the situation as quickly as possible. And to never, ever, ever run from the police.

In some communities, minority parents even go so far as to warn their children to never, under any circumstances, talk to the police. It feels completely counterintuitive to have to treat an institution that is meant to keep us safe, as oppressors. I have asked most black people

I know, and they have all had this conversation with their parents and guardians, or some variation of it. In contrast, when I asked my white friends about the conversations their parents had with them about the police, it tended to sound something like this: 'The police are here for your protection, so if anything bad ever happens or you feel in danger, call the police immediately.'

The power of the police to stop and search is an important one; the problem arises when the police don't adhere to the codes of practice and disproportionally target black and other minority communities. According to the *Guardian* newspaper, a report by the Inspectorate of Constabulary, which oversees the police in England and Wales, found that thirty-two out of forty-three forces failed to meet government rules aimed at stamping out abuses in stop and search.

According to 2019 Home Office internal data reported in the Guardian, black people in England and Wales are 40 times more likely than white people to be stopped and searched. And if you think this figure is high, you should know that it has increased astronomically in just one year; in 2018, a study by the London School of Economics and a pressure group called the Stopwatch coalition, found that Black Britons were stopped and searched 8.4 times more than white people.

This isn't solely an issue for black communities; the latest Home Office figures reported in the *Guardian* show that BAME (Black, Asian, and minority ethnic) people are three times more likely than white people to be stopped and searched. It's then no surprise that young black people are nine times more likely to be locked up in England and Wales than young white people, according to the Ministry of Justice's Lammy Review.

In addition to the fact that black people are being disproportionately stopped and searched, research shows that the outcomes of those stop and searches largely yield no results! Research released following a Freedom of Information request by the *Guardian*, after a debate between then Home Secretary, Theresa May, and the Met Police Chief over the effectiveness of stop and search, found 'no statistically significant crime-reducing effect from the large increase in weapon searches . . .

This suggests that the greater use of weapons searches was not effective at the borough level for reducing crime . . . Overall, analysis shows that there [were] no discernible crime-reducing effects from a large surge in stop and search activity at the borough level during the operation.'

This is also the case in the United States, where a Columbia law professor, Jeffrey Fagan, testified in Manhattan Federal Court that just one gun was recovered for every thousand people stopped. He notes that: 'The NYPD hit rate is far less than what you would achieve by chance.'

IMPACT OF POLICE'S HISTORICAL ACTIONS

After explaining to me what actions I should take whenever stopped by the police, my cousin ended the lecture with, 'Man, fuck tha police!' Hell, yeah; I was pumped. He had managed to summarise my feelings about the whole encounter in just three words – 'fuck tha police'. It wasn't till later that I realised it was the name of a popular song from rap group, N.W.A., and one of the most quoted songs when it comes to the relationship between black people and the police.

Only in the 1980s, following the height of the Civil Rights Movement, could a song called 'Fuck Tha Police' be released to such critical acclaim. It was a very tenuous time in race relations between not only black and white people, but just as important, the police. With lyrics like, 'So police think they have the authority to kill a minority . . . it's gonna be a bloodbath of cops dying in LA,' it's certainly easy to see why this was a hugely provocative song.

It was so provocative that it was enough to incur the wrath of law enforcement agencies across jurisdictions such as the LAPD, Police Unions, the FBI, and even the Secret Service. It actually prompted the then assistant director of the FBI's bureau affairs, Milt Ahlerich, to send a letter to Priority Records, the group's record label, condemning the song and noting that it encourages violence against law enforcement officers. The Minnesota attorney general, Hubert 'Skip' Humphrey, was also inspired to act: he threated to prosecute record stores that sold the track to minors.

However, Ahlerich's letter, the threat of prosecution, and the overreaction from the judiciary had the opposite effect on the popularity of the record. Priority Records leaked the letter to the press, which increased brand awareness – the CBS television network produced a news special called, 'Gangsta Rap lyrics under attack', further boosting the track's popularity and notoriety. Again, we see the long arm of the law disproportionately being extended towards the black community.

The reality is that 'Fuck Tha Police' was not released as a single. So, if you wanted to own this song, you had to buy the entire album. It didn't even appear on the censored version of the album. Back in the 1980s, record labels knew better than to blatantly insult the police on a $2.99 single. Another thing to consider was that the members of N.W.A. weren't fearless campaigners against police brutality, who sought to fight daily for the plight of minorities in society. They were only recording artists who wanted to make money, and felt the best way to do that was to rap about controversial things that were happening in their lives and their communities.

Whatever feelings of animosity N.W.A. had towards the police, maybe 'Fuck Tha Police' and the rest of their albums were less about the social attitudes of black people when it comes to the police, and more about the perceived life of a gangster. After all, did any of them go on to be civil rights activists? No. Dr Dre went on to be one of the biggest producers in hip hop worth around $550 million. Eazy-E is deceased. DJ Yella hasn't really been heard from since 1996. Ice Cube is now doing family-friendly comedy movies. So, it was less about the specific lyrics of the songs and more about the feeling and activism that it inspired.

In those three simple words, N.W.A. had managed to summarise what a lot of black communities were feeling at the time about the police, and galvanised people to speak up and express this mistreatment at the hands of the police. And this was something of which the authorities were painfully aware, or why else would the FBI get involved? If you want an example of how this was yet another way in which the police and law enforcement were institutionally racist, think about all the songs written by brave white artists that have been critical of law enforcement and their brutality – and which law enforcement did nothing or very little to stifle out:

- The Dicks, 'Hate the Police', with the lyrics:
  Daddy, daddy, daddy, proud of his son. He's got him a good job, kills niggers and Mexicans. Dicks hate policemen and it's true, you can't find justice, it'll find you.
- Alkaline Trio, 'Cop':
  Wonder what it was that made you this way . . . Unhappy wife, shitty life, hit the bottle. Left you with meaningless things to prove – like why you became a cop.
- Le Tigre, 'Bang! Bang!':
  In New York, the shooting of another unarmed black man, raises further questions about NYPD tactics. On Friday an undercover policeman, shot and killed Patrick Doorsman . . . Who gave them the fucking right, to run around like they own the night?
- The Clash, 'Know Your Rights':
  You have the right not to be killed. Murder is a crime. Unless it was done by a policeman or aristocrat.
- Or 'The Guns of Brixton':
  When the law break in, how you gonna go? Shot down on the pavement or waiting on death row.
- Sinéad O'Connor, 'Black Boys on Mopeds':
  England's not the mythical land of Madame George and roses. It's the home of police who kill black boys on mopeds.

As embarrassing and painful as my first interaction with the police was, there have been other black kids who have faced much worse; not to mention very public and obvious instances of racism by the police. There were three events that were widely discussed in the black community when I was growing up, which helped me to understand the dynamics between the police and black communities.

THE BRIXTON RIOT (BRIXTON RISING), 1981

The Brixton Riot started as a peace march by members of the Afro-Caribbean community in response to the (perceived) inadequacy of the police's investigation into a (believed) race-related house fire. However, it came to a head when police officers were dispatched into Brixton, and within five days around one thousand people were stopped and searched, and eighty-two were arrested under the stop-and-search rule in Section 4 of the Vagrancy Act 1824. As with the Rodney King riots, this didn't sit well with members of the community, but the real spark that lit the fire was an additional, separate incident.

On 10 April (during the riots), a police officer saw a black youth named Michael Bailey running away, apparently from three other black youths. Bailey was stopped and found to be bleeding, but managed to run away from the officer. When he was later found by the officer, it was revealed that he had a stab wound. This drew the attention of a crowd, who didn't think that the police officer was providing aid quickly enough, and they then proceeded to fight with the police. Much later, rumours ran rampant that Bailey had been left to die by the police, or that the officer himself had stabbed him.

It is certainly no surprise that a town-spread riot resulted from this. One could ask why it was necessary to send police officers in to arrest members of a peaceful march? Also, stopping and searching over two hundred people a day, resulting in those eighty-two arrests, could be construed as gross misuse of power. A very important thing to know is that the law under which they were stopping the youths – the Vagrancy Act 1824 – was written more than 150 years ago at that time.

To put that into context, the law was in existence fifty-nine years before the abolition of slavery (Slavery Abolition Act 1833). So not only were the police misusing power, they were also doing it under the guise of a law that was written at the time when black people were slaves, with absolutely zero rights.

I was born three years after the Brixton Riots, so I was literally born in an era of mistrust of the police in London. Why then should

I change my mind about the police? Why should I and every black person in my age group not view the police as a racist, power-hungry institution, which only exists to make our life worse? And despite the ridiculousness of the stop-and-search laws being practically ancient, what sense is there in an angry mob attacking a police officer when a kid is lying there bleeding? Here, we can clearly see a gross misuse of power and neglect that significantly and negatively impacted members of the black community.

RODNEY KING RIOTS (LA RIOTS), 1992

Most black people are already familiar with the Rodney King story. In fact, pretty much every black comedian in the States during the golden age of black comedy (with acts such as Richard Pryor, Eddie Murphy and Martin Lawrence) have used the Rodney King story to highlight police brutality in their acts. For those not in the know, here are the Cliffs Notes: a black construction worker, Rodney King, was speeding on an American highway and despite being asked to stop by the chasing police, refused to do so. After a high-speed chase at eighty miles per hour, involving several police cars and a police helicopter, King was finally cornered and asked to surrender.

When he came out of the car, four police officers Tasered him and proceeded to beat him mercilessly with batons. Hospital reports showed that he suffered a fractured facial bone, a broken right ankle, and multiple bruises and lacerations. What caused the subsequent riots in Los Angeles was the fact that the four officers were acquitted of the charges of assault with a deadly weapon and use of excessive force.

Naturally, the acquittal spurred feelings of injustice among the black community. The resulting riot lasted over six days; involving widespread looting, assault, arson and murder; and resulted in over $1 billion worth of property damage. It was termed one of the largest riots seen in the United States and the worst in terms of death toll.

The black community at that time argued that this was the legacy of the police – one of brutality. Rodney King wasn't armed at the time of his arrest, he made no move to attack his captors and according to reliable reports, he was only a construction worker and not the Incredible Hulk,* so the excessive force that the police used to bring him in was unnecessary.

I was eight at the time of the Rodney King arrest. An age where realistically you start to understand the functions of the police and other emergency services providers. Imagine the impact that would have had on an eight-year-old black kid in America. What is a black parent supposed to say to their young kids in 1992, after seeing that on the TV? Which ethnic minority is going to feel comfortable calling on the police for help after witnessing that? Under what part of 'to serve and protect' does this fall under? Bearing in mind that the people who were young or old enough to partake in the riots are now parents; this is how the legacy of mistrust is passed on from generation to generation.

As a black man, it is often hard to see beyond the fact that an African American was beaten up indiscriminately by the police, but it is also important to put these reactions in context, and to look at the facts of these situations objectively. If we want to dispel this notion that the police's response to crime in the black community is inappropriate, we must also examine what could have caused the police to act in the first instance – not to justify their actions, but rather to critically examine their response and determine if it was race-related.

In the case of Rodney King, the mitigating circumstances that the police offered included:

1. King had been drinking and smoking weed before he got behind the wheel of the car.
2. King was speeding and continued to do so even after being asked by the police to stop.

---

* Can you even begin to imagine what the police would do to a black Hulk?

3. In addition, the severity of the chase called for multiple police cars and a goddamn police helicopter.

4. There were two other people in the car with him when the car was stopped, who were believed to have been arrested and taken into custody without incident.

5. Once the car was surrounded and officers asked King to come out of the car, he refused.

6. At the time of the incident, King was already on parole for a previous robbery conviction.

7. Two of the officers involved were eventually convicted by a grand jury and found guilty of 'wilfully and intentionally using unreasonable force' and sentenced to thirty-two months in prison.

These were the facts presented by the police (or as close to facts as one can get on a racially tense issue such as this). While these mitigating circumstances don't justify the actions of the officers, it is interesting that in all the cultural renditions of this incident, these factors are barely mentioned – the only prevalent fact was that police officers excessively beat up a black man. While stereotypes can have a tremendous negative impact, especially if based on wrong information, this can also be true in the instances of victimisation. If growing up, all a young black person learns about the Rodney King incident is the beating he received at the hands of the police (just as I did), it will most certainly have an impact on perceptions of the police.

When examining perceptions of the police in the black community, it is always important to heed the facts and not rely solely on stories that are woven to incite a reaction, or to discriminate against a group of people or organisation. I want to be able to trust law enforcement. I want to believe that they are a force for good. But growing up, I couldn't escape from the reality that these stories exist, because they were true. In almost every case of police brutality, they showed time and time again that there was a problem with institutionalised racism that affected people of colour – and black communities the worst.

But I was always relying on stories and retellings of what happened to people in my community. The first time that I truly delved into how the police treat people in my community was the Stephen Lawrence investigation.

STEPHEN LAWRENCE, 1993

The biggest example I can point to that underlines the scepticism of black people with the police in the UK is the Stephen Lawrence murder and its subsequent investigations. Eighteen-year-old Stephen Lawrence was murdered in April 1993 in an unprovoked attack by a gang of white youths, while waiting for a bus in Eltham, south-east London, with his friend, Duwayne Brooks. According to Duwayne, they had yelled 'nigger' at them and then attacked Stephen with a rounders bat, before stabbing him and running off laughing.

When the police arrived, Duwayne claimed that one of the officers threatened to handcuff him because he was 'getting hysterical'. He also said that another officer asked him if he or Stephen had a criminal record and then said, 'Are you sure they called you niggers?' I understand the need for the officers to take control of the situation and it's pretty damn hard to take a statement when someone is 'hysterical', but is it really necessary to threaten to handcuff someone who has not only narrowly escaped death, but witnessed his friend being stabbed? How calm did the police expect him to be? I'm no crime scene investigator, but I'm pretty sure that the dead body of the victim is enough to get the ball rolling on an investigation, rather than needing to confirm that there was indeed a racial slur uttered.

What followed is a series of investigations and trials that can only be accurately described as a continuous round of colossal racist fuck-ups, which prove unequivocally that not only was there an institutionalised racism problem, but the police sought actively to undermine the investigation. Here is an abridged timeline that helps put the resulting police investigations and subsequent trials into light:

1. Despite an anonymous letter naming the suspects and the presence of an eye-witness, it took the police about three weeks to arrest the suspects.

2. Despite Duwayne identifying the culprits in a police parade, his testimony was deemed unreliable because his father had died the night before, and so the charges against the suspects were dropped.

3. The Crown Prosecution Service refused to prosecute, so the Lawrence family had to bring a private prosecution.

4. In the subsequent trial, the judge instructed the jury to consider Duwayne's testimony inadmissible.

5. Finally, in 1997, the Kent Constabulary launched an inquiry into police conduct during the investigation and found that it had 'significant weaknesses, omissions and lost opportunities'.

6. In 1998, the Met Police Commissioner apologises to the Lawrence family, admitting there had been failures.

7. In 1999, the Macpherson Report, which looked into the investigation, was published, accusing the Met Police of institutional racism.

8. The CPS announced there wasn't sufficient evidence to prosecute anyone for Stephen's murder following a review.

9. In 2011, the Court of Appeal decided there was enough new and substantial evidence to allow one of the defendant's acquittal to be quashed and for a new trial to begin. The jury heard that Stephen's DNA was found on the defendants' clothes.

10. In 2012, the suspects were found guilty of murder.

11. In 2013, it was revealed that an undercover police officer worked within the Lawrence family's campaign for justice looking for 'disinformation' to use against the family and those criticising the police.

These are just a few examples, where we can see that there has been a historical problem with how the police deal with black people and crime in our community. So when we cry out and are hurting that there has been another case of police brutality, or murder of a black person, regardless of the facts of the case, it is because this is not new. We have been suffering from this pain for time immemorial and it is exacerbated when we are faced with the response that it is simply the police doing their job, or that we are playing the race card. There are clear examples that this is not the case and until we start to recognise and address this, our faith in the police force will remain shattered.

THE PREVALENCE OF HATE CRIME IN THE UK

Is it any wonder that this generation of black people have an inherent suspicion of the police? The investigation into the most famous black murder case of our generation was ultimately revealed to be institutionally racist. Inherent hate crimes are increasing in the UK – the Institute of Race Relations, which records deaths of a known or suspected racial element, found in its 2012 report that since the death of Stephen Lawrence in 1993, at least ninety-six people have died in such attacks. Of those, four were white and the rest were from black or other ethnic minorities.

This is supported by the Home Office's crime survey reported in the *Independent*, which shows that 278,000 hate crimes are committed a year and 154,000 had an element of racial motivation. Despite this, not only are the police not solving these crimes, they are not even reporting them as hate crimes in the first instance. Official police figures recorded only 42,236 hate crime offences in the past year and just 30,000 racially aggravated crimes – fifteen per cent of the total reported in the crime survey.

In 2016, the BBC wrote about a Freedom of Information report that suggested hate crimes increased by twenty per cent over the past year, to more than 60,000, yet police referrals to prosecutors fell by 1,379. Jon Burnett, a researcher at the Institute for Race Relations, believes that one of the reasons that the police don't label crimes as hate crimes is because there is a belief that it will be more difficult to get a conviction. So, we are having a significant increase in hate crime that is not being labelled as such, nor is it being reported to the Crown Prosecution Service. And this is without the added increase in hate crime since the 2016 Brexit Referendum. Additionally (and this should come as no shock considering the points made in this chapter), most black people don't trust the police and tend not to report a lot of crimes.

But are black communities completely blameless in this? After all, research from the Ministry of Justice in 2012 showed that of the ethnic minorities, black people commit the most homicides. The Met Police in the Home Affairs Committee report revealed that seventy-nine per cent of all suspects of gun crime were from the African/Caribbean community. That does beg the question, however – if black people are more likely to commit a certain crime, does that mean that they should be the first suspects? Is this a fair assessment?

As a black person, it's not that I care that much about being stopped and searched on suspicion of a crime that is mostly committed by black people. I would care more if I was the only one singled out from my group of white friends. Consider this, statistically white people are more likely to embezzle money than black people, but would a white person feel comfortable if only the white employees were questioned in the event of company fraud? Or because ninety per cent of child abuse offences are committed by white men, as reported by Fullfacts, does it mean that white men are the first to be questioned? Just because black people statistically commit more of a certain crime than another race, doesn't mean we are all inherently criminal.

Given all these observations, it's not unreasonable to understand that the way black communities feel about the police today has a lot to do with the way black people have been treated in the past. They say that the sins of the father are paid by the son and this seems to ring true for the black communities in the UK today. Indeed, it must be incredibly difficult for good police officers today to be shackled with the prejudices of years past. The core to good policing is trust of the community, and the police have a long way to go to build the trust of the black community; particularly when you look at the present relationship between black people and the police.

It's hard to look at the police and not think of them as the paradigm of good and justice. It is how they have been pitched to us, it's how we see them every day on our screens and in our media. But like any institution, they are not perfect. They suffer from the same biases and prejudice as individuals, and because they are in a position of great power, we need to examine their actions closely and dispel this idea that when we speak up against police brutality, we are playing a race card or a victim card.

As we can see, there are long and historic examples of the police actively targeting the black community and when we speak up against this, they have taken actions to discredit us, as happened in the Stephen Lawrence case. We need allies in this fight; we need the good men and women in the police force to stand up to their colleagues who perpetuate this bad behaviour, and we need allies in the white communities, who statistically face little to no bias from law enforcement.

A Pew Poll on race and inequality showed that half of white people surveyed don't believe black people are treated unfairly by police – this needs to change. Our voices grow ever louder and harder to ignore if we all sing from the same hymn sheet. In addition to this stereotype, there is also the notion that law enforcement action in our community is warranted, because of increased numbers of crime. This is certainly not the case and I will address this later in the book in Chapter Seven.

Answer to pop quiz: Black Britons are stopped and searched 40 times more than white Britons.

SEX
IS IT TRUE WHAT THEY SAY ABOUT BLACK GUYS?
YOU KNOW . . . DOWN THERE?

Stereotype/negative narrative: That all black men are well-endowed, which leads to the fetishisation of black men.

Pop quiz:

When and from whom was the stereotype of black men being well-endowed believed to have originated?

From sixteenth-century slave owners and trades

From twentieth-century KKK members

From twenty-first-century black men,
who were finally allowed in the porn industry

As a black man living in England, I've become accustomed to racism and stereotypes in varying degrees; ranging from the worst (fuck off back to Africa, nigger) to the completely benign and micro-aggressions (oh wow, you're so well spoken). But one of the infrequently spoken about stereotypes are the so called 'positive stereotypes'. These are the stereotypes that might be considered a compliment to the person saying them, but to the person on the receiving end, it is another stereotype used to generalise and cause harm.

In particular, I'm talking about the stereotype that black men are extremely well-endowed. I can't even recall the number of times someone (male and female) have insinuated or outright said that I (and all black men) have a huge penis. And they say it with the self-assured confidence of Clark Kent proclaiming that he's Superman. But here's the thing, when I ask them if they have ever slept with a black man, or seen a black man naked in real life, nine times out of ten the answer is no!

This is a continuous source of amazement to me; the fact that this stereotype is so prolific in the cultural zeitgeist that we have completely adopted it as truth, regardless of no evidence whatsoever. And I believe that one of the reasons why it has remained such a prevalent and preconceived notion is that it is considered a positive stereotype, which cannot possibly be harmful.

Me, drinking in a bar with three female, white friends looking at one's Tinder profile: 'Hey, what about this guy? It says in his profile he likes rock climbing. You went rock climbing once, right?'*

Friend 1: 'Ooh and he's black.'

Friend 2: 'You know what that means.'

Me: 'Er, you know that's just a stereotype.'

Friend 3: 'Totally swipe right.'

Friend 2: 'Hmmm, what if he's like . . . too big?'

---

* Yep, for men it really is that simple.

Me, continuing even though they're not paying attention to me at all: 'I mean, there have been no conclusive studies to suggest that black men are . . .'

Friend 1: 'Well, you've just got to do your muscle exercises before then. LOL.'

Friend 2: 'Hmmm, I don't know. I don't want him to like . . . ruin my vagina.'

Me (can they even hear me anymore?): 'Actually research has shown that when aroused, the vagina can expand up to two hundred per cent, so you really don't have to worry. Besides, just because he's black, doesn't mean . . .'

Friend 3: 'Hmmm, good point, better leave it then.'

Friend 1: 'Yeah, totes not worth it.'

Me: 'What?! You just prematurely rejected a guy because of some stupid stereotype that you don't know for certain is real?'

Friend 2: 'Come on, everyone knows black people are hung.'

Me, ever the voice of reason: 'Do they? Do they though? Do they actually know or just assume?'

Friend 1: 'It's common knowledge.'

Me, resigned: 'I'm definitely going to need another drink.'

WHY ARE WE ALL SO OBSESSED WITH SIZE?

So, do all black men have huge penises? There is an incredibly widespread and frankly unnecessary obsession with the male reproductive organ. In almost every myth, religion or tall tale, there is a reference to the might of the penis. From the Judeo-Christian focus on circumcision to the rampant dalliances of the Greco-Roman gods, the penis has a (rather unusual) part to play in our historical storytelling. In fact, you'd be hard pressed to walk away from a museum anywhere in the world without seeing a picture or sculpture of a penis.

A Bible story that has always concerned me is the one where David wanted to marry the daughter of a king, and as a dowry, the king demanded one hundred foreskins of his enemies.* What he wanted with one hundred foreskins is anyone's guess,† but I think we can all agree, that's a pretty fucking weird request. The power of penis obsession is, according to Freud, enough to make you want to kill one parent and have sex with the other.

Nowadays, the obsession is not so much with the penis, but with its size. And as with most things in life, the perception is that bigger is most definitely better. For men, no matter how lovingly our partners tell us that we are the best they ever had, there is always this imp at the back of our minds, constantly making us question the size of our manhood. In fact, early man was thought to have had spikes on his penis to anchor it to the vagina for efficient distribution of sperm – scientists believe that we evolved to have smooth penises as we started to adopt monogamous relationships.

As with all areas of sex, it's not just with humans that penis size is crucial. Pygmy chimpanzees engage in penis fencing – length being a huge advantage in this situation. The male garter snake has gone so far as to have two penises so that they can more effectively mate with a female using the one closer to the female at the time. The dolphin penis is not only retractable, but is also prehensile. In fact, even early man had spikes on his penis to anchor it to the vagina for efficient distribution of sperm – scientists believe that we evolved to have smooth penises as we started to adopt monogamous relationships.

But historically, why has penis size always been an issue? Well, ever since the late Mesozoic era about 250 million years ago, primate sex has always been based on the philosophy of a female choosing between rival males. Women can experience multiple orgasms and so it has been theorised by evolutionary anthropologists that women seek multiple partners to satisfy their sexual needs, and to meet the biological imperative to reproduce surviving offspring.

In layman's terms, the bigger the penis, the more likely it is to reach

---

* 1 Samuel 18:25.
† Perhaps to make a nice pashmina?

the G-spot and please a woman; as well as the better chance of your sperm making the journey to fertilise her egg. But this has led to men going to extreme lengths to try to increase the size of their penis. Indian mystics known as Sadhus have been known to stretch their penis from an early age by hanging weights on it, while the Topinama tribesmen of Brazil encourage poisonous snakes to bite their penises to enlarge it.

DOES BLACKER MEAN BIGGER?

A widely quoted study looking at average penis sizes by country was conducted in 2012 by Dr Richard Lynn, professor of psychology at Ulster University. The study seems to perpetuate the common stereotype when it comes to penis size, as African countries dominate the top twenty, and all of the bottom fifteen are from Asian countries. This is as much information I will share on that study, because it is completely bogus. The study has been discredited so much by the scientific community, it might as well have been written by Kim Kardashian.

One of Lynn's justifications in the differences between races in penis length is on the basis that European and Asian males have lower levels of testosterone than Africans. Evidence he discerned, by the way, from a much earlier study on the effects of hormones on rats. Not to mention the fact that he uses a lot of questionable sources – very few of whom are actually scientists.

In March 2015, the most conclusive study into penis size titled, 'Am I Normal', was published in the *British Journal of Urology*. It concluded that the average penis is 5.16 inches in length and 4.6 inches around when erect, and 3.6 inches long and 3.7 inches around when flaccid. The paper also conclusively notes, 'It is not possible from the present meta-analysis to draw any conclusions about any differences in penile size across different races.' The reality of the situation is that there is no, I repeat, no conclusive association between racial background and penis size.

There have been a couple of instances, however, where it could be inferred that certain races' penises might be bigger than others. In 2011, a South African court blocked its government from buying 11 million

Chinese condoms, because they found them to be too small. It should be noted that this wasn't the sole reason. The other two (and I'd wager more important) reasons were that they were made from the wrong material and were not approved by the World Health Organization.

Additionally, according to the Indian Council of Medical Research reported by the BBC, about sixty per cent of men have penises too small for the condoms produced by the WHO. Before Indian men start jumping off tall buildings in despair, you should know that the survey was conducted when the penises were flaccid.* There were considerable challenges in getting the subjects of the study excited for perfect size measures, and as anyone who has tried putting on a condom while flaccid can attest, it's a lot easier to disarm a nuclear device. Blindfolded. With one arm.

IMPACT OF PORNOGRAPHY ON THIS STEREOTYPE

Pornography also has a huge part to play in the perception that black men are bigger. Most pornography videos feature black men with almost exaggerated penis sizes; and this is very misleading, because many people (young men in particular) think pornography is an accurate representation of how sex or romance should be.

So, when they see predominantly black men with huge penises, they believe that is how it must be in real life. But the truth is that the men in porn are specifically selected because they are well-endowed, so yes, they are bigger than average – and black men even more so. This can be explained by a historic lack of diversity in porn. Black men typically weren't featured in pornography and even when they were, they were subject to roles of servitude (such as the servant or even slaves), or were objects of rebellious fantasy (storylines where white women would sleep with black men to feel dangerous, or rebel against their father's wishes).

In fact, interracial scenes are so rare that they are given their own

* Never has the saying 'grower not shower' been more important in India.

category at pornography industry award ceremonies. According to the Internet Adult Film Database reported in XO Jane online, black people account for only about twelve per cent of porn, compared to more than sixty-eight per cent of white people. So, in order for certain black men to break into an industry that wasn't readily accepting of them, they had to offer something different, i.e. a larger penis size.

If you are white and the only black penises you've ever seen are in porn, it is therefore not illogical for you to assume that all black men are as well-endowed as those in the pornography you watch.

TRICKING THE BRAIN

As there is no conclusive proof that black men are more endowed than other races, why does a majority of people believe it? Well, it all has to do with the way the brain works. The conscious human mind doesn't like uncertainty and when it is faced with something it doesn't know or understand, it guesses – by predicting and assuming based on previous information. This is called confabulation. So, the more you hear something (no matter how ludicrous it is), the more you start to believe it.

If someone is constantly being told that black men are well-endowed, and they slept with one or two black men who just so happened to be well-endowed (or at least bigger than anyone else they had slept with), there is a huge chance that they would accept it as the universal truth. Even if those black people hadn't been well-endowed, because they had heard it so often, it is likely that they would go ahead and assume that anyway.

This has been proven scientifically – whenever we think about something or hear it often, the brain creates new neural pathways and establishes it as fact, even if you initially knew it to be untrue. The psychologist, Elizabeth Loftus, managed to prove this when she convinced her adult subjects that they had got lost in a shopping mall at the age of five, even though they hadn't. In fact, the subjects started to add unprompted details to the false story all on their own.

And what if it was proven that black penises are bigger? Would it matter? In fact, most women don't consider size to be a deal breaker at all. A well-circulated study from 2007 by urologists Kevan R. Wylie and Ian Eardley found that forty-five per cent of men longed for a longer penis, and yet eighty-five per cent of their female partners had no complaints. In fact, given that vaginal sex almost always causes tears in the vaginal mucosa, especially in the posterior fourchette, women might prefer an average sized penis to a larger one for long-term partners.

Research published in the *Journal of Sexual Medicine* also shows that when provided with eight aspects of penis appearance (penile length, penile girth, position and shape of meatus, shape of glans, appearance of scrotum, shape of penile skin, appearance of pubic hair, and general cosmetic appearance), women found size to be only the sixth most important – general cosmetic appearance was found to be the most important thing. And while we're at it, according to the doctors at UCL and St Mary's hospital, there isn't a statistically significant relationship between one's height or foot length and penis measurement.

Penis size is just one of the many things that women are interested in when it comes to sex and it is men who are more concerned with penis length (and sex in general). For instance, analyses of Google searches by former quantitative analyst at Google and now contributor to the *New York Times*, Seth Stephens-Davidowitz, showed the following:

- Men Google more questions about their penis than any other body part: more than about their lungs, liver, feet, ears, nose, throat and brain combined.
- Men make more searches asking how to make their penises bigger than how to tune a guitar, make an omelette or change a tyre.
- Men's top Googled concern about steroids is whether taking them might make their penis smaller.
- Men's top Googled question relating to how their body or mind changes as they age is whether their penis gets smaller.

So really, it is all in our minds; the more you hear something and start to believe it, the more your brain will register it as fact, even though it sounds ridiculous. In truth, believing that all black men are well-endowed is as silly as believing all white men can fly. And frankly, commenting on this in public or when company is around doesn't always come across as a compliment – it can often make us feel uncomfortable and fetishised. And if you don't believe this way of thinking doesn't have origins in slavery, think again.

ORIGIN OF THIS STEREOTYPE AND WHY IT IS HARMFUL

It will come as no surprise to you that, like many others, this stereotype has its origins in slavery. Historians such as Herbert Samuels, professor at LaGuardia Community College in New York, report that this stereotype most likely became established from the sixteenth-century opinions of slave traders and owners. In order to discourage their wives and daughters from fraternising with the slaves, they painted this picture of black men being bestial, animalistic and hypersexual. During this period, we know that slavers regularly raped the enslaved – sex for them was expressed through rape – and so they cast the same aspersions on black men, to prevent them from having any sexual contact with white women at that time.

This 'positive' stereotype of the well-endowed black man was originally a ploy to justify slavery and oppression. They positioned black men as strong, athletic, muscular breeders (promoting the Mandingo stereotype) in order to fetch a better price at slave auctions, but when bought, then the narrative became: 'black men are animals with huge penises who cannot control themselves' and so, they had to be enslaved to protect powerless white women from rape. The historian, Philip Dray, supports this theory in his book, *At the Hands of Persons Unknown: The Lynching of Black America*, noting that the slavers couldn't grasp or tolerate the idea of a white woman wanting to have sex with a black man, so any physical relationship between a white woman and a black man had, by definition, to be an unwanted assault.

For the longest time, any black man found with a white woman was accused of rape. Black men were beaten, castrated and even lynched for so much as glancing at or greeting a white woman, as in the case of Emmett Till, who was kidnapped, tortured, and shot for whistling at a white woman – more on him in Chapter Ten. Slavers used the oversexualisation of black men as a means to continue using lynching as a punishment for any form of interaction between black men and white women. In the 1920s, white men still used this stereotype as a form of racial discrimination. In 1921–22, the United States House of Representatives and Senate debated the Dyer Bill, an anti-lynching bill. The Dyer Bill passed in the House of Representatives, but it was rejected in the Senate. Here's a statement from representative Sisson of Mississippi who fought against the bill: 'We are going to protect our girls and womenfolk from these black brutes. When these black fiends keep their hands off the throats of the women of the South, then lynching will stop'.

This stereotype even led to harmful pseudoscience, in which media professionals bought into this racial stereotype – then Baltimore doctor William Lee Howard noted in an article: 'When education will reduce the large size of the Negro's penis as well as bring about the sensitiveness of the terminal fibers which exist in the Caucasian, then will it also be able to prevent the African's birthright to sexual madness and excess.'

The idea of the hypersexualised black man was given further credence thanks to the media. For example, the 1915 silent movie called *Birth of a Nation* (originally called *The Clansman*) about the founding of the Ku Klux Klan, depicted a black character, Gus (played by a white man in black face) aggressively pursuing a white woman, who committed suicide by jumping to her death in order to avoid him. Gus is then tried and killed by members of the Ku Klux Klan, who are portrayed as the good guys of the movie. In our modern, post-slavery era, we still see the same blatant fetishisation of black men.

Another example is in *Hustler*, a pornographic magazine published in the US during the late 1980s. *Hustler* frequently reduced black men to caricatures of mindless animalistic creatures, whose sole purpose was to have sex with white women. Here are a couple of examples of cartoons in the magazines, as reported by Gail Dines in her article 'Gender, Race, and Class in Media':

- *Hustler*, July 1984, p. 23: A picture of Barbie dressed in black underwear, on her knees with ejaculate around her mouth, next to her is a black male doll pulling a very large penis out of her mouth.
- *Hustler*, November 1988, p. 100: A naked white woman is sitting on a bed, legs open, and her vagina has red stars around it, suggesting pain. Also sitting on the bed is a dark, ape-like man with a huge erect penis.
- *Hustler*, December 1988, p. 32: A large black male is looking at his new-born son and screaming at the white nurse, 'Never mind how much he weighs, bitch! How long's my boy's dick?'
- *Hustler*, February 1989, p. 95: A black and white man are walking next to a fence with the white man making a noise by dragging a stick along the fence. The black man is doing the same, only he is using his large penis, which is much bigger than the stick. The black male, who is walking behind the white man, is laughing at the white male's stick.

Why this stereotype is harmful is evident enough, and if you think that it is simply an outdated notion (after all, the examples above are from a racy magazine in the 1980s) and no one believes the racial elements of it now, let me remind you that in 2016, the Governor of Maine in the US said this in a town hall meeting about drug dealers: 'Now the traffickers . . . these are guys with the name D-Money, Smoothie, Shifty, these types of guys. They come from Connecticut and New York, they come up here, they sell their heroin, and they go back home. Incidentally, half the time they impregnate a young, white girl before they leave.'

If that is not evidence enough that this stereotype has permeated to modern times, before the terrorist, Dylann Roof, shot and killed nine people in 2015 at the historical black church, Emanuel African Methodist Episcopal Church, in Charleston, South Carolina, he reportedly said: 'You rape our women, and you're taking over our country, and you have to go . . . Well, I had to do it because somebody had to do something because, you know, black people are killing white people every day on the streets, and they rape white women, a hundred white women a day.'

So you see, stereotypes reinforce human biases and ultimately our behaviour. This stereotype – aside from having roots in slavery and racism – reinforces the notion that black men are hyper-sexualised and dangerous, whether you mean it or not.

THE SEXUALISATION OF BLACK WOMEN

Despite not being the focus of this stereotype, it will be remiss to not mention the fact that black women have also been victims of gross sexualisation. The way we as society sexualise women in general is a massive problem, but very few races have been put through the ringer more than black women. One of the earliest clear examples is that of Sarah Baartman, the European 'freak-show' act, Hottentot Venus. She regularly attracted a huge crowd in 1810 because of her dark skin and significantly large bottom. Even after she died in 1815, her brain, skeleton, and genitals were put on display until 1974, and her remains were finally taken back to South Africa in 2002.

LOVE and BEAUTY – SARTJEE the HOTTENTOT VENUS.

Baartman was used as a sexual tool for the amusement of Europeans – she was a human being! – and a vulnerable one at that. She was brought to Europe under false pretences by a British doctor, and her large bottom was as a result of a disease called steatopygia, which caused a build-up of fat in her bottom.

As in the case of black men, during slavery, black women were perceived as promiscuous and hypersexualised. This was how the slavers could justify raping black women and yet keep their illusions of racial superiority –

because black women being so desperate to have sex was a much better explanation than rape, or the fact that the slavers were simply attracted to them. And this isn't just a thing of the past, today black women are more likely to be sexually harassed in the workplace. A study published in the Gender, Work & Organization journal found that black women experience an increased risk of sexual harassment, even as overall reported harassment claims are down.

Black women had no protection under the law, as the existing laws at that time protecting women from rape didn't apply to black women. In fact, when cases of sexual relations between black women and white men were brought to the courts, black women were perceived to have seduced the slavers and were subjected to harsher punishment. Another way in which the law benefited the raping slavers was that it decreed that the free or enslaved status of a child was to be determined by the mother. This meant that a slave owner could rape a black woman, and then get the additional 'benefit' of more free labour when the child came of age, as they would not be considered a free citizen.

We also see evidence of this today, where black women are often presented as overly sexualised in music videos, or as 'hos' or 'baby mamas', who have children by multiple fathers. The reality is that black women have and continue to be sought after for their presumed hypersexuality. There are countless articles about the provocativeness of Rihanna's choice of clothing, but no comparative articles when it comes to other white female artists such as Lady Gaga, Miley Cyrus, or Ke$ha, who are also known to dress similarly 'provocative'.

For example, look at images online of the outfit Rihanna wore in her music video 'Work' and notice how differently she is described by the media compared to when Bella Hadid wore the same dress. Hadid is referred to as 'edgy', while Rihanna is 'almost naked'.

Or when Kylie Jenner wore dreads, *Fashion Police* host Giuliana Rancic called them 'edgy', but when biracial actress Zendaya rocked dreadlocks, Rancic said they made her look as though she smelled of 'weed or patchouli oil'.

To be perfectly clear, this does not mean if you are white or another race other than black, you can't find black men or women attractive; that would be a ridiculous notion and one I will address in Chapter Ten on interracial dating. What it does mean is that we have to acknowledge the racist origins of the fetishisation of black people and the harm it can cause. We know there is a difference between fantasy and fetish, and that the fantasy of the well-endowed black man exists. We also know that the intentions behind it aren't always malicious, but most times, we just don't want to hear it, because it comes across as more of a fetishisation than a fantasy.

We don't want to have to adhere to someone's fetish about what a black man should be. Black masculinity is often viewed as masculinity on steroids – we are expected to be big, fast, and strong – very often in contrast to how as black men we see ourselves. Well, we are human, and can live quite happily without some outdated view of how we should present ourselves sexually, thank you very much.

Answer to pop quiz: The stereotype that black men are all well-endowed is believed to have originated from the sixteenth-century opinions of slave traders and owners.

FOOD
ALL BLACK PEOPLE LOVE CHICKEN
AND WATERMELON

Stereotype/negative narrative: That all black people love chicken and watermelon.

Pop quiz:

Which popular institution in the States today still uses the melody of a song titled, 'Nigger Love a Watermelon Ha! Ha! Ha!'?

KFC

Roscoe's Chicken n Waffles

Ice Cream trucks

Oxtail with rice. Curry goat, rice and peas, and plantain. Fried catfish. Pounded yam. Jerk chicken. Signature dishes of the Afro-Caribbean community. These meals that seem exotic to other ethnicities, and they would have to go out to restaurants to eat, were meals that we had every day growing up in a black household. And let's not forget the holy grail of African food: *Jollof Rice*. God's own dish. For the those who don't know, the closest you can come to jollof rice are Spain's Paella, Louisiana's Jambalaya, or Charleston's Red Rice; you can even venture as far as Asia to savour the perfect Biryani – but never will anything compare to the mixture of rice, tomatoes, spices, and meat that come together in perfect harmony to make jollof rice. Jollof rice is so good, there is even a friendly rivalry between Nigerians and Ghanaians as to who makes the better jollof rice dish, culminating in the friendly 'Jollof Wars'.

In the United States, 'soul food' is the common term for African-American cuisine, traditionally prepared and eaten by the black community in the southern United States. Soul food originated during slavery, where black slaves were given the undesirable cuts of meat (known as chitterlings), or the leftovers of their masters; essentially, they had to make do with whatever food was available to them. For centuries after the abolition of slavery, many African-Americans continued to make use of these ingredients and recipes to feed their families and communities, and it became a staple of their culture.

This style of cooking and food became prominent in the South because it hosted the two major ports of entry for African slaves: the Chesapeake Bay and Charleston, in South Carolina. Although there is no conclusive proof as to the origins of the term 'soul food', it is believed to have originated in the mid-1960s, when 'soul' was a word commonly used to describe Black and African-American culture. As terms like 'soul brother', 'soul sister' and 'soul music' started to become popular, the word was also used to describe the food that African-Americans had been cooking for generations.

It is believed that the term was first used in 1962 by civil rights activist and poet, Amiri Baraka, in his essay, entitled 'Soul Food', where he argued that African-Americans have their own language and style of cuisine. Given its origins in the South, it's no surprise that most soul food is from ingredients that are commonplace in the South – beans, greens, black-eyed peas, okra, cornbread, grits, sweet potato pie, chicken, and pork.

RACIAL ORIGIN OF BLACK DIETARY STEREOTYPES

Given the ingenuity and diversity of Afro-Caribbean cooking and food, why is there a persistent stereotype that black people love fried chicken? After all, it isn't the most consistent dish among all food within the black community, so why has chicken become the staple of the stereotype – and a persistent one no less? From as far back as 1898 when slavery in the United States was abolished, the racist establishment, who were angered at losing their slaves, were eager to keep the status quo.

Although they did that primarily by segregation, they also embarked on a propaganda campaign by producing an ongoing series of anti-black imagery – depicting black people through Jim Crow and Coon imagery as unintelligent, savage, and obsessed with eating fried chicken, as evidenced by these images.

It is widely believed that this stereotype really took hold in the modern age because of the movie *Birth of a Nation*, which we looked at in Chapter Four. One scene in the movie shows black elected officials (played by white actors in blackface) acting rowdy and irresponsibly in a legislative hall, with one of the black officials enthusiastically tucking in to fried chicken.

According to Claire Schmidt, a professor at the University of Missouri who studies race and folklore, in an interview with NPR: 'That image really solidified the way white people thought of black people and fried chicken.' She also claimed that the love for fried chicken was a good vehicle for racism, because of the way people eat it: 'It's a food you eat with your hands, and therefore it's dirty. Table manners are a way of determining who is worthy of respect or not

. . . it's still a way to express racial contempt without getting into serious trouble.'

Enslaving black people had been a huge source of revenue and economic power for the pro-slavery establishment, but as this had been taken away from them, they needed to reinforce the notion that black people were uncivilised and savage (and therefore worthy of nothing but enslavement) to somehow re-establish slavery and their revenue stream. When it became clear that slavery was not going to be legitimised again, they used the negative notions and anti-black imagery of black people to profit in other ways.

For example, starting in 1925, a restaurant chain called the Coon Chicken Inn flourished for almost twenty years, with locations in Utah, Seattle, and Oregon. The chicken joint's motif consisted of a racist 'coon head' that served as the entrance to each one. The restaurants were staffed by black waiters, who served a predominantly white clientele in a room filled with the chain's hallmark logo. Essentially, black people had to serve white people, with an effigy of a black face with huge red lips, a bellhop's hat, and over-exaggerated features portraying African-Americans as mere cartoon characters, not humans.

Another enduring dietary stereotype directed towards black people is our supposed love for watermelon. Much as with chicken, there doesn't seem to be one particular instance from which this stereotype originated. Prevailing theories include the fact that it was one of the few fruits accessible to slaves in the South and that it was easy to grow. Another is that it is a good and affordable source of nutrition and hydration for slaves working in the fields, who didn't have ready access to water.

But interestingly, we can draw a connection between the popularity of watermelon among black people and the racist origins of the stereotype. After the slaves were emancipated, they started growing (due to its ease) and selling watermelons as a means of economic freedom. However, this was seen as a threat to white people during the Jim Crow era and so much like with chicken, they decided to turn the fruit into a symbol of poverty and poor manners (much like chicken, watermelons are eaten by hand, without cutlery, making it near impossible to eat without making a mess). White people would distribute propaganda and postcards showing black people stealing or fighting over watermelons. This was so ingrained in white people's belief that some of them even stopped eating watermelons. When a white family in Houston's black nanny was freed due to emancipation in 1865, their son, Henry Evans was devastated for he had come to think of the nanny, Clara as a second mother. But when he bumped into her on the street one day and she offered him some watermelon, Henry told her that 'he would not eat what free negroes ate.'

And so, we see evidence of the watermelon stereotype originating from the anti-black propaganda in post-slavery America, with minstrel shows also depicting the watermelon-loving black man. For example, one minstrel song recorded by Harry C. Browne in 1916, titled, 'Nigger Loves a Watermelon, Ha Ha Ha!'* proclaimed there was 'nothing like

---

* Bloody Hell, Harry. That's a bit on the nose, don't you think? Also, the Ha Ha Ha is just overkill. You dick.

a watermelon for the hungry coon'. Interestingly, the melody has become commonplace in America today; most Americans or fans of ice cream would recognise it, for it's the song that most ice cream trucks have played for decades to attract neighbourhood children – 'Turkey in the Straw'.

Interestingly, the first derogatory movie portraying African-Americans' love for watermelon came before *Birth of a Nation*, with Thomas Edison's 1896 production of the silent movie, *Watermelon Eating Contest*. The eighteen-second video depicts black men having a competition over who can eat a watermelon the fastest; and as they eagerly tuck in, they eventually start to sabotage the efforts of each other by pulling the fruit away from their competitors' mouths.

After the video was circulated by Thomas Edison, this stereotype became prominent in society alongside other Jim Crow and Coon propaganda that were being disseminated at the time; postcards, greeting cards, and even nursery books would depict black children grinning from ear to ear with a huge slice of watermelon in their mouths. This continued into the 20th century with Edwin S. Porter's

(famous for directing The Great Train Robbery) 1903 movie, The Watermelon Patch, which featured 'darkies' sneaking into a watermelon patch, men dressed as skeletons chasing away the watermelon thieves (à la the Ku Klux Klan, who dressed as ghosts to frighten blacks), a watermelon-eating contest, and a band of white vigilantes ultimately smoking the watermelon thieves out of a cabin.

The author St Claire Bourne discusses this in her book, *The African American Image in American Cinema*, suggesting that movies such as these helped fuel the idea that black people were childish by nature, unintelligent, and lazy, noting: 'If your goal is to prove that blacks should not have rights because they are inferior, you must warrant some proof of how they are inferior; which the Edison film did.' Unfortunately, like most of the other stereotypes that originated as a result of slavery, we are still seeing evidence of the stereotype that black people love chicken in today's media and society narrative:

A Korean fried chicken company, KyoChon, ran an advert in which it depicted a Korean man on an island kidnapped by black savages (dressed in grass skirts and with painted faces), who are about to cook him in a pot. Fortunately for the Korean man, he manages to conjure up fried chicken, which soothes and distracts the black savages and gives him enough time to escape his captors.*

Professional golfer Fuzzy Zoeller was quoted in an article about the black golfer Tiger Wood's historic victory at the 1997 Masters, which he won by twelve strokes: 'That little boy is driving well and he's putting well. He's doing everything it takes to win. So, you know what you guys do when he gets in here? You pat him on the back and say congratulations and enjoy it and tell him not to serve fried chicken next year. Got it? . . . Or collard greens, or whatever the hell they serve.'

This wasn't the only chicken-related comment directed at Tiger Woods. Another golfer, Sergio Garcia, who had a professional feud

---

* Which makes absolutely no sense. If I were a savage who somehow managed to get hold of a magical Korean who could conjure up fried chicken, that guy's never going free.

with Tiger, had said, 'We will have him round every night. We will serve fried chicken.'

In 2014, the *Boston Herald* and its cartoonist had to apologise for a cartoon that depicted an intruder into the White House sitting in President Obama's bathtub, asking him if he has tried the watermelon-flavoured toothpaste.

A private girls' school in Northern California apologised after serving fried chicken and watermelon to its students to celebrate Black History Month.

In early 2017, a Nevada ranch owner, Madeleine Pickens, hired an African-American chef to cook 'black people food' – not 'white people food' – according to a federal lawsuit accusing her of racial discrimination. The chef claimed that he was told to cook fried chicken, BBQ ribs and corn bread, as it would be perfect for the guests wanting to experience 'black food'. Ms Pickens' lawyers have said that even if the allegations were true, none of her comments were racially motivated and that at the very worst, Ms Pickens' remarks reflected 'a non-racial personality conflict' and amounted to discourtesy, rudeness or lack of sensitivity.

Also, in 2017, Andre Ferro, a Rhode Island firefighter, was fired for making racist remarks to an elderly black woman after responding to a medical call. The *Providence Journal* reports that Ferro was responding to a call to assist an elderly African-American woman suffering from consistent nosebleeds. While the other firefighters attended to the nose-bleed, Ferro made a comment, saying that the woman should 'stop eating fried chicken'; even though (according to the report), there was 'no fried food or fried food smell' in the apartment.

Even the BBC was accused of perpetuating stereotypes after publishing a video asking: 'Is it true all black people like chicken?' The video was released during Black History Month in 2016 and featured individuals of different races discussing a stereotype about black people eating fried chicken. In the video, a white man says, 'Loads of black people I know love chicken . . . there's a stereotype but it's true'; and two white girls claim that the black girls they know eat lots of chicken, because 'apparently it makes your bum bigger'.

In 2018, a Michigan bar owner and his staff reportedly gave a biracial employee a watermelon for Martin Luther King Jr. Day. After the employee's mom complained and raised this racist treatment on Facebook, the owner issued a statement claiming the 'gift' was a 'friendly joke'.

Perhaps one of the biggest indicators of this stereotype permeating today's cultural zeitgeist is its recognition in Urban Dictionary, the go-to online dictionary of slang words and phrases. One of its definitions of watermelon is that it is 'a food that white people who live in a 1%-or-less black neighbourhood think that black people like.'

Time and time again we are seeing that stereotypes heralded as 'only jokes' have their origins in slavery. While at first sight, you might be thinking, well, slavery is over, why is this still offensive – it is important to note that this helps to reinforce the racial stereotypes of that era and lump black people into a negative delineated box. As we can see from the example mentioned above, where the school in Northern California served chicken and watermelon for Black History Month. This type of food serves little to no purpose in further education on black history. Instead of using that opportunity to serve authentic African or Caribbean food, and broadening the students' horizons on how food played a significant part in African history, the school resorted to stupid stereotypes.

And to make matters worse, politicians and government officials buy into this stereotype, which inevitably leads to discrimination of black people. In 2019, the UK Home Office launched a chicken shop-focused anti-knife initiative, repackaging chicken takeaway boxes with messages of young people who successfully went '#knifefree'. The advertising agency, All City Media Solutions who advised the Government claimed that "never has there been an opportunity to target the ethnics" of which they identified 45% to be Afro-Caribbean and the others to be Asian and Middle Eastern. Chicken boxes were their solution – the assumption of course being that knife crime is committed by black people or 'ethnics' and of course we love chicken.

LAYING THE STEREOTYPE TO REST

There is absolutely no scientific, anthropological, or societal proof that black people love chicken any more than other races do. The reality of the situation is that chicken is tasty as fuck,* comparatively affordable compared to other meats, and is readily available across the world. According to Yuval Hariri's book on the history of mankind, *Sapiens*, there are more than 25 billion chickens in existence today, making the domesticated chicken the most widespread fowl ever. Another reason for the mass popularity of chicken is that it doesn't have the additional religious restrictions on it that other meats have, such as those from cows or pigs.

According to UC Davis professor and poultry expert, Dr Rodrigo Gallardo, there are a few reasons why the world is eating more chicken than ever. He notes: 'If you think about several years ago, most people ate beef or pork, because there was more availability and because it was cheaper. But chickens have become more attractive as options over time: they're lean, they've been bred over time to produce more meat, and raising them takes up much less land than raising cows or pigs.'

So, it is reasonable to assume that chicken is simply a meat or meal that is beloved by all races and creeds. And although statistics and research aren't needed to explain how ridiculous it is to assume that all black people love watermelon, data from the US Department of Agriculture reveals that African-Americans actually eat less watermelon than other races. It shows that white people eat it the most, and the largest consumers of watermelon per capita are Asians and Hispanics.

But given chicken's appeal and popularity worldwide, could there be any scientific explanations to the stereotype with black people? Current thinking suggests not. Tom Vanderbilt, author of *You May Also Like*, a book about our preferences in life, notes in an article in the *Atlantic*: 'There's no silver bullet theory for explaining anyone's taste. It's always a mixture of exposure, of culture, of a person's personality. And none of these are particularly static or fixed. The nice

---

* Shout out to Nandos. Cheeky or otherwise.

thing about tastes is that they are subject to change. We can kind of always be reinventing them and reinventing ourselves a little bit.'

Vanderbilt also discusses in this book the idea that taste is not congenital – meaning that we neither inherit it nor is it consistent. So, there is no logic to the stereotype that all black people would like fried chicken. A behavioural scientist at Cornell, Brian Wansink, conducted research which showed that people in our current society face around two hundred food decisions a day. The study also indicated that not only are we aware of a fraction of the food decisions we make, but we are also unaware of how our environment influences these decisions, or we are unwilling to acknowledge it. So, it is also scientifically impractical to suggest that an entire race likes one food out of two hundred.

There have been suggestions that the stereotype is about familiarity; we tend to like what we are used to. And if we are used to having chicken as a readily available option for meals, then that would be something we'd eat continuously. However, this is a fallacy, because if it were strictly true, nothing in food would ever change – people would eat the food they have always eaten, and there would be no evolution of black food over the years.

Vanderbilt does make an interesting point about repetition of food choices as an indicator of preference; as we tend to like things better when we become more familiar with them, whether it's a type of food, song, or even person. However, Vanderbilt points out that this applies to disliking food as well; noting how ridiculous it is for someone to say, 'I don't want Thai food, because I had some yesterday,' forgetting that people in Thailand eat Thai food every day.

SHOULD LOVE FOR CHICKEN JUST BE A HUMAN STEREOTYPE?

The fact that chicken is beloved across all races and creeds further highlights the fact that its negative association with black people is a racial stereotype, perpetuated by pro-slavery America. Fried chicken as a concept is something that has taken hold worldwide and is an increasingly booming industry. In the UK, chicken shops have evolved from simply being a place where you could get a cheap, greasy meal, into becoming as popular as the big fast-food franchises – and often a necessary stop on the way home after a messy night out.

Fried chicken is the fastest growing of all fast foods, representing four per cent of the UK's eating-out market, as well as a sector estimated to be worth £15bn–£20bn. Fried chicken retailers saw their sales grow by thirty-six per cent, compared with only twenty-two per cent in the whole fast-food sector. Americans are expected to eat about ninety-two pounds of chicken per person in a year, the most on record, according to the USDA – dwarfing the demand for beef and pork.

Of the one hundred biggest restaurant chains in the US, three of the five fastest-growing are chicken restaurants. The chicken sector has been the number one category in the fast-food business by purchase consideration, eclipsing the burger sector. Such is the popularity of fried chicken as one of the most marketable types of fast food, that chains are experimenting with adding more of it to the menu.

For instance, in 2017, Taco Bell, a Mexican restaurant chain in the US, launched its 'Naked Chicken Chalupa', which consisted of a tortilla shell made from fried chicken instead of the traditional corn or flour, as well as also testing out fried chicken chips. In 2016, Shake Shack, a US burgers and milkshakes joint, rolled out a fried chicken sandwich, which became one of its top sellers – spurring the company to add a barbecue version to the menu.

McDonald's expanded the test of its Chicken McGriddle breakfast sandwich and Arby's relaunched its fried chicken in 2016, with plans to add more chicken sandwiches to the menu in 2017 after seeing significant growth. In 2015, Burger King launched its Chicken Fries and McDonald's reintroduced Chicken Selects. Jack in the Box even added a fried chicken egg sandwich to its new 'brunchfast' menu.

But it's not just the business growth that demonstrates the love of fried chicken; chicken shops have transcended themselves to become a significant part of the local identity. In the UK, particularly in London, along with betting shops, pound shops and loan shops, they are one of the most recognisable features and symbols of the community – for instance, Morley's in south London, and Sam's in the north of the city. You can practically tell what side of the river someone is from based on their local chicken shop preference, be that a Morley's, Sam's, Chicken Cottage or Perfect Fried Chicken.

Additionally, it has become a recognisable staple of cultural zeitgeist in the UK. You can regularly hear shout-outs from grime artists, acknowledging their local chicken shops; from Stormzy's 'Big for your Boots' music video to Ray BLK's 'My Hood', which includes the line, 'Meet me at Morley's, best fried chicken is in South'. Grime artist Tinie Tempah can even be seen on Morley's Instagram page, helping to promote the business and its branded merchandise.

Perhaps most telling of its injection into the cultural zeitgeist is a YouTube series called 'The Pengest Munch' by Elijah* Quashie, a.k.a 'The Chicken Connoisseur', in which the twenty-five-year-old visits different fried chicken shops in north and south London and reviews the meals and their locations. Quashie's videos have been viewed millions of times on YouTube and garnered mass attention – to the point where he has been commissioned to present a TV show on Channel 4 called *The Peng Life*, in which he will sample food, fashion, and other items at the 'street' and 'elite' level, and decide which is best.

Chickens also have significant economic benefit, particularly for people in the poorer parts of the world. They are an incredible source of income and economic wealth for people in developing countries, because they tend to be relatively inexpensive and widely available. Bill and Melinda Gates, through their charity foundation, which focuses on philanthropy efforts in Africa, have been very vocal about the importance and benefits of chickens to developing countries.

Bill Gates explains in his blog that as little as five hens is enough to net a family in West Africa more than $1,000 a year (compared to the poverty line of about $700 a year). Additionally, he notes that chickens help keep children healthy. Malnutrition kills more than 3.1

* Yeah, yeah, I know.

million children a year and eating eggs, which are rich in protein, calcium, vitamin A and other nutrients, can help fight malnutrition. Such is the value of chickens to developing countries that they are known in international development circles as the 'ATM of the poor', because they are easy to sell on short notice to cover day-to-day expenses, according to his wife, Melinda Gates.

Not only is this beneficial in keeping poor families afloat financially, but it is also empowering for women. Melinda Gates explains in an article that in most developing countries, raising chickens is considered women's work, and the money from selling chickens and eggs belongs to women to spend as they choose. This is empowering, because evidence shows that when women control money, they are more likely than men to spend it on priorities that help to fight poverty, like education, health, and nutrition. In fact, when a woman controls the family's income, her children are twenty per cent more likely to live past the age of five.

So, ultimately, a lot of people like and eat chicken, and some happen to be black. And while it is easy for someone who isn't black to look at this fact and wonder why such an innocuous stereotype could cause so much offence, they need to understand that the nuance is in understanding that the problem stems from the way fried chicken is associated with black people, and the historical baggage that comes with it. The same way blackface recalls minstrel shows, the 'black people love fried chicken' image recalls negative portrayals of black people.

The fact that the negative narrative of black people loving fried chicken has had no positive effect on the community, unlike the corporations that benefit from its mass consumption (which are not owned by black people, by the way), only makes it hurt more. As Claire Schmidt notes in the aforementioned interview with NPR: 'How it's possible [for chicken] to be both a taboo and a corporate mainstream thing just shows how complicated race in America is.'

Answer to pop quiz: Ice cream trucks in the United States today still use the melody of a song titled, 'Nigger Love a Watermelon Ha! Ha! Ha!'

WORK

BUT I WORKED MY WAY UP FROM NOTHING; WHY CAN'T YOU?

Stereotype/negative narrative: That black people have got where they are due to affirmative action and positive diversity and inclusion initiatives.

Pop quiz:

On average in the UK, how much do black employees with degrees earn per hour compared to their white counterparts earning £18.63 for doing the same job?

£14.33

£10.75

£17.24

One of the best episodes of the critically acclaimed TV show, *Master of None*, by Aziz Ansari, is the 'Thanksgiving' episode in season two. Not just for depicting how difficult it is to be a minority within a minority (lesbian within a black household), but also for shining a detailed light on how our values, beliefs, and biases change over the course of different generations. The premise of the episode is that the protagonist, who is a lesbian, brings different dates to Thanksgiving dinner with her African-American family over the course of many years.

It's fascinating to see how each member reacts to the idea of a woman bringing home another woman to meet the family, as well as how those reactions are a product of their time. For example, the ridiculousness of the grandmother dismissing the dates as mere 'gal pals'* at first, or the pain and hurt that the god-fearing mother feels when she realises her daughter is gay, going as far as blaming herself for her daughter's sexuality. It's a thoroughly enjoyable episode and one of the most poignant representations of minority culture on TV today.

One of the lines in the episode that sticks with me as a black man is when the mother (played to perfection by Angela Bassett) explains to the young Indian male and young black female characters what being a minority means: 'Both of you are minorities . . . a group of people who have to work twice as hard in life to get half as far. And Denise, you're a black woman, so you're going to have to work three times as hard.'

I don't know of any black or BAME person who at some point in their lives has not been given some iteration of this speech by their parents or guardians. For most of us whose parents came to this country with literally nothing to their name, getting by was a perpetual struggle, let alone getting ahead. My mum and dad moved to England and Scotland respectively to study, because they wanted more from their lives than what was on offer in Nigeria. While they had perfectly good educations and lived reasonably happy lives, they were concerned with the economic and political situation there and desired a life with more stability.

---

* Because obviously, there were no lesbians in the 1940s – Duh!

When they came to the UK, they studied hard and took shitty jobs* to ensure they could make a comfortable life here and build a family. And this was the price they were willing to pay to ensure that my sister and I had a much easier time of things. Still, they never let us forget how difficult it was for them to forge a life here, and they explained to us that it was very likely to be difficult for us too, being black and children of immigrants.

The notion that we had to work twice as hard as white people was ingrained in us from day one, meaning that our parents held us to much higher and often unrealistic standards compared to white British kids. It was drummed into us more often than the Lord's Prayer and enforced ruthlessly: we had to excel in everything we did.

One year in secondary school, I got a 'B' in English. I was freaking the fuck out that my parents were going to be disappointed, or even worse, angry.[†] And I distinctly remember that one of my white friends, Mike, was so confused that I was upset at getting a 'B'. He told me that if he had got even a 'C', his parents would be overjoyed and if he got a 'B', they would have taken him out for a nice dinner.

Oh Mike, my sweet summer child. What do you know of fear? Fear is for the underachieving black children, whose parents don't tolerate anything but the very best. And sure enough, when I got home, instead of a well done, I got a 'you know you can't be a lawyer if you keep on getting "B"s in English'.[‡]

For most BAME parents, pushing their children to be better, smarter, and more driven than their white counterparts is based on the fundamental belief that this is the only way for children of colour to be successful in life. Have you ever wondered why most first-generation BAME children go on to study and eventually work in law, medicine, accounting, or engineering? Our parents push us into these

---

* Literally, most of our folks used to clean toilets. And I put it to you that there is no worse job than having to clean other people's shit.
† Black parents don't play that 'I'm not angry, I'm disappointed' shit. They get fucking angry, son.
‡ Yes, you fucking can! And you know how I know this? That friend who got a C . . . now a lawyer!

professions, because during their time – i.e. the 1950s and 1960s, which were during the height of economic expansion – becoming a doctor or a lawyer was the pinnacle of success for most black and minority communities. Even today in the States, research from New American Economy shows that African immigrants are more likely to have graduate degrees, with sixteen per cent having a master's degree, medical degree, law degree or doctorate, compared with eleven per cent of the US-born population.

I literally had another black person deduce that I was of Nigerian heritage simply because I told him that I had studied law. Essentially, educated and professional minorities were the celebrities of their time. Even today, the prospect of not wanting to pursue these traditional professions that are atypical to black communities is enough to give a black parent a coronary. Here's how the conversation went when I told my mother that I was quitting law for a career in Public Relations:

Me: '. . . so basically, I'm working all the time, I don't feel like I am really enjoying my twenties, and constantly listening to couples who want to get divorced is not great for me . . . mentally.'

My mum: 'What do you mean – you're working all the time? You're supposed to be working all the time. That's what a job is!'

Me: 'But it's not good for me mentally!'

Mum: 'Having a job is not good for you? *Omode yi o* serious!* Do you know how many people would love to have your job?'

Me: 'Loads probably, but it's just not good for me.'

Mum: 'But Seun's a lawyer and he isn't complaining.'†

Me: 'Yes, but Seun is an insufferable bore who wouldn't know the meaning of fun if it came up and slapped him in the face. You want me to be like that?'

---

* Translation: This boy can't be serious.

† In arguments, Nigerian parents will always reference another family member who's doing well or better than you. Your best bet is to get dirt on all your family members. Kill or be killed, baby!

Mum: 'I want you have a good job.'

Me: 'PR is a good profession!'

Mum: 'What is PR? I don't know anyone who does PR.'*

Me: 'Well then, it can't possibly be a good career then.'

Mum: 'Don't sass me boy! How can you not want to be a lawyer? It is one of the most respectable professions. How else would you be able to provide for a family? I've never heard of a professional PR person.'†

As much as I thought my mother was being unreasonable at the time, in truth, she just cares about me and wants me to do well in life.‡ Given the fact that she was one of eight siblings (not counting step and half-siblings, or the myriad of cousins that Nigerians seem to collect like Pokémon), she didn't have the upbringing she dreamed of: she always had to wear hand-me-down clothes, her toys were second-hand, and her options for a professional life were significantly limited.

Therefore, it was incredibly important to her that I ended up in a profession that would afford me choices and ensure that I wanted for very little in life. And because she didn't have evidence of there being anyone successful in PR (or had even heard of PR before then, come to think of it), she was naturally sceptical.

PROFESSIONAL INEQUALITY COMPARING WHITE AND BLACK PEOPLE

Today, is the lesson still relevant? Is my mother, along with other minority parents, right to be sceptical, or they are unfairly burdening the new generation with their baggage? The reality is that it is still harder for minorities to get ahead professionally and academically compared to their white counterparts. In almost all skilled professions,

---

* If there isn't another family member successfully doing something, then it doesn't exist.
† Clearly my mother wasn't a big fan of Samantha Jones from *Sex in the City*.
‡ Love you, ma.

there is a distinct inequality between white and BAME individuals, and that gap widens even further when you look at management positions in those professions. But what accounts for this inequality?

The first issue here is that there simply aren't enough BAME employees in professional, skilled roles. When you look at the comparative numbers objectively, it is easy to attribute this to a hiring problem and claim that they aren't getting enough BAME applicants for skilled professional roles. However, this notion does not reflect the Department of Work and Pensions' estimate that of the ethnic minority population aged sixteen to twenty-four, sixty-two per cent are eligible and in full-time education or work.

This is also mirrored by the eligibility of the black community in the United States; research from the Economic Policy Institute shows that black job seekers are even more resilient than their white counterparts, staying in the job market longer, despite persistent frustrations in their search for employment.

Another rationale that professional organisations offer for the lack of BAME employees is that if they had to focus on hiring BAME individuals (or had diversity quotas that they had to meet), they risked ignoring talent from white candidates, which would dilute the overall talent pool. But this notion presumes that talent is a zero-sum game; that talent and minorities are mutually exclusive – meaning they couldn't possibly find the right talent among BAME candidates. This excuse is more prevalent in the tech industry, which has staggeringly low diversity figures.

However, there has been research to debunk this myth of the lack of qualified black candidates: a study by *USA Today* showed that both black and Hispanic students are graduating with degrees in computer science and computer engineering at twice the rate that they're being hired by the top tech companies. Additionally, a study from the diversity programme at the National Institute of General Medical Sciences showed a significant increase in the number of black, Hispanic and American Indian students obtaining a PhD in scientific fields. This comes as no surprise, given the fact that the sciences (medicine, engineering, and so on) is one of the areas in which first-generation minorities are encouraged to study and excel.

So, given that the talent pool is available within the BAME community, why are they not being hired for professional roles? It is because businesses favour white candidates for these roles. This has become such a problem for BAME job applicants that they have taken to altering any information on their CV that indicates their ethnicity, a process known as 'whitening'.

A study from the University of Toronto Mississauga found that minority job applicants who resort to 'CV whitening' are more than twice as likely to receive a call-back than those who don't. It showed that while more than twenty-five per cent of CVs received call-backs if African-American candidates' names were 'whitened', only ten per cent received a call-back if they left their name and experience unaltered. For Asian applicants, twenty-one per cent heard back if they altered their CV, and only about eleven per cent of candidates did if their CVs were not 'whitened'.

Another study, this one conducted by professors at the University of Chicago and MIT, sent 5,000 fictitious CVs in response to help wanted ads. Each CV had identical qualifications except for one variation – some applicants had Anglo-sounding names, such as 'Brendan', while others had black-sounding names such as 'Jamal'. Applicants with Anglo-sounding names were fifty per cent more likely to get calls for interviews than their black-sounding counterparts.

This is also a problem in the UK. A study by experts based at the Centre for Social Investigation at Nuffield College, University of Oxford, found applicants from minority ethnic backgrounds had to send 80 per cent more applications to get a positive response from an employer than a white person of British origin.

These studies completely demolish the argument that there is not enough black talent coming through the pipeline and demonstrate that, instead, there is a preference for white candidates. The BBC online cites an IPPR report which notes that immigrants from certain ethnic backgrounds have (on average) had to make up to 150-per-cent more applications than a non-migrant to get a call-back from a job application. So, aside from a preference for white candidates, these studies also suggest the presence of a systemic racist perception against black and minority candidates.

A study by RHR International, a global firm of management psychologists and consultants, suggests that white leadership in business tends to view black workers as incompetent or overly aggressive, while Hispanic employees are often seen as uneducated and lacking ambition. The same study also shows that this accounts for delays in promotions of black employees. This notion of systemic racism is further demonstrated by studies showing that white men, fresh out of prison, were as likely to be called back for a second interview as black men who had no criminal history at all.

According to sociologist and Harvard professor, Devah Pager, in her book, *Marked: Race, Crime and Finding Work in an Era of Mass Incarceration*, 'Being black in America today is just about the same as having a felony conviction in terms of one's chances of finding a job.' These studies all affirm the conclusion that the system is institutionally racist – an important distinction from outright racism, because for starters, institutional racism is not illegal and just as important, it isn't clearly identifiable. For example, an HR manager can be brought in front of an employment tribunal if they have refused to hire a candidate because they are black (outright racism), but a company cannot face that same tribunal if they have deliberately had an incredibly low number of black employees (institutional racism).

The lack of significant black and minority hiring during recruitment eventually snowballs into a bigger problem, because if there isn't a healthy pipeline of black or minority talent coming into the company, there are very few minority employees to recommend other minority candidates for roles within the organisation.

In pretty much every professional job I've had, the majority of new hires have come from existing employees recommending friends, family members, and previous colleagues. If this percentage is more or less the same across all professional roles, it skews the numbers in favour of white candidates, because fewer minority employees will mean there are likely to be fewer recommendations for black candidates.

For instance, according to the Public Religion Research Institute, white Americans have ninety-one times as many white friends as black friends, and three-quarters of white people have entirely white social networks without any minority presence. So, if a majority of the current employees are white and don't know any people of colour, then they can't possibly have any minority person to recommend. Additionally, if an organisation or a business is not diverse, then it is virtually impossible for them to reach out genuinely to an ethnic community of which they are not a part.

Minority candidates want to see people who look like them, or are from the same culture, represented in the company that they are being approached to work for, and if companies can't produce diverse leaders or employees who have been successful in their company, then the candidates are more likely to seek employment elsewhere.

If the first major problem is that there aren't enough black (and minority) employees in professional, skilled roles, the second is the discrimination faced by those that make it into the roles. Firstly, research has shown that employees of colour are statistically paid less by a considerable margin. The American Institute for Economic Research reports in a *USA Today* article that black employees earn $3,656 less than white employees and Asians make $8,146 less.

In the UK, the Equality and Human Rights Commission revealed that overall, people from an ethnic minority background earn on average nearly six per cent less than white people. When it comes to black employees specifically, the Trades Union Congress showed that black employees with degrees earned an average of £14.33 per hour, while their white equivalents earned an average of £18.63 for the same amount of work. And this is not only limited to the West; a study reported in Okay Africa online revealed that in South Africa, despite accounting for over eighty per cent of the country's population, black South Africans earn five times less than their white counterparts, who constitute only eight per cent of the population.

Imagine how despondent you'd feel if you finally managed to squeeze into a job where you were part of a smart minority, only to find out that on average you were paid less than other members of your team for doing the same work. And that's not all – despite the comparatively low compensation, minorities in the workplace are also frequent victims of bias and abuse. A report from the charity Business in the Community found that thirty per cent of black, Asian or ethnic minority workers have witnessed, or experienced, racial harassment in the workplace in the past year alone.

If you are not a minority, or work in a liberal company or environment, you might be forgiven for thinking that these numbers are suspiciously high, but it is important to remember that not every instance of discrimination is blatantly obvious, or even reported. Some of them might come in forms of 'microaggressions', a word used to describe the casual, everyday slights and insults that serve to remind minorities they are different from the majority.

This could take the form of asking someone of a different ethnicity where they're 'really from', after they've said they were born and raised in Manchester (as discussed in Chapter One), or putting on an (exaggerated) accent when mimicking someone, or even expressing surprise that a colleague from a different ethnic background is so fluent in English.

Now I know that these might seem fairly innocuous and a number of readers might be thinking, where's the line, are we no longer allowed to make jokes in the office? Of course, jokes between friends and colleagues are obviously okay, but it is also equally important to understand and check your privilege to realise how your actions may make someone feel who hasn't had the same advantages in life as you.

It is also vital to recognise your unconscious bias – the little snap judgements and unfair conclusions your brain makes without you even realising it. Everyone has unconscious or implicit biases, which are influenced by our background, culture, and personal experiences. While we may not be aware of these views and opinions, we need to understand how they impact our decisions and translate to comments about friends and colleagues.

As hard as it is to be a black or minority man in the workplace; it pales in comparison to what it's like being a black or minority woman. Women (of all races) are at a disadvantage in the workplace, because they are constantly having to prove that they are just as good as men; they have to walk the fine line between not seeming too feminine, so as not to be considered incompetent, but then not too masculine so as not to be disliked (or called bitchy or bossy). At the same time, they have to deal with the 'motherhood issue' – the perception that they are not as committed to their jobs compared to men when they have children.

These are all nightmare scenarios for women that are amplified if directed at a woman of colour. According to a report by the United States' National Partnership for Women and Families, black women's wages range from forty-eight to sixty-nine cents for every dollar paid to white men. One in four black women live in poverty, a rate more than double white women's poverty. Additionally, it would take nearly two black women college graduates to earn what the average white male college graduate earns by himself ($55,804 vs. $100,620).

The tech/science industry is a good indicator of the bias faced by women – a report, *Double Jeopardy: Gender Bias Against Women of Color in Science*, found that one hundred per cent of the scientists interviewed reported experiencing bias and discrimination. And this was to the extent where African-American and Latina scientists said they were routinely mistaken for janitors. To the point above regarding competency, more than three-quarters of the African-American women scientists surveyed reported having repeatedly to provide further evidence of their competence for their roles.

Another huge problem for the black employees is that even if you manage to clear the hurdles of getting a job and a fair wage, the chances of you succeeding to a leadership role in your job are extremely low, given current figures. In 2016, an independent review into the ethnic diversity of UK boards found that out of 1,087 director positions in the FTSE 100, only eight per cent of positions are held by directors of colour, of which only one-and-a-half per cent are from the UK.

The review also found that only seven companies account for over one-third of directors of colour in the FTSE 100, while fifty-three of the FTSE 100 do not have any directors of colour at all.

The numbers are distressing, and this is a huge problem for the UK. Ethnic minorities make up around fourteen per cent of the total UK population and yet nowhere near similar representation can be found in positions of leadership. There is also a similar situation in leadership positions in the United States. As of 2016, there have been only fifteen black CEOs in the history of the Fortune 500, of whom five are currently in the role (with Ursula Burns, CEO of Xerox as the only woman).

According to a corporate diversity survey reported in *Fortune* magazine online, black men and women account for only about five per cent of executive team members in the Fortune 500 and hold an estimate of almost seven per cent of the nation's 16.2 million management jobs in smaller companies, even though they make up twice that share of the population at large. And just as expected, the issue is much more prevalent for black women.

The Center of American Progress, as reported in *USA Today* reviewed that the percentage of white women moved into upper-positions at work were around thirty-five per cent compared to a mere nineteen per cent of black women. Incidentally, it reported thirty-five per cent of Latina women in leadership positions – so even within minorities, it seems that black women are drawing the short straw.

The direness of this situation is summed up in a quote from Ronald C. Parker, president and CEO of the Executive Leadership Council, in a report looking at diversity in leadership: 'Almost seventy per cent of board seats in the Fortune 500 are still held by Caucasian/white men, and at the current rate of progress, we won't likely see the number of women and minorities increase to ABD's target of forty-per-cent board representation until the year 2026.'

And this lack of black employees in leadership roles isn't just prevalent in the professional industry, it is also a significant problem in the academic space. According to figures released by the Higher Education

Statistics Agency, no black academics have worked in senior management in any British university since 2014. Among the 535 senior officials who declared their ethnicity, 510 were white, fifteen were Asian, and ten were recorded as 'other including mixed'. Overall, universities employed around 158,000 white people as academics compared to just 3,205 black people. A 2018 study by the Royal Historical Society recently found fewer than one in a hundred history professors working in the UK today is from a black background, while ninety-four per cent are from a white background. And when the BBC sent a Freedom of Information request to twenty-four research-based universities, it found that black and Arab academics at the UK's top universities earn an average twenty-six per cent less than white colleagues.

In the light of such overwhelming evidence about the disparity of black talent in professional and leadership roles, you'd think that professional and academic institutions would act to redress this issue. After all, there is overwhelming research which proves that diverse businesses are the most profitable: McKinsey reports that companies in the top quartile for racial and ethnic diversity are thirty-five per cent more likely to outperform their respective national industry averages.

However, much like the preconceived notions that there is limited black talent overall, or to focus on black talent would dilute the overall talent pool, there is one main discriminatory and racist notion centred on the black community that we need to address, to ensure that there is a future for black talent in professional and academic skilled roles. And this is the prevailing narrative that black people just aren't as smart as white people.

ARE WHITE PEOPLE SMARTER THAN BLACK PEOPLE?

Throughout the history of psychology, one of the most persistent questions is what impact, if any, does race have on cognitive ability. And for as far back as we can look, scientists and researchers have cast black people as cognitively inferior to white people. *The Brief History of Modern Psychology* reports that in 1912, psychology graduate Frank

Bruner characterised black people in a psychological bulletin as: 'lacked filial affection, strong migratory instincts and tendencies; little sense of veneration, integrity or honor; shiftless, indolent, untidy, improvident, extravagant, lazy, lacking in persistence and initiative and unwilling to work continuously at details. Indeed, experience with the Negro in classrooms indicates that it is impossible to get the child to do anything with continued accuracy, and similarly in industrial pursuits, the Negro shows a woeful lack of power of sustained activity and constructive conduct.'*

While you might excuse those conclusions as a product of a 'different time',† this was still a prevailing belief as late as the early 90s: the controversial book, *The Bell Curve*, by psychologist Richard J. Hernnstein and political scientist Charles Murray, published in 1994, suggested that the average IQ for African Americans was lower than those for Latino, White, Asian, and Jewish Americans. And as recent as 2007, James D. Watson, a Nobel laureate in biology, was quoted in an interview to the *Sunday Times* magazine, stating that he was 'inherently gloomy about the prospect of Africa, because all our social policies are based on the fact that their intelligence is the same as ours – whereas all the testing says not really.'

Now these individuals are not rubes; they are incredibly smart people, who sought to show through research and study that there is a genetic difference between races when it comes to intelligence – which ultimately puts black people at a disadvantage today. Having said all that, it's important to remember that these books and research have been heavily criticised by both peers of their time and even more recently. For instance, columnist Bob Herbert described *The Bell Curve* in the *New York Times* as 'a scabrous piece of racial pornography masquerading as serious scholarship . . . It's an ugly stunt. Mr Murray can protest all he wants; his book is just a genteel way of calling somebody a nigger.'

* Well, fuck you too, buddy.
† Lord knows, we do for everything else.

It is also worth noting that even the research seeming to suggest that white people are smarter than black people states that the notion is not conclusive. In chapter thirteen of *The Bell Curve*, the authors note that: 'If the reader is now convinced that either the genetic or environmental explanation has won out to the exclusion of the other, we have not done a sufficiently good job of presenting one side or the other. It seems highly likely to us that *both* genes and the environment have something to do with racial differences,' as well as stating, 'The debate about whether and how much genes and environment have to do with ethnic differences remains unresolved.'

In truth, there is no conclusive research to prove that intelligence has any significant correlation with race, ethnicity, or gender for that matter. We know more about genetics and our biases towards race today than we ever have done and we've discussed in Chapter One how race is nothing more than a social construct, and how biologically we are more similar than we are different. So surely any differences in IQ would be because of social issues, rather than biological or genetic.

This is no surprise really; particularly given the history and treatment of black people in the West – enslaved for centuries, deprived of basic human and civil rights, made to live in segregation and abject poverty, deprived of education, victimised by law enforcement, and generally treated as second-class citizens – so, it's no wonder at all that we do not measure up on a social scale. As such, the negative narrative around black people and intelligence seems to be a 'self-reinforcing cycle of cause and effect', according to Yuval Noah Harari in his book, *Sapiens*. He uses African Americans in the southern United States as an example for this theory, noting: 'After the Civil War, in 1865, the 13th Amendment to the Constitution of the United States outlawed slavery and the 14th Amendment mandated citizenship and equal protection under the law regardless of race. However, after two centuries of slavery, black families were poorer and far less educated than white families. As such, a black person born in Alabama in 1865 had much less chance of getting a good education and a well-paid job than did his white neighbours. Similarly, his children, born in the 1880s and 1890s, started life with the same disadvantage – they too were born into a poor uneducated family.'

So, at that time, it was taken as fact that black people were less intelligent (not to mention, more violent prone); and as time went by, these prejudices became more entrenched. Since all the best jobs were held by white people, it became easier to believe that black people really were less intelligent. He claims that an average white citizen would hold a view such as: 'Blacks have been free for generations, yet there are no black professors, bankers, or tellers. Isn't this proof that blacks are simply less intelligent and hard-working?'

Trapped in this circle, black people were less likely to be hired for skilled jobs, because they were deemed less intelligent, all the while basing proof of this inferiority on the fact that there was a lack of black people in white-collar jobs. Evidence of this could be found in the case of Clennon King, a black student who applied to the University of Mississippi in 1958 and was forcefully committed to a mental asylum – with the presiding judge ruling that a black person must be surely insane to think they could be admitted to the University of Mississippi (incidentally, he was also the first African-American man to run for the office of President of the United States).*

Ultimately, what characterised the differences between black and white people is not a difference in work ethic or intelligence, but historical social, political, and economic systems engineered to place one on top of the other. We can see evidence of this 'vicious circle' still evident in our societies today. One of the most decisive events of our time that impacted race relations was the presidential campaign of Donald Trump. Given that Americans had just had their first African-American president, and Trump's campaign was controversial when it came to race relations, it was a perfect time to study the attitude of voters towards race relations.

The American National Elections Study (ANES) survey, reported

* Damn, this brother just doesn't quit!

in the *Salon*, provided a unique opportunity to examine the attitudes of voters, because it was completed before Trump had won the Republican nomination. Within the survey, there was a question addressed only to white people, asking, 'How likely is it that many whites are unable to find a job because employers are hiring minorities instead?' Respondents could answer: 'extremely likely', 'very likely', 'moderately likely', 'a little likely' and 'not at all likely'. To draw a connection between Trump supporters, respondents were also asked to place their feelings about Donald Trump on a scale from 0 (coldest) to 100 (warmest).

Rather unsurprisingly, the survey revealed that eighty-four per cent of white respondents who believed it is 'extremely likely' that white people can't find a job because employers are hiring people of colour supported Trump, compared to twenty-three per cent of those who think it is 'not at all likely'. Incidentally, among white people who believe the word 'violent' describes black people 'extremely well', seventy-eight per cent support Trump, compared with thirty-four per cent of white people who believe 'not at all well'.

Another survey by political scientists Spencer Piston and Ashley Jardina, reported in *Slate* online, found that more than half of Trump supporters dehumanise black people, describing them as less evolved than white people. Some examples of their responses included, 'I consider blacks to be closer to the animal kingdom,' while another respondent said black people 'lack the intelligence and morals' of other races, another stated that black people 'carry and conduct themselves' in ways that are 'almost animalistic', and others replied that blacks are 'people who act like animals'. Remember, as we saw in Chapter Four, this is how black people were described in the slavery era and so we can see a direct link from stereotypes of the past being harmful today.

Ironically, the negative narrative and 'vicious circle' is also prevalent in the education system. A study from the Upjohn Institute for Employment Research showed that non-black teachers have significantly lower educational expectations for black students than do black teachers – as low as twelve percentage points. This in turn materialises as less opportunities for black students.

For example, studies reported by the BBC show that only three of Oxford's thirty-two colleges made an offer to a black A-level applicant every year between 2010–15. Additionally, statistics from Cambridge revealed a quarter of colleges failed to make any offers to black British applicants during that time. However, this hasn't impacted black people. We remain as committed to overperforming in our education and our professions. Contrary to the narrative that we are lazy, we excel at school and are especially proud of our results.

Dr Ivory Toldson, senior research analyst for the Congressional Black Caucus Foundation, and editor-in-chief of *The Journal of Negro Education*, notes in an article for *The Root* that it's actually white male students who express the most ambivalence about the impact of good grades on their social standing. By contrast, ninety-five per cent of black female students reported that, if they did well in school, they would be proud and tell all of their friends about it. Similarly, black students were most likely to report that their friends would be happier if they went to college than if they didn't. Most white students said their friends wouldn't care either way.

Additionally, in 2009, James W. Ainsworth-Darnell and Douglas B. Downey concluded in an *American Sociological Review* article, 'The Search for Oppositional Culture Among Black Students', that high-achieving black students were in fact especially popular among their peers, and that being a good student increased popularity among black students even more so than for white students.

To the earlier point about black candidates wanting to work at businesses where they see examples of people who look like them succeeding, we are also seeing this trend in academia. Research from the IZA Institute of Labor Economics reported that the risk of dropping out of school decreases forty per cent for low-income black students who have a black teacher for at least one year. So, an important component to black success in academia and professional spaces is having a role model that we can aspire to.

Education remains an important aspect for any community; allowing its habitants to succeed in the labour market, attain financial stability, and accumulate wealth. So, outwardly or implicitly impacting black people's access to education impacts the community's ability to thrive socially.

TURNING TO SPORTS

As discussed in Chapter Two, black people appear to dominate certain sports and the popularity and success of black individuals in this area has led it to be viewed as a lucrative avenue for many black people. Indeed, given that black parents by and large believe the educational and professional system to be rigged against minorities, they (and in turn their children) are increasingly seeing professional sports and entertainment as a possible way to improve their conditions in life. Unfortunately, young black kids are starting to believe that it is easier to make it into professional sports than it is to have a 'proper job'. They look to the popularity of most black athletes today as a reassurance that the stakes are not so skewed against black folk in sports as they are in academia, or in the professional world.

Secondly, even if you are one of the few that make it, there is no guarantee that you will be successful in the long run. Studies show that less than two per cent of college football or basketball players go on to play in the NFL or the National Basketball Association. Just 8 out of every 10,000 high school football players get drafted by an NFL team. The research from the Institute for Diversity and Ethics in Sport showed that of the thirty-two quarterbacks in the NFL, only five black QBs were projected to start in the 2017 season. And for those black athletes who do make it in professional sports, it's not like life is all champagne and high-fives. They suffer tremendous amounts of racism.

In 2015, Kick It Out, football's anti-discrimination campaign, recorded a thirty-five-per-cent increase in racial abuse. We've all seen bananas being thrown at black footballers, or heard monkey chants directed at them – particularly in the Italian Serie A league and English Premier League. In fact, a study by Kick It Out found that the black Italian footballer, Mario Balotelli, was the most abused Premier League player on social media: he received, on average, 8,000 abusive posts directed at him between August 2014 and March 2015.

This is not only indicative of top-level football. The Football Association's head of judicial services estimated that the FA had received seventy-per-cent more reports of racist abuse and other discrimination in just one season in grass-roots amateur football. And in December 2018, a video of a black high-school wrestler, Andrew Johnson, went viral after he was forced to cut his dreadlocks seconds before his wrestling bout, or forfeit the match. Our hair is a symbol of our pride and our heritage, and to be forced to cut it off is one of the most blatant forms of racism.

Another key point to note is that while *black athletes* may dominate sports, the *black community* do not. We don't own or lead major sports teams in virtually any of the major sports franchises; whereas there are at least a handful of black CEOs of Fortune 500 companies. As comedian Chris Rock says in his comedy special, *Never Scared*: 'Shaq is rich; the white man who signs his cheque is wealthy.'

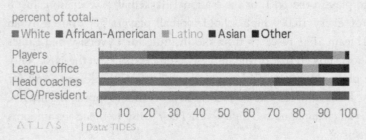

Racial breakdown in the NBA

percent of total...
■ White ■ African-American ▨ Latino ■ Asian ■ Other

Players
League office
Head coaches
CEO/President

0 10 20 30 40 50 60 70 80 90 100

ATLAS | Data: TIDES

For example, the NBA basketball league is a sport in which black people usually dominate, but as we can see from the bar graph, while we dominate playing the sport, our numbers start to decrease when you look at coaching and ownership. And as of January 2019, there are only three minority head coaches in the National Football League. If we look a little closer to home at the Football League, as of December 2018, there are fewer than six black managers at the seventy-two Football League clubs in the UK and only one in the Premier League – Chris Hughton of Brighton and Hove Albion.

So yes, black people tend to turn to sports, but it is easy to see why. In the States, the NFL is nearly seventy per cent black, so we feel we belong in this sport – compared to the tech industry, which is around eight per cent black. So we can see why there might be a lack of interest to move into this industry compared to sports.

ENTERTAINMENT AS AN OPTION FOR BLACK PEOPLE?

At first sight, entertainment is a lucrative industry that is favourable to black people. Indeed, the popularity and prevalence of hip hop, R&B, soul, and rap music is testament to the opportunities for black artists. However, we see only the successes, who had to suffer through serious adversity to reach where they are today. Making it in the music business is tremendously difficult and black people face the same issues here that they do in academia and their professional lives.

As of 2016, the most recent *Billboard* magazine's 'Power 100' (list of the most influential people in the American music industry) shows a staggering lack of black inclusions – particularly given black contribution to music. Of the 141 individuals on the Power 100 (more than one person can share a single ranking), less than ten per cent are even people of colour.

We also see this similarity in the TV and movie industry, as brought to light rather significantly by the #OscarsSoWhite movement in 2016. This movement originated from the anger at the absence of actors of colour from the twenty nominees at the Oscars, resulting in a boycott from celebrities such as Ava DuVernay, Spike Lee, Michael Moore and Will Smith. This wasn't a one-off; there were no nominees of colour the previous year either.

It's not as if there were no options. *Creed* starred the black actor Michael B. Jordan and was directed by Ryan Coogler, but both were ignored; the film's only nomination went to Sylvester Stallone for Best Supporting Actor. *Straight Outta Compton*, a hit film about a black hip-hop group with a black director and producer, was nominated only for its screenplay, the writers of which were white. *Selma*, a film about the civil rights movement was nominated but did not win Best Picture, and neither its director, Ava DuVernay, nor its star, David Oyelowo, were recognised by the Academy of Motion Picture Arts and Sciences at the awards.

When you look at the industry, you see that this issue is systemic. According to *The Economist*, black people account for more than twelve per cent of the American population, and yet ten per cent of Oscar nominations since 2000 have gone to black actors. And only three per cent of nominations have gone to Hispanic people (who represent sixteen per cent of the population), and one per cent to those with Asian backgrounds.

This is not just an issue for Academy nominations, but appearances in film altogether. According to a study by the Annenberg Center for Communication and Journalism, which looked at around 900 popular movies from 2007–2016, black actors account for less than fourteen per cent of characters – a number that hasn't changed since 2007. Additionally, twenty-five films of the 900 have no black or African-American speaking characters at all, and nearly half of all the 100 top films of 2016 evaluated were completely missing black female speaking characters.

This is not a problem limited to the United States; it is equally dire in the UK. Research conducted by the British Film Institute (BFI) revealed that as of 2016, fifty-nine per cent of British films over the last ten years featured no black actors at all in a named role. Additionally, a recent report from the USC School of Journalism shows that despite the box-office success of *Black Panther* and *Crazy Rich Asians*, only about twenty-nine per cent of characters in the top 100 grossing movies of 2017 were from communities of colour. The research further showed that of the movies with black actors in them, the themes and subjects tended to be overly negative – black actors were playing the roles of gangsters and slaves. Leading themes included: slavery, religion, homicide, civil war,* gangsters and organised crime, hip hop, Martin Luther King/civil rights, engagement/wedding, Nelson Mandela/South Africa, and athletics/competitions.

Not only is the lack of representation a concern, but it also becomes a problem when we look to our screens and mostly see negative representations of ourselves. The reality is that TV is a very important medium in the cultural zeitgeist, through which we can get our diction, our belief in what is considered as attractive, our values, and even our sense of self-worth.

A study called 'Racial and Gender Differences in the Relationship Between Children's Television Use and Self-Esteem' found that television exposure predicted a decrease in self-esteem for black boys and girls (also white girls), but an increase in self-esteem among white boys. The researchers explain that black boys can be disturbed by their TV counterparts, who are often criminalised, or shown as hoodlums and buffoons. They add that white boys may experience the opposite effect, because they tend to identify with powerful characters who don't seem to work very hard for their accomplishments.

One of the main excuses that movie studios have offered for lack of diversity in leading roles is that minority stars do not have the appeal for drawing audiences and getting financing that white stars do. For instance, following the movie, *Exodus: Gods and Kings*, where white actors played the principal parts (Christian Bale as Moses, Australian actor Joel Edgerton as the Pharaoh Ramses II, John Turturro as Pharaoh Seti, and so on), its director Ridley Scott said in an interview with *Variety* magazine about casting minority actors: 'I can't mount a film of this budget, where I have to rely on tax rebates in Spain, and say that my lead actor is Mohammad so-and-so from such-and-such.†

---

* Nope, not *Captain America: Civil War*.

† Shows what he knows. I would totally pay money to go and see a movie with Mohammad so-and-so from such-and-such. He's such a dynamic actor.

I'm just not going to get it financed. So, the question doesn't even come up.'

Aside from this being incredibly insulting and borderline xenophobic, it is factually incorrect. Movies with minority actors do have the ability to do well financially and draw audiences; in fact, minority audiences are more likely to show up if they feel that they are being represented on the big screen.

In 2017, the comedy movie, *Girls Trip*, about four black women who reconnect over a fun trip to the Essence Festival, featuring Regina Hall, Jada Pinkett Smith, Queen Latifah and Tiffany Haddish, took the number one spot in its opening weekend, beating the likes of *War for the Planet of the Apes* and *Spider-Man: Homecoming*. The movie has grossed $138 million worldwide, including over $100 million domestically (the only comedy of 2017 to do so) and was chosen by *Time* magazine as one of its top ten films of 2017.

So not only did it do well financially, it managed to draw an incredibly diverse crowd: according to Box Office Mojo, a movie-tracking website, around fifty-nine per cent of the audience that went to see the movie was black, nineteen per cent was white, seventeen per cent was Hispanic, and three per cent was Asian. We saw similar success with the movie *Get Out*, starring Daniel Kaluuya* and directed by Jordan Peele. Despite being a film about the black experience when it comes to subtle and disguised racism, starring a relatively unknown black actor and a first-time movie director, the movie received critical acclaim and was chosen by the National Board of Review, the American Film Institute, and *Time* magazine as one of the top ten films of the year. Additionally, it grossed $254 million worldwide on a $4.5 million budget.

CNN Money reported that Marvel's *Black Panther*, a movie about a black superhero from a fictional African country, with a predominantly black cast, outsold every previous superhero movie in advanced

---

* Damn, if they had a problem with a name like Mohammad, Lord knows how they managed to finance a film with a name like Kaluuya.

ticket sales as of February 2018. In fact, the number of black people attending movies overall, regardless of whether there is a minority in the leading role, has increased since 2009.

According to a report by the Motion Picture Association of America, minorities overall made up a larger percentage of ticket buyers: for example, Hispanics represented twenty-one per cent of ticket buyers, even though they make up only eighteen per cent of the population in the States. African Americans, who represent twelve per cent of the population, purchased fourteen per cent of all tickets. Asian and other minorities, who make up eight per cent of the population, bought fourteen per cent of all tickets sold. Caucasians bought only fifty-one per cent of all tickets, even though they make up sixty-two per cent of the population.

So, all this shows that there is absolutely no denying there is a problem with adequate representation in the entertainment industry. And much like the representation of black people in academia and professional industries, this creates unrealistic expectations when black and BAME parents encourage their children to enter different professional fields.

ACCUMULATING WEALTH: AN UNLEVEL PLAYING FIELD FOR MINORITIES

The starting point to the premise of inequality is acknowledging that there is one. We touched on this briefly in Chapter Two as to why black people are not able to afford swimming pools. And it all boils down to wealth. Wealth equals opportunity. Wealth equals freedom. Wealth equals power. And there is a significant lack of wealth in the black community.

I don't use 'significant' lightly. The black community has been plagued by lack of wealth resulting from the victimisation of slavery; and this remains the foundation for the inequality. A very common response (retort mostly) from (white) people to this suggestion is, 'Well, I wasn't handed anything for free. I worked my way up from nothing; why can't you?', which may very well be true, but for black and other minorities, the systematic problems in our educational and social systems, not to mention the history of racial preference, mean that we are not operating from a level playing field.

It took white people four hundred years of slavery, segregation, and institutionalised racism and discrimination to build the wealth gap that we see today. If you were to take two dirt-poor individuals of similar circumstance: one black and the other white, statistically, the black person is going to be worse off, because there is always the possibility that they will be seen as inferior, unfairly oppressed by the police, or handed unfair judgment if they happen to commit any societal wrong. It is essentially a handicap – hence the quote from the novel *Americanah* by Chimamanda Ngozi Adichie: 'Yes, it sucks to be poor and white, but try being poor and non-white.'

The premise of 'I worked my way up from nothing, why can't you?' is flawed, because it presumes blame on the individual who hasn't been able to work their way up. This is based on a concept called 'fundamental attribution error': the natural tendency to see the behaviour of others as being determined by their character, while excusing our own behaviour based on circumstances. In other words, to a white person who 'worked their way up', a black person on welfare is poor, because they have simply made bad choices in life. This sort of thinking arises from a lack of understanding of the circumstances that afflict a certain group or minority, the challenges they have had to go through, and the realisation that there is not an equal playing field when it comes to race and wealth.

We are seeing evidence of this still today. In the UK, BAME families earn as much as £8,900 a year less than their white British counterparts, according to a study from the Resolution Foundation. Black African families were found to earn typically a fifth less than white families, while Bangladeshi and Pakistani households earn about a third less on average. This is similar to the income gap between races in the United States – according to the Federal Reserve, the typical African-American family had a median net worth of $17,600 in 2016.

In contrast, white households had a median net worth of $171,000, which shows a significant disparity.

A study by the Institute of Policy Studies supports the notion that there isn't a level playing field across races, reporting that if current economic trends continue, the average black household will need *228 years** to accumulate as much wealth as their white counterparts hold today (for the average Latino family, it will take eighty-four years). Even the rate of growth is inconsistent between black and white households; the study says that if current trends persist for another thirty years, the average white family's net worth will grow by $18,000 per year, but black and Hispanic households would see theirs grow by only $750 and $2,250 per year, respectively – which is a ridiculous income gap.

Another bit of research that challenges this notion of a level playing field is provided by Richard Reeves, a Brookings Institution economist, in a YouTube video titled 'Is America Dreaming?: Understanding Social Mobility', where he discusses 'getting ahead in America and the chances of making it from the bottom to the top', by breaking society into five groups from bottom to top. In a perfectly equal world, each of the five

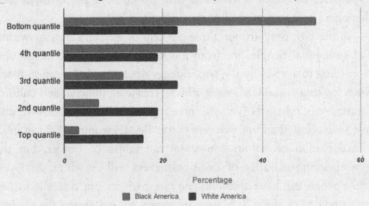

Chances of moving from bottom income quantile to the top in America

* Bear in mind that this is just seventeen years shorter than the 245-year span of slavery in the United States.

groups would consist of twenty per cent of the population. He notes that in reality, there is a thirty-six-per-cent chance of an American born in the bottom quintile of society remaining at the bottom and a ten-per-cent chance of making it to the top. For white Americans, there is actually a better chance than average: a twenty-three-per-cent chance of remaining in the bottom and a sixteen-per-cent chance of making it to the top.

Not only is it better than average for white Americans, but they come close enough to the ideal world scenario, i.e. sixteen-per-cent chance of making it to the top out of twenty per cent. However, for African Americans, there is a fifty-one-per-cent chance that they'd remain at the bottom and only a three-per-cent chance of making it to the top. So even if all Americans were placed at a level playing field at the bottom, the chance of success will still be extremely more difficult for black people.

So, wealth inequality is a huge concern. And when I refer to wealth, I don't just mean average income; the story is the same for the upper echelons of wealth. For example, even though 2017 was a record year for the richest people on earth, with the number of billionaires jumping to 2,043 from 1,810 in 2016; according to *Forbes*, only ten of these billionaires are black. That's less than half of one per cent! In fact, there isn't even a black billionaire in the top 100.

In the UK, only around three per cent of Britain's most powerful and influential people are from black and minority ethnic groups. According to a study by the *Guardian* newspaper and Operation Black Vote, looking at the UK's top political, financial, judicial, and cultural figures, only thirty-six (around three per cent) were from BAME and just seven (less than one per cent) were BAME women. Yes, an individual person of colour can sit at the tables of power, but the overwhelming majority of decision-makers will be white. And yes, white people can have problems and face barriers, but systemic racism won't be one of them. It is very important to understand the distinction between individual prejudice (which white people sometimes face) and a system of unequal institutionalised racial power (which white people never face).

HOUSING DISPARITY BETWEEN BLACK AND WHITE FAMILIES

One of the most obvious indicators of wealth and ensuring it remains in the family is house ownership. Think about it: if you own property, you don't have to worry about exorbitant rent fees, or being homeless. It is also a nest egg that you can tap into for a rainy day through re-mortgaging, or simply pass on to children and descendants. But the disparities in home ownership also fall along racial and ethnic lines.

According to the UK Department for Communities and Local Government, of the estimated 14.3 million homeowners in the UK, ethnic minority householders were less likely to be in owner-occupation than white British households (except for Indian, mixed white, and Asian and Pakistani households, who have similar rates of home ownership). The report also showed that when comparing all other ethnic groups – across every socio-economic group, income band, region and age group – white British people were just more likely to own their own homes.

In the US, studies from the Institute of Assets and Social Policy show that seventy-three per cent of white people own a home, compared to forty-seven per cent of Latinos and forty-five per cent of blacks. And it is not only in the ability and means to own a home where we are seeing a lack of representation, but also in the type of home. The median white homeowner's house is worth $85,800, compared to $50,000 for black homeowners and $48,000 for Latino homeowners.

But what accounts for the disparity in home ownership and in the value of homes – particularly in the States, where the Fair Housing Act made discrimination in housing illegal in 1968? Well, aside from the twenty years that it took to fully implement the law, whereby people of colour missed out on the robust growth of the housing markets, we are still seeing methods of discrimination in recent years.

According to The Justice Department, Wells Fargo Bank, the largest residential home mortgage originator in the United States, as well as Countrywide Financial Corporation, engaged in discrimination against qualified African-American and Hispanic borrowers, in that they were charged higher fees and rates, or were placed improperly into subprime loans; all the while offering prime mortgages to white borrowers with similar credit profiles. This is essentially an example of the redlining that was prevalent in the States – where black and other minorities were denied access to housing in 'white neighbourhoods' through denial of financial services, or generally, racist landlords.

While there doesn't appear to be any significant proof that UK financial institutions have had mortgage lending policies as overtly racist as shown in the US, the former Deputy Prime Minister, Nick Clegg, has accused financial institutions in the UK of racism, citing in a *Guardian* article that ethnic minority businesses have historically had a more difficult time in receiving finance from banks, with black African businesses being four times less likely to be approved for loans and being subject to higher interest rates.

As we've mentioned the notion of 'white neighbourhoods', it's also important to touch on the impact of gentrification, because historically, it's black and minority neighbourhoods that tend to be impacted by the influx of wealthy (often white) people. I mentioned in the chapter looking at the impact of drugs on the black community what Brixton used to be like. And even though it was considered a 'rough neighbourhood' with high crime numbers, for the black community, it was something else. It was home. On any given day, you could walk down Brixton, head to the market, and see representations of Africa and the Caribbean: from the people to the music to the smells of the delicious meals that reminded you of mama's cooking. And the businesses were black-owned businesses.

With gentrification and arrival of the wealthy, there has been a negative impact on the black community. But this isn't a narrative about the identity of Brixton, or that it is now populated with more white people then there were previously. After all, neighbourhoods change and evolve constantly over time. This is a narrative about wealth. Because in almost all examples of gentrification, it is often initiated by the wealthy, who see opportunities to become even wealthier by buying up real estate at prices that current residents can't afford.

We have seen how this has affected black wealth in Brixton. Increasing rent and housing rates have meant that the local black businesses that once flourished in Brixton are no more, replaced by the name-brand retailers. Brixton natives are no longer able to afford living in Brixton, and are having to move south to Croydon and Norbury for (comparatively) reasonable rent.

According to the local campaign, Save Brixton Arches: 'Network Rail proposes to evict over thirty units occupied by independent shops and businesses, in order to complete a facelift, estimated to take over a year. Once completed, tenants will face massive rent increases of around three hundred per cent, which in effect, will exclude them from the area where generations of these families have served the local community for over eighty years.'

This speaks to the wealth issue: if a society or a neighbourhood is to progress and accumulate wealth, shouldn't some, or arguably most, of that wealth be reserved for the inhabitants of the community? As of late 2017, it will have been well over a year since planning permission was awarded to Network Rail, but none of the main refurbishment works have even started – further delaying the opportunities for local businesses to return. And that's one of the main issues that locals have against gentrification; it doesn't merely signal the arrival of another Starbucks, or ironic hipster café, it impacts the local culture and distributes wealth unfairly to the disadvantage of minorities.

We've seen examples of this in the States as well; in Brooklyn, San Francisco, Chicago, Washington, DC and elsewhere. One of the prevailing arguments in favour of gentrification is that it brings wealth to the whole community. However, research from writer Dax-Devlon Ross, who views north-west DC as a 'centre of the city's black intellectual and cultural life', suggests otherwise.

He notes: 'In 2011 alone, condos accounted for fifty per cent of total home sales (276), most at triple the 2000 median price. The zip code now boasts an Ann Taylor, a Brooks Brothers, an Urban

Outfitters, enough bars to serve several university populations at once, and a mind-boggling ten Starbucks . . . What's telling about the zip code's "new build" makeover is that it did not move the poverty needle. The zip code's poverty rate is exactly what it was in 1980, 1990 and 2000 – twenty-eight per cent – and the child poverty rate is nearly twice what it was in 1990 (forty-five per cent).'

So, how can the black community escape this vicious circle: this lack of wealth, discrimination in academia, and negative narrative about our ability to learn and generate business? This is a huge problem, because wealth accumulates wealth. The major source of wealth for the wealthy is inheritance and the ability to transfer to the next generation.

Hell, the richest African is Aliko Dangote (with an estimated wealth of $12.2 billion, according to *Forbes*) who founded Dangote Cement, Africa's largest cement provider; but even he inherited his wealth. He is the great-grandson of Alhaji Alhassan Dantata, who was the richest African at the time of his death in 1955. So accumulated wealth becomes an efficient mechanism for carrying on success from generation to generation, and community to community; the wealth of a child's family is the single greatest predictor of that child's future economic prospects. So, what then do all black parents have to pass on to their children, but an understanding of how the system works, the challenges that you'll have to face, and the drive to ensure that you are always the best – no matter what the circumstance. I will always be grateful to my parents for instilling that in me.

However, I would like to add an addendum to this lesson. BAME children don't have to limit themselves to the stereotypical professions that our parents succeeded in. We can create our own destiny. We can demand a seat at the table; in fact, we should scream and shout until we get it. We can be writers, graphic designers, opera singers, and ballet dancers. There are a load of creative industries that we can break into, if not for our own gratification but for the next generation – so that they can read books written by BAME writers and see more BAME representations on our TV screens.

Most importantly, we need to gift our children with the knowledge that not only are they free to do whatever it is that would make them happy and successful in life, but it is also a genuine possibility. Only then, can we truly progress. But we do *need* programmes and initiatives in place to give us a helping hand. We have had an over two-hundred-year handicap and the fact that we have managed to progress to this point is damn near impossible to contemplate.

This is why the notion that if we just worked a little harder, we'd be more successful in life is so harmful. It blindly ignores the institutional inequality among races and belittles the progress that we have made as the black community. We need that helping hand to make things not simply equal, but equitable. There is a significant difference between equality and equity – equality assumes that everyone is operating from the same starting point, whereas equity tries to ensure that everyone gets the same opportunities and benefits.

So as a member of a privileged group, if you see that opportunities are being offered to a minority group and aren't being offered to you, remember that it is to address a larger systemic problem in the institution that you operate in, and not giving an unfair advantage to that minority group.

Answer to pop quiz: Black employees with degrees earn an average of £14.33 per hour compared to their white equivalents who earn an average of £18.63 for the same amount of work.

TARGETS

IS IT CUZ I'M BLACK? PART 2

Stereotype/negative narrative: That crime is overly prevalent in black communities and actions taken by police to combat this are appropriate. Complaints from the black communities that they are unfairly targeted and mistreated by the police are unfounded.

Pop quiz:

How much more likely are the Met Police to use force against black people than white people in London?

8 x

2 x

4 x

One evening in 2016, I cried uncontrollably for the first time since my dad passed away years earlier. There had been yet another shooting of a black kid in America, and in this instance, there was footage of the shooting. I managed to hold it together, but after work that day, I was in the pub with a few black friends and we got talking about the increase in fatalities of black men at the hands of American police officers. It was quite a sober conversation and at one stage, one of my black friends asked, 'What did we do? What have we ever done as a people to deserve this?'

That was it; I couldn't hold it together anymore. I rushed to the toilet and burst into tears. I was worried, angry, and scared about the unfairness of it all. Because we hadn't done anything to deserve the treatment we've been given. We have always been the victims: taken from our ancestral home, enslaved, and made to suffer all manner of indignity; only to be finally emancipated, yet still treated as second-class citizens: demoralised, abused, and killed. And therein lies the crux of the dilemma for black people today: the feeling of not being safe, accepted, or welcome in a country that you call home, and not being protected by the institutions that are meant to keep you safe.

The years 2016 and 2017 had been a truly horrible and troubling time with regards to black people being increasingly shot (and often killed) by the police in the States. The stats from numerous sources about black fatalities at the hands of the police are overwhelming. Regardless of the numbers, they all show that black people (mostly males) are more likely to be victims of police violence than white people.

In the UK, we have seen an increase in knife crime in highly populated black communities, the failure of law enforcement to properly respond to the threat, and the demonisation of these communities as a result. Here are the stats:

- The Met Police are four times more likely to use force against black people than white people in London.
- Also, black people are at least eight times more likely than white

people to be stopped and searched, even though it is statistically less likely for drugs to be found.

- In the US, young black males are twenty-one times more likely to be shot dead by police than their white counterparts.
- Sadly, they are also four times as likely to be shot in the back.
- Ethnic minorities made up about thirty-seven per cent of the general population, but they made up nearly sixty-three per cent of unarmed people killed by police.
- Black people were also twice as likely to be shot after being pulled over for a traffic violation, or for suspicion of a minor crime like smoking weed, or not committing any crime at all!

Interestingly, this points to a larger problem with the police as opposed to *just* institutional racism. As a police force, the perception that black people and communities are the first port of call for crime is so inherent that it has become an implicit bias. A Department of Justice report looking at the use of deadly force by Philadelphia police revealed that police are susceptible to implicit bias, even if the officers were themselves black or Latino. One could even argue that this might be indicative of the police force in the United States overall, given that in March of 2015, police officers in the United States killed more people than police officers in the UK did in the entire twentieth century.

More evidence of this implicit bias is the case of a white Louisville, Kentucky, police officer, who was forced to resign after he was found to be instructing recruits to shoot black kids if they are caught smoking marijuana, saying, 'Fuck the right thing, if black, shoot them.'

THE PLIGHT OF BLACK YOUTHS IN AMERICA

Since 2016, there has been a lot of news coverage about homicides at the hands of the police in America involving black youths, such as Jordan Davis and Trayvon Martin. While not all these cases involved incompetence or racism on behalf of the police, it does perpetuate the notion that police officers disproportionately see black youths as a threat – and the best way to deal with this threat is with extreme force. Let's look at some of these cases.

One of the most dominant news stories of police brutality over the past couple of years was the Michael Brown shooting in Ferguson. On 9 August 2014, Ferguson Police Officer Darren Wilson shot and killed Michael Brown, an unarmed, black eighteen-year-old, and left his body on a street for four and a half hours. Brown was a (seemingly) college-bound student with no criminal record, who was accused of robbing a convenience store, moments before the shooting. Officer Wilson claimed that Brown was violent during the attempted arrest and even tried running at him after the shots were fired.

One of the things that make the story so controversial is the dispute in different accounts. Eye-witnesses claim that there was an initial confrontation between Brown and Wilson. Brown ran, Wilson chased after him, and shot him to death as Brown attempted to surrender. Wilson claims Brown didn't attempt to surrender and instead attempted to take his handgun during the initial confrontation. The following grand jury decided not to indict Wilson for the shooting, which led to series of protests in the town of Ferguson.

Considering that the police were accused of using excessive force in the shooting, it's even more surprising that they responded to the protests with so much greater force. Police turned up equipped with military-grade weapons, including tanks, tear gas, rubber bullets and military rifles. All for a protest in Ferguson, Missouri – population 21,203. A town so small, you could have gone your whole life without knowing it exists. The subsequent report by the Department of Justice into the Ferguson Police Department found that at each juncture in the criminal process, the law is enforced more harshly against black people than others, and there was substantial evidence of intentional discrimination.

Worryingly, the situation in Ferguson escalated, as in March 2015, two police officers were wounded by gunfire outside the Ferguson police headquarters while providing security at a protest. To make the situation worse, further investigation into the Ferguson Police Department has revealed significant racism, not only on the black community, but other ethnic minorities. A Department of Justice report into the arrest and summons practices in Ferguson revealed that they are incredibly biased and frivolous.

Some examples include: a Latino boy and girl being given a summons for being in the park after dusk at 11 p.m., even though it was actually 8 p.m.; a police officer arresting a sixteen-year-old Latino boy for trespassing, while the boy was standing in the lobby of the building he lives in; and police officers approaching seven rickshaw drivers who were on break and telling them that they each needed an arrest. Since there were more drivers than officers, the officers told the drivers to play a game to determine which one of them would be arrested. The drivers were arrested for unauthorised parking and spent fifteen hours locked up before a judge dismissed the charges.

Since the investigation, it has been revealed that senior police officers and a city official in Ferguson exchanged emails that likened ethnic minority welfare recipients to dogs, and joked about stoning Muslim women. One of those emails depicted Barack Obama as a chimpanzee in the arms of former president Ronald Reagan, another doubted his ability as a black man to hold a job for four years, while a third labelled a photograph of a black tribal gathering with topless women as Michelle Obama's high-school reunion.

It is not just in Ferguson that fatal police brutality in the States has been an issue over the past years. A similar situation happened in July 2016 in New York, where a black man, Eric Garner, died after a police officer, Daniel Pantaleo, put him in a chokehold. Pantaleo attempted to arrest Garner on suspicion of selling cigarettes on the street. It's alleged that Garner swatted Pantaleo's arms away when he tried to arrest him, resulting in the officer putting him in the chokehold. Garner lost consciousness and remained on the street surrounded by police for seven minutes, until the ambulance arrived. He was pronounced dead on arrival at the hospital, where the medical examiners concluded that Garner was killed by 'compression of neck (chokehold), compression of chest and prone positioning during physical restraint by police'. In this case also, a grand jury decided not to indict Pantaleo.

The incident that made me cry was the fatal shooting of a black youth, Laquan McDonald. In this case, police were called to investigate McDonald, responding to reports that he was carrying a knife and breaking into vehicles. When he was confronted by police officers, he used the knife to slash the tyres of the police officer and damage his windshield. After several calls from the police to drop the knife, he was then shot sixteen times in approximately fourteen to fifteen seconds by the officer, Jason Van Dyke.

Video of the shooting shows that McDonald fell to the ground after the first shot was fired, and even the first responding officer stated that he did not see the need to use further force, and that none of the eight or more other officers on the scene fired their weapons. This would mean that Van Dyke emptied the entire clip of his 9mm semi-automatic gun shooting a teenager, who according to witness reports wasn't being threatening and was shying away from the police when cornered.

What is even more horrific about this case is the information that has subsequently been made public under a Freedom of Information request: the initial police report of the incident was ruled a 'justifiable homicide and within the bounds of the department's use of force guidelines', and the fact that the officer who shot McDonald had at least twenty citizen complaints filed against him, with none resulting in disciplinary action. Van Dyke has since been found guilty of second degree murder and the McDonald family has been given a $5 million settlement.

INCOMPETENCE OR RACISM?

In the cases above, the victims allegedly took some threatening action that they shouldn't have: McDonald slashed police tyres, and Garner swatted the police officer's arms away; but there have also been some cases where it would be hard for any reasonable person to conclude that the police should have taken fatal action, and it was not racially motivated.

For example, Walter Scott was stopped for a non-functioning brake light by Michael Slager, a white North Charleston police officer. When Scott tried to flee, Slager shot him fatally five times in the back. In Slager's report, he claimed that he feared for his life, because Scott tried to grab his Taser. The incident was caught on camera and it showed that when Slager fired his gun, Scott was approximately fifteen to twenty feet (five to six metres) away, so couldn't possibly have been reaching for his Taser.

In 2014, police responded to a noise complaint in Florida at the home of Gregory Hill, and fatally shot him. They claimed that when they announced themselves, Hill refused to grant them entry and raised a gun towards them. Consequent investigations found that Hill's gun was found unloaded and inside of his back-right pocket after he was killed. So, it was impossible for him to have raised it at police officers. Additionally, the officers shot him through the door, so it is hard to see how they could have known he had raised his weapon. To add insult to injury, when Hill's mother, Viola Bryant, filed a lawsuit regarding the death, the jury determined that the family should receive just $4 – the sum of $1 to Hill's mother for funeral expenses and $1 for each of Hill's three children.

Charles Kinsey, a therapist who worked at an assisted living facility, was trying to help an autistic patient that had escaped from a group home, when he was shot by an officer from the North Miami Police, despite being unarmed and pleading with the officers with his hands in the air. The police had arrived in response to a 911 call regarding an armed man who was threatening suicide, so there really wasn't any need to shoot anyone. When Kinsey asked the police officer why he had shot him, he replied, 'I don't know.'

In another instance, police officers in New Mexico handcuffed Ben Anthony C de Baca, threw him on his stomach, pulled a mask over his face, and planted their knees in his back. While he cried that he couldn't breathe, the officers were busy laughing at a joke. Consequently, Mr de Baca died, and two police officers were caught on camera fist-bumping.

In 2018, Californian police officers detained three black friends leaving an Airbnb after a neighbour called 911 and reported them as possible burglars. A simple misunderstanding, right? So how does one explain why the police sent seven squad cars and a goddamn helicopter to detain them?* They were just three black people, yet all of a sudden the incident turned into a scene from the game *Grand Theft Auto: Vice City*.

That same year, a white police officer in Dallas, Texas, Amber Guyger, shot and killed her black neighbour, Botham Jean, inside his own flat. Guyger claimed that she mistook Botham Jean's flat for her own and thought Jean was an intruder, leading her to shoot him twice. Witnesses, however, say that they heard Guyger knocking on Jean's door and demanding to be let in before the shooting.

Moving towards this side of the Atlantic, in France, investigators concluded that police officers in Paris who sodomised a young black man with a baton did so accidentally, and that the incident did not constitute rape. The victim was a twenty-two-year-old youth worker, who claimed that officers sodomised him with a truncheon, spat on him, beat his genitals and called him names, including 'negro' and 'bitch'. He had to be taken to the hospital for an emergency surgery. The investigation by France's national police force concluded that the incident, while 'very serious', was 'not a rape' due to the 'unintentional character' of the officers' actions.

Now compare these treatments of black suspects to the arrests of murderers who are white – actual murderers, and not suspects or individuals who had committed minor crimes, like in the examples of the black men mentioned above. Dylann Roof killed nine worshippers in an historic black church in Charleston, but when he was arrested, police officers took him to go and get a hamburger. The Oklahoma City bomber, Timothy McVeigh; the Planned Parenthood shooter, Robert Lewis Dear; and the Aurora theatre shooter – all managed to end up alive after carrying out mass murders.

---

* This is why I don't check into any Airbnb without my half-British, half-Spanish friend, Ricardo. He's doubly white, that should keep me safe.

This racism is not limited to arrests, but sentencing as well. For example, a black kid, Cory Batey, raped a woman and was found guilty and sentenced to fifteen to twenty-five years in prison – as well he should. It's less than he deserved. But compare that to the case of Brock Turner, a white kid at Stanford, who raped a woman and was found guilty, but given only a six-month jail sentence and told he could be released on good behaviour in as little as three months. He won't even go to an actual prison; he will remain in the local jail. We see a similar situation with Jacob Walter Anderson, accused of drugging and raping college women, who was handed only a $400 fine and three years' probation!

If you're still not convinced, in 2016, Lieutenant Greg Abbott, a police officer from Georgia, USA, pulled over a white woman he suspected of driving under the influence. Upon approaching the car, the woman refused to move her hands, because she had 'seen way too many videos of cops . . .' Before she could finish, Abbott cut her off, saying, 'But you're not black. Remember, we only shoot black people. Yeah, we only kill black people, right? All of the videos you've seen, have you seen the black people get killed? You have.'

UK INSTANCES

A lot of the publicity and awareness of police brutality among black youths has been focused on American instances, so it is sometimes easy to forget that we also face this issue closer to home. The UK is most certainly not immune to institutional racism by the police that leads to fatalities. In 2017, a police officer had to admit that he had failed to follow safety rules in arresting a black man, Rashan Charles, who died in custody.

In 2016, Sarah Reed, a black thirty-two-year-old woman suffering with mental health issues, was found dead in her cell in north London's Holloway prison, where she was on remand awaiting trial. What was more terrifying is that she reported being sexually assaulted while being detained under the Mental Health Act, and in 2012 she was ruthlessly beaten up by a police officer, with the attack caught on camera – she was thrown to the ground, grabbed by the hair, and punched three times in the head as she was arrested.

In 2015, Sheku Bayoh, a British-Sierra Leonean man, died after being arrested by police in Fife, Scotland. He was detained, handcuffed, pepper-sprayed, and put in leg restraints following an alleged altercation with a police officer. According to the Bayoh family's lawyer, post-mortem evidence suggests that Bayoh died of positional asphyxia, after being pinned to the ground by four officers.

While UK instances of police discrimination and brutality generally get less mainstream media visibility than incidents in the US, it's important to know that of all the people who have died in, or following, police custody in the UK since 1990, more than five hundred of these were BAME individuals. Yet, not a single police officer has been successfully prosecuted, despite the fact that a large proportion of these deaths involved undue and excessive force. Often, the individuals detained suffered from a severe mental illness.

Historically, one of the most high-profile black British victims of police brutality was David Oluwale, who died in 1969, and was the first recorded black person to have died in police custody in the UK. Oluwale's case appears to be the only instance in contemporary British history in which police officers were held responsible for a death in police custody. In this case, the officers had beaten David Oluwale with truncheons and then kicked him into the River Aire in Yorkshire. His lifeless body was pulled from the river two weeks after the attack. Reporting on this incident, *Fader* magazine notes: 'In the UK, a black person is less likely to be shot dead on the streets than their counterpart in America. But we are more likely to be detained with brute force and left to die at the hands of neglectful officers. The racism in Britain's justice system is insidious, but deadly nonetheless.'

More recently, one of the most important cases of police brutality and racism towards a black man was the case of Christopher Alder. Alder was a black British man of Nigerian descent, born in the UK. He joined the British Army at the young age of sixteen and served in the Parachute Regiment for six years. In April 1998, he got into a physical altercation with a man outside a club after drinking, got hurt, and was taken to the hospital. Alder was deemed to be uncooperative at the hospital and so the hospital was unable to administer aid. He was eventually arrested to prevent a breach of the peace.

On arrival at the police station, he was left lying down in the cell with no examination from the police officers. The officers could see a pool of blood around his mouth on CCTV and one of the officers could be heard on the CCTV footage saying that Alder should be taken to the hospital, but the other officers complained that they had just come from there and claimed he was acting. When they eventually went to examine him, Alder could be heard making 'gurgling noises' as he tried to breathe through the pool of blood. Instead of calling for aid, the CCTV footage revealed that the officers were making monkey noises at Alder. By the time they called the ambulance, Alder was already dead.

As we've seen with a lot of these cases, the actions that followed the brutality were atrocious. It was revealed that Alder's clothes were destroyed by a West Yorkshire Police team and never subjected to forensic examination; the Crown Prosecution Service initially declined to pursue criminal charges against the officers; when they finally did, the judge in the case ordered the jury to find the officers not guilty on all charges; and following the acquittal, an internal police disciplinary inquiry cleared the officers of any wrongdoing.

LACK OF REPERCUSSIONS FOR POLICE'S UNLAWFUL KILLINGS

If there is anything more ridiculous than these examples of the police assaulting and killing black men and women, it is that generally there are no repercussions for the officers involved. In fact, police officers are indicted in less than one per cent of these killings, but the indictment rate for citizens is ninety per cent. And this is my fundamental problem with the 'Blue Lives Matter' movement. Of course, police officers' lives matter, and we shouldn't forget that they are doing a dangerous job; but there isn't a system of institutional racism against police officers in the black community. Black people by and large do not consciously or unconsciously target police officers to murder. Additionally, if a police officer is murdered, they get a dedicated police funeral (as well they should) and the perpetrator is hunted down.

However, if a black person is killed by the police, the police officers aren't always indicted. The 'Black Lives Matter' movement was born in the USA out of fear at the institutional racism in the police forces, the need to educate the population about this dire and immediate situation within the black community, and frustration at the lack of outrage from media and our government. It wasn't a proclamation that other lives don't matter or aren't as important – in the same way that when you run a fundraising campaign to support the victims of Hurricane Harvey in Texas, it doesn't mean fuck all other States, or that you don't care about the victims of other natural disasters.

The sheer amount of racial crimes that had been perpetrated in the African-American community at the hands of the police had reached

saturation point: the victims' families were still not getting justice and there were no ramifications for the officers involved. Let's look at some examples.

In the UK, PC Katie Barratt was allowed to come back to the force and given £15,000 back pay after she was sacked for racially abusing takeaway staff. She had reportedly called staff in the Spice of Punjab takeaway 'Pakis' and 'Niggers'. The panel overturned her 'unreasonable' dismissal and apparently, her remarks 'were not the worst kind of racism'.

The shooting of Timothy Russell and Malissa Williams in 2012 caused a huge uproar in the black community. According to reports, a plain-clothes police officer spotted the car carrying the two victims in an area known for drug deals. When the officers tried to pull them over, Russell sped away and the police gave chase. It was reported that the chase went up to speeds of 100 mph, and a total of sixty-two police cars and six law enforcement departments were involved at one point. After a twenty-two-mile chase, police officers believed they saw a firearm in the car and that Russell was planning on running them over. One officer opened fire, followed by thirteen other officers, who fired a total of 137 bullets into the car, with Cleveland officer Michael Brelo firing forty-nine of those shots.

Subsequent investigations revealed that no weapon was recovered from the vehicle. Michael Brelo was acquitted of all charges against him in the shooting deaths of Timothy Russell and Malissa Williams, despite reports that not only did Brelo reload at some point during the shooting, he took his final fifteen shots when he jumped on the hood of the car to fire at the victims – even after all the other officers stopped firing. It wasn't until 2016 that six officers including Brelo were fired from the Cleveland Police, but hey, at least the Cleveland Police Patrolmen's Association said that they would work to get the six reinstated to their positions, so good news for racists everywhere.

Freddie Gray was arrested by the Baltimore Police Department for possessing what the police alleged was an illegal switchblade. While being transported in a police van, Gray fell into a coma and died. The medical examiner's office concluded that Gray's death was a homicide, because officers failed to follow safety procedures – the officers hadn't secured him while transporting him in the van. There were also eye-witness accounts, which suggested that the arresting officers used unnecessary force during the arrest. Two Baltimore officers, Caesar Goodson Jr and Edward Nero, were found not guilty on the charges relating to Gray's death.

I mentioned Michael Brown's fatality earlier in this chapter. What is of additional note (outside of the fact that the perpetrator Darren Wilson was exonerated of the crime) was the fact that within two weeks of the killing, a GoFundMe page set up to support Wilson raised $225,000. A second GoFundMe page was created after initial outrage from the black community, raising the total to $433,000. In fact, according to website QZ, a Wilson fundraising organiser revealed that an outpouring of additional donations had raised Wilson's total to roughly one million dollars. One million dollars for taking the life of a young, black boy. And this is not an isolated incident; the gun that George Zimmerman used to kill unarmed black teenager Trayvon Martin, sold for $250,000 at auction.

The stats and the examples are clear: black people (and males in particular) have historically and overwhelmingly been targeted and victimised by the police. As I have indicated, you can see how this erodes our faith in law enforcement and the harm it does to the idea and perceptions of black communities at large. There is a direct corre-lation between the idea that our communities are crime-ridden, and the amount of force used against black people – but to delve deeper, we must understand how this has come to be.

SEEING BLACK AS A THREAT

So, this brings up the question of why? After all, it is rather unrea-sonable to assume that all the police officers involved in these scenarios are outright racist. So, what is it about being black that makes us such a target for police shootings and outright attacks? There have been many researchers trying to understand this issue. A study by John Paul

Wilson, PhD, of Montclair State University, suggests it has to do with the perceived threat of black people.

Wilson and his colleagues conducted a series of experiments in which people were shown photographs of white and black males (the individuals were all equal height and weight). The participants were then asked to estimate the height, weight, strength and overall muscularity of the men pictured. The experiment showed that participants judged the black men to be larger, stronger and more muscular than the white men, even though they were the same size. Even black participants judged the black men in the photo to be larger and stronger.

This lends itself to the stereotype around black people being comparatively well-endowed compared to white people – pure perception based on no facts (see Chapter Four). What's more worrying about this is that some police officers have gone to great lengths to reinforce this stereotype of black men as threats; such as the officers in North Miami Beach's police department, who were caught using mugshots of actual black people for target practice.

So, given the research, studies and experiments, why does this keep happening? And equally, why isn't there a much larger outrage from white communities? Why is the response to a legitimate movement like Black Lives Matter being met by All Lives Matter, or Blue Lives Matter? It's because their communities don't see it as an issue – a Pew Poll on race and inequality showed that half of white people surveyed don't believe black people are treated unfairly by police.

There have been numerous studies which show that everyone has an unconscious bias, no matter how liberal or well-meaning you are. It could be something as simple as crossing the street when you see someone whom you perceive to be dangerous, to assuming that someone is going to speak with a thick ethnic accent before they even open their mouth. The huge difference being that not everyone's prejudice results in the immediate death of another.

In some instances, there isn't even implied racism or stereotyping, but rather outright racism. For example, in 2015, almost the entire police force of Parma, Missouri resigned following the election of a black mayor.

Before Tyus Byrd was sworn in as the town's first black female mayor, eleven of the town's municipal employees had quit, including five out of its six police officers, which consisted of its entire police force.

BLACK ≠ CRIMINAL

Something that black people constantly have to challenge and refute is the notion that 'black culture' is somehow synonymous with crime and poverty. The general perception or stereotype that we constantly face is that because we are black, we must have had a poor upbringing, must love hip hop, must talk like a drug-dealing gangster from *The Wire*, and have gotten in trouble with the police. And when you don't fit into this delineated stereotype, you get the insult disguised as a compliment: 'You're not like other black people.'*

This is an overall perception that is even believed by the police themselves; the phenomenon of 'driving while black', where most black men driving a nice car are stopped by the police because they believe it to be stolen – for, of course, black people certainly can't afford a nice ride. 'Black culture' shouldn't automatically mean crime, any more than Italian culture should scream 'Mob'. People tend to conflate 'crime' with 'black' and 'poor', and criminality with 'young and black'. But there is nothing uniquely black about crime, or the propensity to commit crime – and it is only when we start recognising and understanding this about black and other marginalised communities that the inherent racism and unconscious bias can stop.

So, despite depictions in rap music videos, movies, TV shows and other forms of fiction, crime is neither inherent nor a source of pride for the black community. Donald Braman, law professor and author of *Doing Time on the Outside*, spent four years conducting interviews with prisoners, ex-prisoners, and their families in Washington, DC, and found that black families regarded going to prison or returning from prison with anything but pride. Instead, he found a sense of

---

* If you ever think of saying this to a black person, seriously, DON'T.

shame: families of those in prison hid the truth from even their extended family and closest friends.

When interviewing around fifty families, Braman reported that not one ex-prisoner had revealed to their families that they had been in prison. In fact, research into child development between black and white kids has shown that black families place an even greater emphasis on following the rules, compared with white families – arguably due to the sit-down talk black parents have with their children at an early age about the police.

One of the responses you are bound to hear about police brutality towards black people, or the notion that black culture doesn't equal crime, is the 'black on black crime' argument. 'If black communities are so safe, why is there so much black on black crime?' you'll hear them say. In a 2014 'Meet the Press' segment, *Wall Street Journal* editorial writer, Jason Riley, said, 'Let's not pretend that our morgues and cemeteries are full of young black men because cops are shooting them. The reality is that it's because other black people are shooting them.'*

Firstly, it's important to acknowledge that the current social conditions of the black community, which often lead to crime, are a direct result of slavery, segregation, and racist housing policies that prevented black and other ethnic minority communities from achieving sustainable wealth or social progression. It would be remiss of me to not mention the increasing level of knife crime in London over the past couple of years, and there is no denying the fact that a lot of that crime is prevalent in communities with a high black population.

But upon closer inspection, we see that a more accurate analysis shows that this sort of crime – knife and street violence – is associated with the most economically deprived areas. There is an increase in overall crime, particularly among youths in areas with families that are at the bottom of the economic ladder. Society has failed these individuals and created the conditions for them to turn to crime. Let me be

---

* Put this book down and Google a picture of him immediately . . . that's right, he's black! How's that for irony?

clear, this is not excusing the actions of the perpetrators – no matter the colour of their skin. If you commit a crime, you have to face the consequences of your actions. But I'm bringing this point up to drive home the fact that social conditions and not race are the drivers of violent crime in these communities.

After all, you would be hard pressed to find a large percentage of crime committed by individuals who feel supported and cared for by the society in which they live. So, you can't talk about the high levels of crime in the black community without addressing the injustices that caused there to be high levels of crime in the black community. One of the main challenges we have to face as a community is that law enforcement criminalise poverty, instead of enforcing policies to help people out of poverty.

In addition, studies have shown that poverty is one of the determining factors that could lead to crime, not being black. For instance if you look at a map showing the areas in London where the highest amount of violent crimes has been carried out, you will also see that it correlates with the areas of London with the highest number of people recorded as living in poverty. And the numbers prove it; for example, according to a House of Commons briefing paper on knife crime in England and Wales, the highest proportional increase of knife crime was in Kent (increased from twelve per 100,000 population in 2010/11 to forty-three in 2017/18), despite having a percentage average of around one-per-cent black population (compared to nearly ninety-four-per-cent white) in the most recent census. Additionally, the paper showed that Surrey, an affluent area, had the lowest rate of violent offences involving a knife with five per 100,000 population.

Another point to dispute the 'black on black' crime fallacy, especially when it is used to defend excessive action by the police in black communities, is that if a black person commits a crime against another black person, it's *not* because he's black; whereas in the case of fatalities at the hands of the police, studies have shown that they *are* racially motivated. Given the failures of the police in the black community, is it any wonder that they lack legitimacy in the eyes of black people?

That black parents are teaching their children to fear the police, instead of reaching to them for help? As alluded to in the previous chapter on stop and search, police officers are more likely to search and harass black people, even though these procedures are less likely to turn up anything criminal than searches involving white people.

As the *Los Angeles Times* writer, Jill Leovy, argues in her book, *Ghettoside*, the law has always existed to help people solve disputes without them taking matters into their own hands and solving it with violence. Black communities haven't had the luxury of the police being on their side and having them solve disputes, and as mentioned earlier, when the police overstep their bounds, there are no repercussions. As such, black communities rely on their own form of justice, which can lead to high homicide and violent crime rates.

Leovy notes in an interview with Vox online in 2016: 'Imagine that you're a student at a school. There are bullies at the school, and the bullies beat you up every day on the playground. But the only time the playground supervisor comes around, he or she says, "Don't chew gum on the playground," and walks away, and ignores the bruises and the fighting. You would be cynical. You would cease to believe in the system.'

At this point, it is worth noting that historically, black communities have been denied support from the government because of this very stereotype – for example, a confidential memo from the 1980s was leaked recently, which revealed that an MP, Oliver Letwin, had advised then-prime minister, Margaret Thatcher, that any social help for black entrepreneurs would only end up in the 'disco and drug trade'. Again, we see a direct correlation between stereotypes of the black community and the harm it causes to the community.

Finally, 'black on black crime' is not a phenomenon unique to the black community. That is, black people aren't uniquely predisposed to commit crimes against each other; crime by and large depends on several factors, and you are more likely to commit a crime against people that you know or live near* – and this applies to every race. For instance,

---

* As I've been reliably informed by literally every episode of *CSI* and *Law & Order* ever.

while the FBI's Uniform Crime Report showed that close to ninety per cent of African-American homicides were committed by other African Americans, it also showed that the majority (eighty-two per cent) of white American homicide victims were killed by other white people.

So, if there is a 'black on black' crime problem, there most certainly is a 'white on white one' too. In fact, according to a more recent report by the Department of Justice, the rate of white-on-white violent crime is about four times the rate of black-on-white crime. As Leovy says in *Ghettoside*, 'Take a bunch of teenage boys from the whitest, safest suburb in America and plunk them down in a place where their friends are murdered, and they are constantly attacked and threatened. Signal that no one cares and fail to solve murders. Limit their options for escape. Then see what happens.'

A BETTER FUTURE OF POLICING

The fatalities and overwhelming discrimination that black (and other minority) communities have faced at the hands of the police over the last few years have highlighted the problems in the perception of these communities and how they impact policing. Fortunately, we are starting to see steps taken in the UK to address the societal issues that are resulting in these crimes, if not the underlying stereotypes. The UK has been looking into how Glasgow went from being branded the murder capital of Europe by the World Health Organization to being heralded as reducing knife crime – the number of people admitted to its hospitals fell by sixty-five per cent between 2004–05 and 2016–17. The Glaswegian police attribute the success to the establishment of a policing unit called the Violence Reduction Unit (VRU), which combined strict enforcement and sentencing for carrying and using a knife with a 'public health' approach.

The officers arrived at the same conclusion I pointed to above, which is that the most vulnerable areas were also its poorest, and so, the knife crime and youth violence was seen as a symptom of the problems of society. They adopted an approach of early intervention, linking policing with social work, education, and employment. The unit focused on finding counselling for victims of violence, partnering with charities to teach and encourage children not to carry knives, working with schools on new education policies, and helping to find jobs for individuals with a criminal record.

By the way, it's worth noting that according to the 2011 UK Census, only about two per cent of Glasgow's population identified as African, Caribbean, black or any other black background. So it is encouraging to see that several English police forces have already been learning about this unit, and there is a forthcoming report by MPs calling for a public health approach to dealing with the knife crime issue in England and Wales.

Law enforcement in the States are also taking action to highlight and solve the problems in the current training and attitudes of the police force. Police in the United States have been progressive in issuing body cameras to its officers with some success. The San Diego Police Department reported that in the past three years of wearing body cameras, overall misconduct allegations were down forty-three per cent. More serious allegations related to criminal behaviour, discrimination, force, and racial or ethnic slurs were down forty-seven per cent, while allegations related to conduct, courtesy, procedure and service were down forty per cent. And though the use of force by officers increased, use of high-level use of force, such as physical takedowns, or employing Tasers, chemical agents or weapons, was down sixteen per cent. Of 520,000 incidents that San Diego officers responded to in 2016, just over 4,600 – less than one per cent – involved the use of force.

In 2015, the city of Chicago became the first city in the US to create a reparations fund for victims of police torture, after the City Council unanimously approved $5.5 million for the fund. Chicago Mayor, Rahm Emanuel, is quoted in NPR, noting that the abuse and torture of mostly black, male suspects from the 1970s to the early 1990s is a 'stain that cannot be removed from our city's history'.

As of May 2017, the Salt Lake City Police Department claimed to have not had an officer-involved fatality since 2015, as a result of retraining their officers to prevent fatal shootings. Their officers have adopted a confrontation tactic called de-escalation, where the officers are encouraged to communicate and empathise with suspects, take stock of the factors contributing to a confrontation, and consider ways to disengage before the situation spirals out of control, leading to the use of force.

Lorie Fridell, a criminologist with the University of South Florida and former director of research at the Police Executive Research Forum, has been working with police officers to help them resist biases, particularly against young black men, and the results show that with training, these biases are reduced. Her book, *Producing Bias-Free Policing: A Science-Based Approach*, has been the basis for this training and seeks to help police officers understand how they categorise individuals according to the stereotypes associated with their group. She notes: 'This does not require animus; it requires only knowledge of the stereotype.'

We tend to think of societal conflict in terms of winners and losers, or good guys vs. bad guys. It wasn't until I studied about the Cuban Missile Crisis in depth, as part of my A Levels, that I truly began to understand how conflict isn't so black and white. I had previously studied the crisis as part of high school history and knew where I stood. America (and by default the West) had won – we were the good guys and Russia were the bad guys. This is the point of view that most people in the West take on the issue, because of how we were taught in high school: that the Crisis was a two-week stand-off between the USA and Russia in 1962 off the coast of Cuba.

After the Second World War, the countries left standing decided that a Third World War was something they could really live without, and nuclear deterrence seemed to be the best way they saw to prevent this. So, the USA placed nuclear missiles in Turkey and Italy, aimed at Moscow, to which Russia responded by shipping nuclear missiles to Cuba, which is just under 2,450 kilometres from the USA (meaning an Intercontinental Ballistic Missile launched from Cuba could hit the States in six minutes). America, not fully understanding the rules of the 'you place nuclear missiles near me and I get to do the same' game, set up a military blockade off the coast of Cuba to prevent this.

The fact that we are currently not living in a nuclear winter means that the conflict was concluded peacefully – Russia retreated. While this is generally considered a victory for America and the West, I learnt later that it was actually a compromise and a few months after the blockade, America quietly removed their Jupiter missiles from Turkey. In essence, both parties walked away, being able to tell their respective parties they had won and the other side, who were the bad guys, had lost.

I think about this analogy a lot whenever I'm faced with another story of police brutality. Do we feel that as the victims we are in the right? The good guys of this conflict? I often try to think what it must be like for the police officers – even if they are unconsciously biased. After all, we all have an unconscious bias, only mine doesn't result in a life or death situation. I know that there is a problem with institutional racism in the police force; at the same time, I know there is a huge problem with crime in black communities. One thing I'm certain of is that we want to feel safe in our communities – whether that is by the reduction of crime or better law enforcement. What we don't want is racial profiling or excessive force.

So how can the next generation have faith and trust in law enforcement? Is it seeing more black and ethnic minority police officers? Is it by the strict and immediate prosecution of hate crime perpetrators? I don't know for certain, but the one thing I do know is that both sides have a lot of work to do and the only way we can succeed is by forgiving old sins and doing better as a community and a police force.

Answer to pop quiz: The Met Police are four times more likely to use force against black people than white people.

DRUGS

YOU KNOW WHERE TO GET WEED, RIGHT?

Stereotype/negative narrative: The intricate association with drugs (cannabis in particular) and its prevalence in the black community.

Pop quiz:

How many more times are black people likely to be stopped and searched for drugs than white people?

8.4

5

6.3

I'm not very cool – never have been and unlikely to ever be. And while I'm comfortable with this status as a man in his early thirties, I absolutely strived for coolness when I was in college. The most frustrating part of it all was that I wasn't a complete loser – it was just that coolness was a little outside of my reach. I basically ticked all the boxes necessary for being cool: I was black,* which was a novelty at our school, good at football, and got on very well with the few girls that attended my Sixth Form College. But I didn't quite make the cut.

Yeah, I was black, but I preferred studying to bunking off and trying to pick up girls from the neighbouring schools, like some of the other kids; I was good at football, but not rugby or basketball, which were the cool sports; and all the girls were friends with me, because I helped them with their homework and didn't touch them inappropriately. As such, I didn't fit nicely into the stereotypical jocks group, but wasn't automatically relegated to the nerd group either.

Me and some other friends who were in this predicament – the half-Spanish, quarter-Italian, quarter-Brit who always got attention from the girls, but only wanted to study maths and play football; and the half-Sierra Leonean, half-Malaysian kid who was hilarious and great with one-liners, but never spoke to anyone other than that; amongst others – formed a splinter group that could easily be described as Switzerland. We weren't bullied or outright ignored, but at the same time, weren't being invited to all the cool parties.

But I remember the day I could have joined the ranks of the cool at my college. We had recently had a girl join from a prep school in France and she was gorgeous. She was nice to everyone – almost as if she wasn't aware of her star status in the Catholic sixth form college, where boys constituted ninety-nine per cent of the student body (having joined from the associated all-boys Catholic secondary school).

I had noticed her, of course, but had not spoken one word to her, because (a) her kind didn't associate with mine and (b) I was really

* Still am, praise Jesus!

getting into quantum mechanics in physics class and didn't have time for girls.* But one day, she walked up to me, introduced herself, and invited me to her houseparty. Man, I was so excited. Mostly because this beautiful and nice girl from a superior social circle had invited me to her house party, but also because the fact she had invited me meant that the quantum mechanics theory of the multiverse was plausible, and I had clearly fallen into a parallel universe, where I was cool and being invited to the cool kids' party.

After about a full minute of trying to remember how to talk in this new universe, I introduced myself and accepted her invitation. She smiled at me and turned to walk away. And if we were in the parallel universe where I was cool, that would have been the end of it. But because we are in this shit universe where Brexit is a thing, Bowie's dead, and there was no proper season three of *Chappelle's Show*, she asked me, 'You know where to get weed, right?'

Well, fuck me! At that point in my life, I was more likely to be able to cross-pollinate tetrahydrocannabinol strands from scratch than to know where to buy the damn thing. But I couldn't say that, because I really wanted to go to the party, so I simply told her that I did and would have no problem bringing it.

Dear readers, I cannot begin to explain the panic I faced as I tried every nerd method to secure weed for this girl's party. A simple Yahoo search† for 'where to buy weed' did not come up with any solutions I was willing to participate in. I asked my friends and they were frankly as clueless as I was. I even asked the 'bad boy' of our year to see if he could help, but he just assumed I was looking to 'grass him up' (I was the deputy head boy at the time) and he told me to fuck off.

So, the night of the party, I went to the only place I could think of to find weed – Brixton. My mother had expressly forbidden me from going to Brixton once the sun set, because Brixton in the early

---

* Seriously, I was really not cool.
† Yep, I'm that old.

noughties after dark was full of 'drug addicts and good-for-nothings"*. I must have hung around Brixton, watching the people who were obviously selling weed for about an hour, trying to pluck up my courage to ask to buy some. But I couldn't shake the feeling that they were going to take my money and not give me the weed, or that I was under surveillance from the police. In the end, I went home disappointed; so much so that I couldn't even bring myself to fantasise about being in another parallel universe – one where the cool beautiful girl wanted me to go to her party, not because I could score her some weed, but because she genuinely wanted me there.

The next day, she didn't ask me why I couldn't make it; the first thing she asked was why I didn't turn up with the weed. I couldn't very well tell her it was because I didn't have a clue how to get some, so I made up some flimsy excuse. That was the last time she ever spoke to me.

I saw that as my one chance to enter the cool kids' crew and, for a few years after that, I couldn't help thinking that she only wanted me to come to her party because she thought I might have weed. It took me a while to realise that she most likely asked me if I could get weed, because I was the only black person she knew at the school. Let's face it, there was nothing about my personality at school that would even suggest I had smoked a regular cigarette, let alone a joint. It was simply a manifestation of another stereotype – this intricate association with drugs (weed in particular) and its prevalence in the black community.

This stereotype rears its head when we are approached by law enforcement, when we are depicted in TV and movies, and even in our social circles. And as a black man, this stereotype hangs over us like the Sword of Damocles, ever ready to deny us opportunities, or cast us in a negative light. And while the movement for the legalisation or decriminalisation of cannabis has gathered momentum over the past years, making it one of the least controversial drugs, it's important to

* And presumably vampires.

remember that the overall association with drugs is something that has deeply impacted the black community for years. The drug policies of our governments and law enforcement have disproportionately targeted black communities and set them back socially, economically, and materially for years.

This chapter looks at the history of these drug policies and their impact on the black community – with a focus on cannabis (weed), because even though it is one of the more commonly accepted and decriminalised drugs, its freedom of use and sale is still not reflecting positive experiences for the black community. So, while these days, a black person enjoying a joint on Hampstead Heath or Dolores Park with the rest of the hipsters may not be as risky as it used to be, you can bet your last penny that if there are any consequences, it'll be the black people paying it.

ORIGINS OF CANNABIS USE
(*SPOILER ALERT, NOT FROM JAMAICA*)

One of the fundamental aspects of being human is seeking escape from pain or discomfort. And while we may sometimes alleviate this through enjoyable social activities with friends, family, or other members of our social circles, synthetic or natural drugs are often the most popular or efficient use to alleviate pain – and this is not limited to humans. Animals also use drugs to escape from the pangs of discomfort. Ever see a cat on catnip? They literally exhibit the characteristics of a human high on drugs. Scientists have observed dolphins carrying puffer fish in their mouths, squeezing them to get the fish to release a small burst of neurotoxin, which gets them high. After enjoying it, they then pass the fish along to other dolphins for them to share in the intoxication.*

In fact, animals experimenting with drugs isn't a recent thing. Ronald Siegel notes in his book, *Intoxication: The Universal Drive for Mind-Altering Substances*, that as early as AD 900, Abyssinian herders

---

* Literally, 'puff, puff, give'!

noticed their animals were energised after eating the bright red fruit of a tree that would later be named 'coffee'. He theorises that man may have learned how to take drugs from watching and emulating animals; noting that man cleaned his wounds after watching animals lick theirs, and observed which plants resulted in pleasurable effects after the animals had eaten them. Then, over the course of time, man learned to sniff, smoke, and inject drugs for pleasure.

Cannabis is among the earliest plants cultivated by man. According to Hui-Lin Li, a Chinese botanist and researcher, the plant had been cultivated for fibres, ropes, textiles and paper since 4000 BC. Textiles and paper made from cannabis were even found in the tomb of Emperor Wu (104–87 BC) of the Han dynasty. It wasn't till around 2700 BC that cannabis was reported to be used to alleviate pain, or used as medicine; in the beginning of the Christian Era, Hua T'o, the founder of Chinese surgery (AD 110–207), used cannabis, taken with wine, to anaesthetise patients during surgical operations.

The first reference to the use of cannabis as a psychoactive drug was reported in the world's oldest pharmacopoeia, the *Pen-ts'ao Ching*, which said: 'the ma-fen (the fruit of cannabis) . . . if taken in excess will produce visions of devils . . . over a long term, it makes one communicate with spirits and lightens one's body.' Later, its use spread to India, where cannabis was used both as a medicine and as a recreational drug. The researcher Mia Touw theorises that such broad use may be down to the fact that it was embedded in religion at the time, as the *Atharva Veda* (a collection of sacred texts) mentions cannabis as one of five sacred plants, referring to it as a 'source of happiness, donator of joy, and bringer of freedom'.*

Barney Warf, a professor of geography at the University of Kansas, believed that cannabis came to the Middle East between 2000 BC and 1400 BC and noted that it was probably used there by the Scythians, a nomadic Indo-European group. According to Warf, the Scythians also likely carried the drug into south-east Russia and Ukraine, given

---

* You can say that again.

that they occupied both territories for years. Germanic tribes brought the drug into Germany, and marijuana went from there to Britain during the fifth century with the Anglo-Saxon invasions.

According to archaeology researcher John Peter Wild, the oldest evidence of cannabis in Britain was in a Viking settlement in York in the tenth century, and it has been theorised that much like its original use in 4000 BC, it was used as a source for rope. Because of its usefulness as rope, in 1533 King Henry VIII mandated that landowners grow it in abundance and in 1563, Queen Elizabeth I decreed that landowners with sixty acres or more must grow cannabis, or else face a £5 fine.

This brief but detailed insight into the origin of cannabis use and its spread across the world is very relevant in this chapter, because it helps dispel the myth that cannabis and its use originated from Jamaica or the Caribbean. And this is a prevailing stereotype – one of the laid-back, dreadlocked Jamaican man, who listens to reggae with a joint in his mouth. Cannabis was in fact introduced to Jamaica in the 1850s by slaves imported from India during British rule.*

The reality is that the prevalence of cannabis in Jamaican culture is based largely on the Rastafarian movement, which allows for its followers to consume and share cannabis as a sacrament and herbal medicine – much like the ancient Chinese and Indians. Rastafarians believe that the Tree of Life mentioned in the Bible (which Adam and Eve ate from) is the marijuana plant; and point to several other biblical passages that they believe promote its use, such as, 'Thou shalt eat the plants of the field' (Genesis 3:18), 'Eat every herb of the land' (Exodus 10:12), and 'The herb is the healing of the nations' (Revelation 22:2).

In fact, most Rastafarians condemn the use of cannabis simply to get high, because it is such an ingrained and important part of their religion. They use it in their religious ceremonies known as 'reasoning sessions' to get closer to 'Jah' (God) and believe that they can see the truth of the world more clearly when smoking cannabis. So, to Rastafarians, cannabis use is no different than Christians participating

---

* I mean, come on. You knew slavery was going to rear its ugly head at some point.

in the sacrament of the body of Christ. To assume Rastafarians are drug-addled because they smoke cannabis is like assuming that Christians are alcoholics, because they drink wine in church first thing every Sunday morning.

So, if cannabis did not originate from Jamaica, the Caribbean, or other black communities, why is there a prevailing stigma and negative stereotype towards black people and cannabis – notably that our communities are responsible for its prevalence? More importantly, why are there more black people in prison for cannabis-related offences compared to other races or ethnicities? The answer is obvious and simple: because the laws and principles targeted at drug users, in this case cannabis, are racist.

THE WAR ON DRUGS IS RACIST

Growing up in Streatham, in south London, meant being around a diverse community with a healthy amount of BAME residents. In writing this chapter, I got in contact with a few of my black friends who also grew up (and some still live) in south London to ask what the main reason was for them having been stopped by the police in the past – to see if their experience mirrored my own, which I described in Chapter Three. They all unanimously cited it was drugs. I tried to replicate this with a few of my white (and to be fair, Indian) friends who also grew up there, but unsurprisingly so few of my white friends had ever been stopped and searched by the police that it was even a moot point to ask if it was for drugs.

Black people always have to challenge the notion that black culture is synonymous with crime and poverty. An extension of that notion is the narrative about drugs in our community, because the storytellers of this narrative are law enforcement, and they are simply spewing out untruths to further their own agenda. In fact, the British police have a long history of spreading disinformation about illegal drugs overall.

In 2007, the Oxfordshire Police Force alerted eighty schools about how drug dealers were selling a new product called 'Strawberry Quik', which was allegedly pink-coloured, strawberry-scented crystal meth aimed at children. However, despite the police warnings and the media reports, there have been no cases of the drug or children using it at all, according to fact-checking website, Snopes.com.

In 2010, the police were behind a *Daily Mail* article: 'Police reveal 180 pupils at one school off sick after taking legal "Meow Meow" party drug', which helped fuel the widespread drug panic at that time. A week after the *Mail* article, a police officer reported that two teenagers in Scunthorpe had died after taking mephedrone – and because of the inaccurate media hype, the government rushed to ban mephedrone. However, in the months following the ban, the BBC reported that the teenagers in Scunthorpe had not even taken mephedrone, and the story about the 180 school kids was dismissed by Leicestershire Council as false.

In 2012, the Northamptonshire Police released an official statement to the media claiming that the odour from cannabis plants causes cancer, declaring that: 'Police are warning that when cannabis plants reach the final stages of maturity the odour they release has carcinogenic properties . . . Officers who deal with the plants use ventilation masks and protective suits, and people who have plants in their home, especially anyone with young children, may be exposing their family to a health risk.'

As this is blatantly incorrect, the police had to retract their statement and the newspapers who reported this had to publish a correction, when Peter Reynolds, who heads a group called Cannabis Law Reform,* complained to the Press Complaints Commission saying there was no evidence to support the claim, and the newspaper had failed in its duty to check the facts.

Given these instances, it's no surprise that the University of Kansas professor, Barney Warf, said: 'Many early prejudices against marijuana were thinly veiled racist fears of its smokers, often promulgated by reactionary newspapers.' So we can see how false narratives can play a part in formulating law enforcement's agenda or perceptions when it comes to exacerbating the drug problem, and while these are separate

---

* And a goddamn hero!

incidences in the UK, the biggest untrue and completely racist narrative on drugs came from America: the so called 'War on Drugs' initiative, introduced by President Richard Nixon.

On 17 June 1971, then President of the United States, Richard Nixon formally launched the 'War on Drugs' in a speech to Congress, saying that: 'If we cannot destroy the drug menace in America, then it will surely in time destroy us.' And while this is a noble endeavour to pursue – after all, the 1970s were rife with drug use among hippies and there was a genuine problem with soldiers coming home from Vietnam hooked on heroin – in the decades that followed, it resulted in an escalation of unnecessary law creation, police enforcement, and mass detention of people from BAME communities, particularly when it came to cannabis.

The author and essayist, Brent Staples, notes in his *New York Times* article, 'The Federal Marijuana Ban Is Rooted in Myth and Xenophobia', that because cannabis was brought to the US by Mexican immigrants (for use as an intoxicant and for other medicinal purposes, as they had done back in Mexico) the negative view of marijuana by law enforcement was shaped by the narrative that drug use is prevalent among brown people from Mexico, and subsequently with black and poor communities. He notes that police in Texas border towns demonised cannabis in racial terms as the drug of 'immoral' populations.

He further states, citing the work of legal scholars Richard Bonnie and Charles Whitebread in their book, *The Marihuana Conviction: A History of Marihuana Prohibition in the United States*, that it was cannabis use among minorities that ensured it a classification as a 'narcotic' alongside far more dangerous drugs like heroin and morphine, and attributed it with addictive qualities it did not have. In addition, in the 1970s, *60 Minutes*, then the most-watched TV news programme in the USA, did a segment on Rastafarianism, portraying it as nothing more than a drug-smuggling business using religion to mask the import of illegal drugs.

To this day, a lot of people (of an older generation) in the black community believe that crack cocaine was introduced into the community by the government to justify incarcerating them in large numbers. While there is no evidence to support this belief, it is not surprising that it exists, given that law enforcement essentially manufactured the narrative of a crack-cocaine epidemic in minority communities. And we see a lot of evidence of this in the media narrative of its day.

For instance, a 1914 article in the *New York Times* warned: 'Murder and Insanity Increasing Among Lower Class Blacks Because They Have Taken to "Sniffing" Since Deprived by Whiskey Prohibition'. The article, by Dr Edward H. Williams, stated: 'Most of the negroes are poor, illiterate and shiftless . . . Once the negro has formed the habit, he is irreclaimable. The only method to keep him away from taking the drug is by imprisoning him. [Cocaine] produces several other conditions that make the "fiend" a peculiarly dangerous criminal. One of these conditions is a temporary immunity to shock – a resistance to the "knock down" effects of fatal wounds. Bullets fired into vital parts that would drop a sane man in his tracks, fail to check the "fiend".' So, according to Williams, cocaine makes black men both murderous and, at least temporarily, impervious to bullets.*

This unnecessary and draconian narrative around the effects of crack cocaine is also exemplified by the Anti-Drug Abuse Act, passed by the United States Congress in 1986, which sets out the penalties for crack cocaine convictions. The penalties for crack cocaine were 100 times harsher than for powder cocaine because, while powder cocaine was regarded as a classy drug and a symbol of luxury associated with white people, crack was portrayed as addictive, dangerous and associated with black people – eighty-five per cent of those sentenced for crack cocaine offences were black, even though most users of the drug were white.

Additionally, the effects of crack were greatly exaggerated; crack cocaine is no more harmful than powder cocaine. The only difference between crack cocaine and powder cocaine is the removal of hydrochloride, which allows for a higher melting point, and the ability to be smoked. Crack cocaine is typically produced by mixing powder cocaine with

---

* If only Pablo Escobar were black, he'd be alive today.

baking soda and water, and then heating it. The process dries the cocaine into a rock-like shape (hence the colloquialism – rocks).* But on a molecular level, crack and powder cocaine are still nearly identical. What makes crack cocaine more potent is the fact that it can be smoked, which provides a quicker high than snorting.† But the mandatory minimum sentence threshold for crack cocaine compared to powder cocaine in America is significantly higher. For instance, you would need to have nearly eighteen times more powder cocaine than crack cocaine to get the five-year mandatory minimum sentence that crack carries.

In case you are still not convinced that this is evidence enough of a racist narrative, an aide to Richard Nixon recently admitted it publicly. In a 2016 interview with *Harper* magazine, former Richard Nixon aide, John Ehrlichman, said when asked about drug policies: 'You want to know what this was really all about?' The Nixon campaign in 1968, and the Nixon White House after that, had two enemies: the anti-war left and black people. You understand what I'm saying? We knew we couldn't make it illegal to be either against the war or black, but by getting the public to associate the hippies with marijuana and blacks with heroin, and then criminalising both heavily, we could disrupt those communities. We could arrest their leaders, raid their homes, break up their meetings, and vilify them night after night on the evening news. Did we know we were lying about the drugs? Of course, we did.'

THE CONSEQUENCES OF THE NEGATIVE NARRATIVE – RACIAL DISPARITY

While the promotors of the negative narrative associating black and minority communities with drugs might have had some form of altruistic motive to fight the drug epidemic, it had some real-life consequences for the black community. It resulted in black people being the de-facto

---

* Don't try this at home – especially if black. The last thing you want is to be convicted as a distributor.
† Did I mention that I kick arse in chemistry also? Walter White ain't got shit on me.

scapegoats and ultimate victims of the 'war on drugs' and overall drug policy. There has been comprehensive research supporting this notion; one of the most prominent by Release, the national centre of expertise on drugs and drugs law in the UK.

It showed that the average search rate for drugs across the UK between 2009 and 2010 was ten searches per 1,000 people. For those identifying as white, it was seven per 1,000, increasing to fourteen per 1,000 for those identifying as mixed race, eighteen per 1,000 for those identifying as Asian and forty-five per 1,000 for those identifying as black. This means that black people are over six times more likely to be searched for drugs than white people, even though statistically, people of African and Caribbean heritage take fewer drugs.

This has also been supported by research in the States, where the ACLU found that while cannabis use is roughly equal among blacks and whites, blacks are nearly four times as likely to be arrested for cannabis possession. And this form of discrimination extends to sentencing, in that black people caught in possession of weed are five times more likely to be charged with a criminal offence than white people, and cautioned three times more. So it comes as no surprise to me that in 2019, a judge in Swansea spared two white drug dealers jail time, because he was impressed with their spelling and grammar in the text messages used in the drug deal.

It's certainly understandable given the prevailing stereotypes of drug dealers, if while reading the previous paragraph, you were thinking of black males. But the racial disparity when it comes to drug arrests affects black women, too. According to a review by the Ministry of Justice (aka the Lammy review), in the UK, for every 100 white women handed custodial sentences for drug offences in 2014, 227 black women were imprisoned. Additionally, for every 100 white women handed custodial sentences at crown courts for drug offences in 2014, 227 black women were given prison terms. And not only are black women more likely to go to prison for drug offences, but according to the Prison Reform Trust, they are also more likely to face difficulty in finding support after their conviction.

Aside from the racist narrative being the rationale behind these actions, in some cases, the police target black and minority communities for drug offences in order to arrest them for other more dangerous crimes. A Vox article reported that in certain cases, '. . . the police have used drug crime as a proxy for violent crime. It's much easier for a prosecutor to guarantee a conviction on a drug charge – where there's physical evidence that the defendant had drugs – than on a violent charge, where proving what happened is more complicated. And police target drug enforcement in high-violence neighbourhoods, which are overwhelmingly black and Latino.'

This is one of the reasons why there is such a large percentage of black people in prison. According to the Institute of Race Relations, ten per cent of inmates are black, even though black people make up only three per cent of the UK population, and there are 141 black men in prison for drug offences for every 100 white men. It is not just the arrest rates that are discriminatory to the black community: once convicted, black drug offenders get longer sentences than white drug offenders.

According to a report by the US Sentencing Commission, drug sentences for black men were thirteen-per-cent longer than drug sentences for white men. Roughly forty per cent of the two million imprisoned men in the US are African American and at any given time, more than ten per cent of black men in their twenties or thirties are in jail or prison. In the UK, the proportion of black people in jail is almost seven times their share of the population. It's no wonder that scholar and writer, Michelle Alexander, notes in her book, *The New Jim Crow: Mass Incarceration in the Age of Colorblindness*, that there are now more African-American men in prison and jail, or on probation and parole, than were slaves before the start of the Civil War.

In a 2015 article for *Vice* magazine, former Secretary-General of the United Nations, Kofi Annan, discusses at length about the negative impact that criminalisation has had on Africans, and the huge mistake of the governments who decided to focus on criminalisation instead of the problem of drug addiction and focusing on treatment.

He notes: 'Governments that focus on drug users and small-time dealers often create an unsustainable burden on their criminal justice systems, while ignoring the health and social problems that have emerged with increasing levels of trafficking, consumption, and production, which goes on unabated . . . the current policies are not only ineffective but actually detrimental to the efforts being made to contain the threats that drugs pose . . . drugs may have destroyed many people, but wrong governmental policies have destroyed many more. Let us not repeat this mistake.'

This is not a problem only prevalent in Africa, the UK or US; another article in *Vice* magazine shines a light on the plight of other vulnerable people in different countries, who have found themselves on the receiving end of the 'war on drugs':

Russia: In Russia, home to the highest number of injecting drug users in the world, trumped-up drug offences are used by police as an excuse to beat, torture and rape vulnerable drug users and sex workers.

Thailand: In Thailand in 2003, thousands of 'undesirables' (mainly the homeless, orphans, drug addicts and petty dealers) were rounded up and locked in rehab centres or prisons as part of a national 'war on drugs' by Prime Minister Thaksin Shinawatra. During the purge, there were 2,800 extrajudicial killings, although half the victims had no connection to drugs.

Iran: In Iran, the war on drugs is quietly used as a way to bump off enemies of the state, or helpless Afghani refugees, by planting drugs on them and then hanging them. Research by human rights charity Reprieve found evidence in Iran – whose drug police are part funded by the UN – that 'drug charges may be used as a pretext for persecuting and executing political dissidents'. It said exiles and human rights monitors allege that 'many persons supposedly executed for criminal offences, such as narcotics trafficking, were political dissidents'. In the first half of 2015, according to a report by drug charity Harm Reduction

International, there were an estimated 570 executions in Iran, of which 394 people (sixty-nine per cent) were allegedly drug offenders. After anti-government protests in 2009 and 2010, execution doubled, with most killed under the banner of being drug criminals.

So, we can see how law enforcement and regulators appear to have formulated the 'war on drugs' to target the most vulnerable. Dan Dolan from Reprieve, which assists those facing the death penalty notes: 'The global drug enforcement system is disproportionately penalising vulnerable and marginalised people. These people are never the drug barons or kingpins [that] governments claim to be targeting. In most cases they are low-level drug carriers or mules, selected for their expendability. In almost all cases they suffer from intellectual disability, addiction or severe economic disadvantage.'

Surely, then, the focus for governments should be on rehabilitation? Fortunately, we are starting to see a bit more movement in this area in the United States. Under Barack Obama, the White House's Office of National Drug Control Policy had planned to increase funding for rehabilitation programmes and approved regulatory reforms like Obamacare, which increased access to addiction treatment through health insurance. Donald Trump's policy also includes grants to programmes that could help communities in their drug rehabilitation. Of note is the 'Drug Court Program', which helps ensure that drug addicts receive help and not punishment, so that instead of sending drug offenders to jail or prison, these courts send them to rehabilitation programmes that focus on treating addiction.

Now the use of these examples is by no means to suggest that the 'war on drugs' was solely driven by racism and xenophobia. As mentioned before, there was an increase in the amount of drug use, resulting in very real economic, physical, and emotional damage. The point is that the 'war on drugs' was founded on a lack of understanding about drug use within minority communities and as such, these communities bore the brunt of the harshest penalties – and for what?

Sources report that the 'war on drugs' cost America around

$1 trillion, causing Harvard University economist, Jeffrey Miron, to note in an Associated Press report that the only sure thing taxpayers get for more spending on police and soldiers is more homicides: 'Current policy is not having an effect of reducing drug use, but it's costing the public a fortune.'

This is all best summarised by Chris Rock in his comedy special *Never Scared*:

'One thing I don't like about America is we've got bad drug policy. We got people in jail for getting high. The Government says drugs are illegal, because they're trying to protect society. But they don't give a fuck about your safety – they sell guns at Wal-Mart. They don't give a fuck about you. No, the Government's like this: they don't want you to use your drugs, they want you to use *their* drugs.

The reason coke and weed are illegal in America is cos the best coke and weed ain't made in America . . . The first reason they will never legalise drugs in America is because the Government makes way too much money putting our brothers and sisters in fucking jail. The second reason the Government will never legalise drugs in America is because, God forbid, some brown people got wealthy.'

ALTERNATIVE SOLUTIONS TO RACIST 'WAR ON DRUGS' POLICY

So, if we accept that the war on drugs policy is racist, we need to look at what alternatives there are to solve the drug problem that would not be prejudicial to black and other minority communities. Much like dealing with the violent crime problem in communities, there is evidence that a 'harm reduction' approach to combating the drug problem could work. This would help by focusing on reducing the negative outcomes of drug use to both individuals and their communities. The goal of harm reduction is not necessarily to eliminate drug use altogether, but to reduce harmful side-effects, such as contracting infectious diseases or overdosing.

The most common way of achieving this is through a treatment commonly referred to as Supervised Injectable Heroin (SIH) treatment, where medical professionals prescribe and administer synthetic, injectable heroin to [opiate] addicts – who have proven resistant to other treatments – in a supervised environment that minimises risk to themselves and others. This treatment allows some addicts to satisfy their drug dependency, without the risk of overdose or resorting to crimes to obtain drugs; overall it benefits the community and saves law enforcement the cost of trials and incarceration.

The SIH treatment programme in Switzerland, the first national scheme of its kind, has been credited as a success and since the introduction of SIH treatment, more countries including the UK, Denmark, Germany and the Netherlands, have tried and tested this clinical approach. According to a report by the EU Drugs Agency, research trials show that SIH treatment can lead to the 'substantially improved' health and well-being of this group; 'major reductions' in their continued use of illicit 'street' heroin; 'major disengagement from criminal activities', such as acquisitive crime to fund their drug use; and 'marked improvements in social functioning', with stable housing and a higher employment rate.

A CRAZY IDEA: LEGALISATION

The case for legalisation is a simple one: cannabis is not more harmful than other legal vices, so legalise it and generate revenue for the economy through taxation. After all, alcohol is perfectly legal, but has been proven to be significantly more harmful than cannabis. In fact, a 2015 scientific study revealed that smoking weed is 114 times safer than drinking alcohol. And think of the economic boost that we'd benefit from in legalising a substance that is readily available, has an established customer base, and is found to be mostly unharmful.

More importantly, legalisation would deal with the discriminatory targeting of black and minority communities by the existing racist drug policies. There have been genuine attempts to drive this notion in the UK. A study commissioned by the Liberal Democrat party reported in *Vice* magazine reveals that legalising cannabis would generate hundreds of millions each year for the UK, as well as save the criminal justice system more than 300 million a year in court and police costs. Not to mention, it is a movement that people actually want and would be good politically.*

The same article reports that a petition on legalisation had over 220,000 signatures and revealed that around 216 tonnes of cannabis was smoked in the UK in the past year and that 2.2 million people aged sixteen to fifty-nine are thought to have used the drug in that time, making it the UK's most widely used narcotic. And this is just on the proactive side of things; think how much money the government would save if it didn't incarcerate on the grounds of cannabis use. For instance, between 2000 and 2009, there were an average of 1,139 cannabis offenders in custody a year. According to a news article by the *Guardian*, it costs around £45,000 a year to house an inmate, so quashing all previous cannabis convictions would result in a potential annual saving of approximately £51.2 million.

This could also have the same effect for the United States. The CATO Institute, an American think tank found that legalising cannabis would provide all levels of government with $17.4 billion annually, with around half of that because of reduced spending (particularly on law enforcement) and the rest would come from taxing marijuana like alcohol and tobacco.

Those worried about the mass effects of complete legalisation, fearing that their streets would be overrun with the prevalence of weed, need not worry. Legalisation could take many forms. For instance, the government could allow citizens to have, use or 'possess' cannabis, but not sell or grow it; additionally, the government could

---

* Lord knows the Lib Dems could use every bit of support they can get.

issue licences to trusted individuals and businesses to sell the drug.
Indeed, the government could create a state-run monopoly that
produces and sells the drug, which would help eliminate potential
black-market sales.

Research by RAND found that US States that maintained a
government-operated monopoly for alcohol kept prices higher,
reduced access to youth, and lowered overall levels of use – all which
are socially beneficial to the public – so they can adopt this approach
with cannabis and benefit from similar results. Just think about how
empowering and freeing legalisation would be for communities where
law enforcement has typically targeted them, and for the most minor
of drug offences.

WILL LEGALISATION SET US FREE?

Given that there appears to be good cause (and effect) for the legalisation, or at least decriminalisation of cannabis, is this enough to be a
solution to the racist narrative and effects of the 'war on drugs'? Will
it be enough for black and brown people to acquire wealth that comes
close to equalling that of the white community? In essence, will it set
us free?

Unfortunately, so far, the evidence points to the contrary. In the
United States, even though we have seen a strong contribution to the
community and the economy at large due to the decriminalisation and
taxation of cannabis, we are also seeing that black people and its
communities are more likely to be excluded from the profitable impact
of decriminalisation. If you accept the premise that the 'war on drugs'
disproportionately targeted, arrested and incarcerated the black
community, then this creates a whole new set of problems when it
comes to acquiring wealth in the post-decriminalisation era.

The reason is that black people are much more likely than any
other race to have a criminal record because of drugs (under the
racist policy), and every US state that has legalised or decriminalised
cannabis bans people with drug felonies from working at, owning,

investing in, or sitting on the board of a cannabis business. So even after having borne the brunt of the 'war on drugs', the black community is now largely missing out on the economic opportunities created by legalisation or decriminalisation. As a result, fewer than thirty-six of the 3,600 (about one per cent) storefront cannabis dispensaries in the United States are owned by black people, according to a report by Buzzfeed.

This sad fact is embodied by a quote from writer and law professor, Michelle Alexander, in a press call arranged by the Drug Policy Alliance: 'When I see images of people using marijuana and images of people who are now trying to run legitimate marijuana businesses, they're almost all white. After forty years of impoverished black men getting prison time for selling weed, white men are planning to get rich doing the same things.' So, it is not enough to end the war on drugs, we must repair the harm that was caused by it, which still reverberates within the black community.

Now it's unreasonable to assume that every black person arrested for a drug offence was disproportionally targeted, so even if we exclude them, even without a criminal record, black people looking to get into the cannabis business face huge obstacles. In an article, Sarah Cross, the chief operating officer of Green Rush Consulting, a business that secures cannabis permits and licences, estimates that it takes at least a quarter of a million dollars to start a legal marijuana business.

After generations of systematic discrimination affecting the wealth, housing, education and employment of black people, African Americans are simply less likely to be able to afford that kind of money. In addition, they can't get loans for their business, because banks are insured by federal agencies, and federal law still considers cannabis illegal – cannabis legalisation is granted by State law.

But hey, this all could be explained by simple economics; besides, there are poor white people who also cannot afford to drop half a million dollars to set up a cannabis business. Why is this only a problem for the black community? Well, if you take economics out of the equation and focus simply on the racist targeting and negative narrative, you'll see that even after legalisation or decriminalisation, black people are still being targeted disproportionately. For example, even though overall drug arrests dropped ninety per cent in Washington DC and sixty per cent in Colorado (states where weed has been legalised) between 2008 and 2014, the post-legalisation arrest rates for black people were still double the rates for non-blacks, according to Mike Males, a senior research fellow at the Center on Juvenile and Criminal Justice.

It stands to reason that because African Americans constituted such an excessively large proportion of cannabis arrests before legalisation, then the fact that the disparity remains after legalisation confirms the existence of racist targeting. After all, black people can't double the amount of crime they are committing if the act itself is no longer legal. Couple this notion with the fact that arrest rates for white people have fallen post-legalisation, which is a more likely effect of legalisation: NPR reported that the marijuana arrest rate for white ten- to seventeen-year-olds fell by nearly ten per cent from 2012 to 2014, while arrest rates for Latino and black youths rose more than twenty per cent and fifty per cent respectively!

Aside from enforcement post-legalisation being unduly targeted towards the black community, the racist and negative narrative is still prevalent. For instance, in 2017, the Metropolitan Police tweeted about a 1 kilo heroin haul they had made in Catford, positioning it as a pre-emptive drug strike ahead of that weekend's Notting Hill Carnival. What makes this tweet part of the racist narrative is that Catford is twelve miles away from Notting Hill and has no obvious connection to the Notting Hill Carnival, so it's hard to understand why the police would make that connection. Unless there were no drug arrests in any of the regions between Catford and Notting Hill, or they had distinct evidence that the perpetrators had planned to distribute it at the carnival, then the tweet was discriminatory.

Notting Hill Carnival is a celebration of black Britain and unfortunately, as a result, has always been associated with drug-related crime by the police and the media. I'm not saying that there is no crime at all at the carnival; in fact, there is a ridiculous amount of pick-pocketing that occurs, but that would happen whenever you have a large number of drunk and happy people concentrated in one area – they make easy targets.

Notting Hill Carnival is simply more associated with drug-crime compared to other events that aren't predominately to celebrate black culture. *Vice* magazine breaks down some of the figures to compare, showing how a few of the UK's biggest summer festivals measure up to the carnival in 2017, which was attended by roughly 1.5 million people across the weekend and saw 450 arrests, 169 of which were drug-related.

In 2016, Glastonbury hosted around 135,000 people. Official figures from the Avon and Somerset Constabulary show that 3,911 grams of illegal substances were seized. That's the equivalent of 43 kilos being seized at Carnival. Yet there were no major articles in the media about drug arrests at Glastonbury.

The 2016 Bestival on the Isle of Wight saw £175,000 worth of drugs seized with an attendance of 50,000 people. There were forty arrests, thirty of which were drug-related. If you scale that up to Carnival numbers, you would have seen 900 drug-related arrests – more than Carnival's 450.

At Boomtown, located near Bristol, £134,000 worth of drugs were seized from an audience of just 46,000. This would be roughly the equivalent of a £5 million haul at Carnival.

Chelmsford's V Festival saw forty-three arrests last year, twenty-seven of which were drug-related from an attendance of roughly 170,000. There would have to be 238 drug-related arrests at Carnival for it to equal this.

There were 137 arrests made at Creamfield 2016 Festival,* a majority of which were for drug-related offences. Given that only 70,000 were in attendance, there would have to be 2,935 arrests at Carnival to equal this.

---

* I've run a Google image search for this event and couldn't find even one black person.

Latitude festival has an attendance of roughly 35,000 and was awarded 'Best Family Festival' at the 2012 UK Festival Awards. In 2016, eight people were arrested for drug-related offences, which at first sight doesn't seem that much, but if you scale up attendance to Carnival levels, that's 342 drug-related arrests – almost twice the amount of 2017's Notting Hill figures.

IS THERE ANY HOPE FOR THE FUTURE?

Drug laws are a funny old thing. In the UK, if you've ever had a joint in your possession, you've committed a crime that could cost you up to five years in prison and a fine. If it was cocaine or ecstasy, then that's seven years plus a fine. To put that in comparison, that's more than you would get if you were found with Gamma-hydroxybutyrate aka GHB, which is a date-rape drug. Given GHB is a Class-C drug, the maximum sentence is two years. Hell, the sentence for possession of a firearm is only five years, so arguably, you are going to get a longer sentence for having cocaine than for having a gun.

In the US, it's even more ridiculous – there's no point doing a gun comparison, because as Chris Rock says, you can simply buy a gun in Wal-Mart. But what's crazier still is the fact that marijuana is considered a Schedule 1 drug under the Controlled Substances Act, alongside ecstasy, LSD, and heroin. But I suppose we are (comparatively) fortunate given how stringent drug laws are in other countries. In China, Malaysia, Iran and Saudi Arabia, you can be executed for any number of drug crimes – in Vietnam, if you're arrested with more than 1.3 pounds of heroin, you'll be automatically executed.

Perhaps being legally compared to these nations (where frankly, you could be put to death for any number of offences) is one of the reasons why the UK has started taking a more lenient approach to certain drugs. For example, in 2009, Britain's Transform Drug Policy Foundation put out a 232-page report called 'After the War on Drugs: Blueprint for Regulation', where the authors suggested issuing licences for buying and using drugs, with sanctions for those who break the law – like the requirement for gun licences in the US, or a driver's licence. It suggested that prices should be high enough to 'discourage misuse, and sufficiently low to ensure that under-cutting . . . is not profitable for illicit drug suppliers.'

Now that doesn't seem to be such a bad idea. But in any case, the police in the UK have seemed to stop giving a shit about your weed. The BBC, through a Freedom of Information request, found that arrests for the possession of cannabis in England and Wales have dropped by forty-six per cent since 2010, which is good news in ensuring that members of the black community will not be unfairly targeted for cannabis offences, but what about in America – how can we start to take advantage of the moves towards legalisation that will benefit the black community?

An interesting solution has been proposed in Oakland, California,* where in May 2016, its city council unanimously approved a programme that gives people with former marijuana convictions a chance to enter Oakland's growing legal cannabis industry. At the time, of the city's eight dispensaries, only one was black-owned. However, Oakland's Equity Permit Program reserves half of its marijuana business licences for the recently incarcerated, and people living in neighbourhoods directly impacted by the drug war.

Also, Californians with marijuana convictions may soon have their offences reduced, or records cleared, if the Assembly Appropriations Committee approves a bill requiring California courts to review marijuana convictions and automatically reduce or expunge them. Think of what a positive impact this will have on black people in California and their ability to own their own businesses.

Much like the actions of the police towards the black community, and the economic status of said communities, we are seeing exactly how much of an impact old, outdated, and frankly racist policies have on the black community today. A huge amount is asked of us to be able to move forward, when it seems like the deck is stacked against

* Because . . . California.

us and has been for generations. When it comes to cannabis, there is no perfect economic and social solution, so we'd need to settle on the best option that gives us a degree of fairness and puts us on equal ground with the white community, because that's all we've ever wanted – equality.

Answer to pop quiz: Black people are 6.3 times more likely to be searched for drugs than white people.

DANCE

YOU'VE GOT THAT NATURAL RHYTHM

Stereotype/negative narrative: That all black people have natural rhythm and white people have none.

Pop quiz:
*As of December 2018, how many black dancers
are in the British Ballet Theatre or at least featured
on their dancers' webpage?*

3

0

5

I remember the first time I was told that I didn't know how to dance. It was 1994 and the R&B sensation, Aaliyah, had just released a song called 'Back & Forth'. It was a hot track, and everyone knew the words and the dance moves that went along with it. Unsurprisingly, it involved moving your hips back (twice) and then forward (also twice), while stepping to the side twice (known as the Two Step).

I was in my living room with my younger sister and my older cousin, when the track came on the radio and we all immediately got up and started dancing. My cousin was two years older and already knew the moves, so was teaching it to my sister, who picked it up quickly. I, on the other hand, resembled a newly born antelope trying to walk for the first time. After being laughed at, my cousin proclaimed with the audacity of a town crier: 'You just don't know how to dance.' Now granted, being able to dance was hardly a huge concern for me at age ten – I was more pissed off because there was something that my annoying little sister could do better than me.

It wasn't until my teenage years when I learnt that being able to dance was something that is supposed to come naturally to black people, whereas white people were meant to be awful at dancing. This theory was given further merit when I attended my first Nigerian wedding and was absolutely mesmerised by the rhythm, the movement, the freedom of black people dancing.

Now that I'm older and thankfully know how to dance the 'black way', I can't help but question why it is that black people dancing is seen as more aesthetically pleasing than white people. I mean, it's ridiculous to presume that white people can't dance; it's not as if there is a 'dancing gene' that is present in black people, which is absent in white people. So I started to wonder if it had something to do with our culture and history? Or was it simply because 'black music', such as hip-hop and R&B, has popularised urban music?

While this is another 'positive stereotype' (like the stereotype about black men being well-endowed), it still remains harmful, for it is founded upon 'race-based thinking' – that you are genetically able to do certain things (or not), because of something as trivial as the colour of your skin. And for some reason,* this always seems to be the case when it comes to black people.

I'll give you an example: statistically speaking, a lot of Chinese children over the last generation are competent at playing musical instruments, particularly the piano and the violin. The BBC reports that over forty million children from China are learning the instrument and China is the world's largest piano producer and consumer, accounting for nearly eighty per cent of the global piano output. But it is widely accepted that this is because they are receiving increased training to learn the instrument, and not because there is something fundamentally Asian or Chinese about playing the piano. So why then can't this consideration be afforded to black people?

To truly understand the origins of the stereotype that black people are great dancers and white people aren't, we must understand that there has always been a difference in the way black people and white people considered dancing. While today, what we consider as music is an important part of both races' cultures, it wasn't always so – as the author, Ruth Stone, noted in her book, *The Garland Encyclopaedia of World Music: Africa*: 'Honest observers are hard pressed to find a single indigenous group in Africa that has a term congruent to the usual Western notion of music. There are terms for more specific acts like singing, playing instruments, and more broadly performing (dance, games, music); but the isolation of musical sound from other arts proves a Western abstraction.'

In Afro-Caribbean history, dance and music played an integral part of everyday life. In some African cultures, dancing was an initiation rite – a necessary part of becoming an adult. For example, in the Liberian region, the Poro and Sande societies perform a dancing ceremony with elaborate costumes. Young initiates in the Cameroons, and adults performing in the Gelede and Egungun societies in Nigeria, are recognised as spiritual beings when they dance in their costumes. And

---

* I mean, the reason is almost always slavery and racism.

in northern Nigeria, the Barawa dancers are said to embody the dodo, the ancestral spirit of the dead.

In some instances, dancing was a sort of language, used to express joy at weddings or births, or sadness at funerals. It was as potent as a specific dialect. In fact, many African cultures did not have a separate word for music and dance; for example, the Kpelle people of Liberia use a single word 'sang' to describe a well-danced movement. Some African scholars such as Caesar Ndlovu were actively against even writing down African music, noting that to do so would compromise the performance of African dance. In short, dancing was viewed as a form of communication and expression, which encompassed different activities. Because this was a means of communication (and writing it down was discouraged), it could be argued that there was the need for African dance to be as expressive as possible.

However, this was not always the case in Western or white cultures – as far back as the Middle Ages, dancing in groups was considered a form of madness or 'mania' in Europe and readily associated with symptoms of the bubonic plague.* The rationale here was that dancing is an expression of joy, and there was nothing to celebrate while friends and family were dying of the plague. Dancing was also severely discouraged because it involved physical contact, to which people were averse, as they didn't want to come in contact with or get infected by the sick and dying.

But there was one thing that played a major role in the way Europeans and therefore white people came to consider dancing – and that was religion.

DANCING AND RELIGION

The Puritans in early seventeenth-century Europe believed that everyday life should be lived per God's will; in other words, pious and consecrated. In this time, dancing was considered evil, promiscuous,

---

* Dance fever being a stage 2 symptom of the bubonic plague.

and the pastime of the devil and his cohorts. As evidence of this, the Puritans would use a biblical passage, referencing that the dancing of Salome, daughter of the Roman king, Herod, was so hypnotic that Herod offered to grant her any wish, enabling her to ask for the head of John the Baptist* (who happened to be Jesus's cousin).

Additionally, the Puritans believed that music led to laziness, which in turn meant that people weren't spending their time honouring God. They even shirked away from using music and dance to honour God because it was common practice for Catholics to use music during mass and boy, did they hate the Catholics. The lives of the Puritans were based on what their religion dictated, so even outside of the church, music in the personal life of early Puritans was minimal, if not non-existent.

From the early sixteenth-century onwards, we start to see various ministers denouncing dancing – the infamous Protestant minister, John Northbrooke, proclaimed dancing to be 'the vilest vice of them all' – as well as books being published warning against the dangers of dancing. Some cult classics include:

- *A Treatise Against Dicing, Dancing, Plays and Interludes*, Minister John Northbrooke, 1577
- *Anecdotes for Girls (with warnings against dancing)*, Harvey Newcomb, 1848
- *Social Dancing Inconsistent with a Christian Profession and Baptismal Vows*, Benjamin Palmer, 1849
- *An Appeal to All Christians Against the Practice of Social Dancing*, Rev. John Jones, 1867
- *From Ballroom to Hell and the Lure of Dance*, T.A. Falkner, 1922

We still see evidence of this in a lot of Catholic and Church of England practices today; worship is formal, still, and pious. Religious scholar,

---

* Mark, Chapter 6, Verses 21–29.

Robert Orsi, discusses in detail the stillness expected in Catholic mass, noting that a 'strict physical discipline' on the body was meant to be reflective of spiritual reverence. Carla De Sola also notes in her book, *The Spirit Moves*, that 'as a dancer, my body is dulled during a long mass with no physical expression.'

Now, let's compare this to worship in 'black churches'. From the mid to late 1960s, most African countries started to gain their independence. However, the impact of colonisation did not dissipate immediately. In fact, most countries adopted some of the traits of their previous colonial masters, such as systems of government, laws, currency, language, names, and religion. But with independence came the freedom to practise Christianity in a way that suited Africans – an opportunity to put their personal stamp on the religion, and thus the popularity of Gospel music and dancing within black culture began.

For most black children growing up in the Christian faith, dancing has always been a huge part of religion. And it is not the solemn swaying that most Roman Catholic and Church of England churches employ; it is loud chanting, clapping, singing and dancing that is so often used as a physical expression of spirituality. In fact, the louder you are and the more fervour you apply to your praise, the closer to God you are meant to be. 'Let the spirit move you' is a frequent saying in a lot of black Baptist and Pentecostal churches.

This freedom of expression during worship differs from the expected stillness in the traditional European-formed Church.* Some scholars have even claimed that stillness in worship represents godliness, compared to the free movement of the body during traditional African worship, which is immoral. Dance scholar, Brenda Dixon Gottschild, notes how the African system of religion was believed to embody deities that render the body as 'vulgar, comic, uncontrolled, undisciplined, and most of all, promiscuous'. Admittedly it is as unreasonable to assume that all Pentecostal/Gospel parishioners are predominantly

---

* The eerie silence of Catholic mass, making your impure thoughts seem even louder.

black, as it is to assume most Catholic parishioners are white. After all, the Pew Research Center estimates that there are more Catholics in the Democratic Republic of Congo than there are in the United Kingdom.

However, given how much of religion still impacts our lives today – holidays, marriage, extremism, and war – it is not at all unreasonable that it could have played a significant part in how, and why, which type of dance is most popular.

MOVIES AND DANCING

Movies provide a widely accepted cultural lens for addressing the stereotype of black people having natural rhythm. While the Puritan's notion that dancing is evil might seem ridiculous to us in the twenty-first century, let's not forget that this notion formed the plot of a hugely popular 1984 movie, *Footloose*, in which a cool teenager from Chicago moves to a small town, where the city council has banned dancing and rock music. The cool protagonist falls for the daughter of the councilman leading the charge against dancing, and through his disturbingly hypnotic dance moves, helps the town see the error of their ways to embrace dancing again.

If this seems ridiculous still,* you'll be surprised to learn that the movie was based on actual events that occurred in Elmore City, Oklahoma. Dancing was banned for almost a hundred years in Elmore City ending in 1980, when the high school graduating class got permission to dance at their prom. After which, then class president, Rex Kennedy, said in an interview with *People* magazine: 'We thought about asking for permission to dance at the next Future Farmers of America meeting, but I guess that's pushing our luck.' Worryingly, he wasn't being sarcastic.

Another worthy movie to help unravel this stereotype is *Save the Last Dance* (released in 2001). The plot revolves around an interracial

---

* The movie grossed over $80m on a $8m budget, by the way.

couple who fall in love through their mutual love of dance – hip hop, in the case of the black male (Derek Reynolds) and ballet, in the case of the white female (Sara Johnson).* One of the standout scenes in the movie is when the white protagonist goes to a hip hop club for the first time and is completely overwhelmed by the level of skill involved in the dancing. This leads to a montage where Reynolds teaches Johnson how to dance to hip hop – incorporating grinding, swagger and, of course, the Two Step – and in return, she introduces him to the choreographed stylings of ballet.

It's a beautiful scene, which helps establish a relationship between the characters, however, it is rather ridiculous that the audience is expected to believe that a Julliard-worthy dancer would struggle to master the simple moves of the Two Step – just so she can fit in at a tacky Chicago club called STEPPS? This reference, and indeed the whole movie, tends to support the stereotype that black people have natural rhythm, whereas white people must choreograph their dance moves. In the movie, the black characters all move to the music; freestyling where necessary, and form their own dance moves from the beat. In addition, the white protagonist had to incorporate the choreography of ballet with the freestyle of hip hop to secure her place at Julliard.

BALLET AS A TYPE OF FORMALISED DANCING

While it appears that historically dance was favoured more among black cultures (even as late as the twentieth century), it wasn't always doom and gloom for the early Europeans. The restrictions to dance were mostly aimed at the commoners, which suited them fine, as they had nothing much to celebrate or dance about really. The royals and their courts readily adopted forms of formalised dancing, and this period heralded dances such as *la volte* and the waltz. However, there was a dance movement that became very popular in the sixteenth

---

* Although I would pay double to see a movie where the musical tastes are reversed.

century that bears significance when it comes to stereotypes about dance. I'm talking, of course, about ballet.

Positive stereotype or not, this type of race-based thinking marginalises us into specific areas of music, because if black people are seen as having a natural rhythm that applies only to the likes of hip hop and R&B, then we are missing out on entire genres of music, and ballet is a good example of this. Ballet is an interesting dance movement to examine in context of the dancing stereotype, in that it's rare to find a black person, or many people of colour, in depictions of ballet – either in real life or in fiction.

The Bolshoi Ballet is one of the oldest and most renowned ballet companies in the world, and looking at their dancers, there is a distinct lack of diversity (to be fair, most of them are Russian and it's not like there is a huge black population in Vladivostok). So let's take the American Ballet Theatre as another example. As of 2018, out of all their principals and soloists, only one black person is well-known – Misty Copeland; there is also one Philippina-American, Stella Abrera. Similarly, as of 2017, there appears to be only two black dancers out of sixty-four in the English National Ballet, and a review of the British Ballet Theatre's website shows that there are no black ballet dancers at all.

The reasons cited for the lack of black people in ballet are a history of non-inclusion and wrong body shape – white people being perceived as being more likely to be thin, petite and lean, compared to black people. However, a rebuttal of that argument would be that much like any other athlete or dancer, performers train to be in that shape, and do not often come naturally prepared for ballet. And if you need further proof of the racial disparity in ballet, it's only in 2018 that the pointe shoes which ballet dancers are required to wear come in the colour brown – two hundred years after white ones. Before this, ballet dancers of colour had to spend at least forty-five minutes dying or painting each shoe, in order to match the colour of their skin.*

---

* Ever wonder why plasters are the colour that they are, i.e. nude? It's to better blend in with your skin colour, which of course doesn't work at all on the skin of people of colour.

Fortunately, we might be seeing a revolution in this area. Homer Hans Bryant of the Chicago Multi-Cultural Dance Center, has created a new genre of ballet called 'Hiplet' (pronounced hip-lay), which is a fusion of ballet with hip hop, performed predominantly by people of colour. So now little black boys and girls can look to ballet as a viable option.

To conclude, we should consider if there is any scientific proof that black people are any better at dancing than white people. As ridiculous as it sounds, there has been some research into the 'dancing gene'. In 2005, the Hebrew University of Jerusalem conducted such research, theorising that the AVPR1a and SLC6A4 genes contribute to creative dance. AVPR1a is a vasopressin receptor, which is non-scientist speak for hormones responsible for water retention and constricting blood vessels. Not very interesting, or at first sight relevant for our case, is it?

What is interesting, though, is that when it comes to behaviour in mammals, AVPR1a has been seen to reduce anxiety-like behaviour and to stabilise social recognition. Equally, SLC6A4 is a serotonin transporter; and serotonin is a neurotransmitter that governs your perception of resource availability — mostly food. But when it comes to social interactions, serotonin is a confidence booster. Research in *Science* magazine indicates that animals injected with high serotonin levels are shown to have an inhibiting fleeing reaction, act like alphas, and become socially dominant. This all makes sense in a human setting, because you are more likely to dance if you have reduced anxiety (AVPR1a), and you're more socially dominant and less likely to run away when approached by a member of the opposite sex to dance (SLC6A4).

Now, to bring it back to the stereotype about black people being better dancers: if high levels of these genes are responsible for better or natural dancing, then it stands to reason that black people would have more of these genes in proportion to white people, right? However, it turns out that assertion is wrong. Research looking at the differences in serotonin transporters in European and African-

American subjects by the National Institute of Mental Health's Collaborative Center for Genomic Studies,* shows that African Americans were seen to have significantly lower rates of the serotonin alleles compared to European Americans. So, this research would suggest that scientifically, it's white people who should have the natural rhythm.

The reality of the situation is that trends change: what was cool or acceptable at one point in time is rarely cool and acceptable in another. The times we live in now place hip hop and R&B at the epicentre of cool. So, dancing to this genre of music will be considered as cool – and naturally, the group or ethnicity that grew up with this type of music will be seen as having the 'natural rhythm'. I grew up in a predominantly black household, so a member of One Direction could walk into my house right now and I wouldn't know who the hell they were. And that isn't because I am not naturally attuned to pop music, but because I was brought up with a different genre (hip hop) and it's one that I like.

At its most basic, dancing is movement of the human body. So, dancing becomes an extension of what we think of the human body. Like the body, dancing can be beautiful or ugly, good or bad, sexual or chaste, expressive or personal. Also, dancing means many things to different people. It can be for fun, exercise, art or pure amusement. In essence, whether people can dance depends on factors relating to much more than race.

Sure, I can dance to R&B and hip hop music, but when I attempted the waltz, I spent a considerable amount of time stepping on my partner's toes. That's not because I'm black, but because I had never given any thought to the waltz. Equally, there are many white people who would be more comfortable on the dance floor of a hip hop club, rather than in a ballroom doing the waltz.

Still not convinced? The next time you're in a club and you see a black person you think is a great dancer, put your hands over your

* Undoubtedly where the party's at.

ears and see how ridiculous they look without sound. After all, as the Puritan minister, Increase Maher, famously asked: 'Is there a difference between a dancer and a madman?'

Answer to pop quiz: As of December 2018, there were no black dancers in the British Ballet Theatre or at least featured on their dancers' webpage.

DATING

WHY DO YOU DATE THOSE WHITE BOYS/GIRLS THOUGH?

Stereotype/negative narrative: That black people with white or other race partners prefer them because they're not black and would forgo a good black partner as a result.

Pop quiz:

According to census data, how many people in England and Wales are living with or married to someone from another ethnic group?

5 million

1.8 million

2.3 million

There is an important rite of passage in the life of every first-generation kid – the moment they stray from the path their family had set out for them. This is a monumental step and one not to be taken too lightly, because a lot rides on that step. You're gonna want to choose something important enough that your parents realise you are independent, capable of making your own decisions, and not be beholden to the traditions of the past, *but* not something so important that they are going to accuse you of forgetting your roots and ship you back to the motherland, so you remember where you came from.*

The first time I 'went against the family',† was in 1997. In fact, I can remember it down to the exact minute. It was 17 May 1997 at 16.45 British Standard Time. Chelsea had just finished playing Middlesbrough in the FA Cup final and had won 2–0. It was the first football game that I had watched from start to finish with a friend, instead of a member of my family. At the end of the game (in which Chelsea midfielder, Roberto Di Matteo scored the then fastest goal in an FA Cup final at Wembley), I decided that I was going to start supporting Chelsea Football Club.

Now, this was hugely controversial, because every member of my immediate and extended family are staunch Arsenal supporters and expected me to be the same. And this preference for Arsenal as a football team within the black community is still prevalent today. The fact is, most black people from London support Arsenal. A survey conducted by the University of Leicester's Football Research Centre, reported on the BBC, revealed that nearly eight per cent of Arsenal's fan base identified as 'not white', compared to the average one per cent of the rest of the Premiership clubs. This could be explained by its location – as the most popular team in north London, it garners support from its neighbouring communities such as Hackney, where there are many Afro-Caribbean residents.

Having spoken to my family members and other members of the

---

* This is not a joke; it has happened before. It's every first-generation kid's nightmare.
† If Nigerians had a mob, it would be just as dangerous as the Mafia or Yakuza, but oh so inefficiently run.

black community, it became clear that one of the main reasons that most black people support Arsenal is because it was one of the first major clubs in London that had several black players. From its first black player, Brendon Batson, in the 1960s, to the 1990s and 2000s period that heralded players such as Patrick Vieira, Kolo Touré, Sol Campbell, Ashley Cole, Thierry Henry, Nicolas Anelka and Nwankwo Kanu – Arsenal football club was considered as the predominant team for black players to progress in the Premier League. So, to say my family were surprised and confused that I chose to support Chelsea would be an understatement.

My father: 'Boy, the Arsenal game is on, hurry up! Oh, and get me a Coke from the fridge.'*

Me, from the safety of my bedroom: 'I think I'll give this one a miss, actually.'

Father, utterly confounded: 'Boy, come down here when I'm talking to you. (*I slink down the stairs.*) What do you mean "give it a miss"?'

Me: 'Erm . . . well . . . I've decided to . . . that is to say . . . I think I am going to support another team . . . just because . . . you know.'

Father, no longer watching the football:† 'You are supporting another team? Why?'

Me: 'Well, I just decided to . . . you know . . . do something different . . . you know?'

Father: 'Must you say "you know" all the time. What kind of lawyer says "you know"?'

Me: 'I'm not actually a lawyer yet, because I'm only thirteen,‡ but I've just decided . . . you know . . . I mean, not you know.'

---

* Every time a Nigerian parent calls for you, they'll always add you getting them something – even if they are closer to the thing you want. 'Boy, the house is on fire, hurry up and get out. Oh, and make me a cup of tea while you're at it.'

† Which was already a bad sign!

‡ Doesn't matter to a Nigerian parent. The moment you express interest in a profession, you had better be the best at that profession.

> *Father*: 'I honestly don't know what's wrong with you? You're such a confusing boy. Well, if you want to support Wimbledon or Crystal Palace, I suppose that's fine. Where's my Coke?'
> *Me, handing him the Coke and about to drop the bombshell*: 'Actually, I've decided to support Chelsea.'
> *Father, does a genuine spit-take*: 'You are going to support Chelsea? You? My son?'
> *Me*: 'Well, yes. Just to see . . . maybe for a while.'
> *Father*: 'But they are racist!'
> *Me*: 'No, they're not.* Their manager is a person of colour, and they have this Jamaican defender called Frank Sinclair . . .'
> *Father, back to focusing on the game as he seriously contemplates disowning me*: 'Fine, it's your funeral.'†

My father (and the rest of the family when they were informed) couldn't seem to wrap their heads around why I would choose to go against the norm, against a tradition clearly set and accepted by the rest of the family. Consequently, I ended up missing some of the crucial father-son bonding moments: going to a game together, or even watching and supporting the same team on TV.‡

Not all stereotypes about the black community are external, some are prevalent within our own communities. In some black families (arguably most), there is a big expectation that their offspring will end up with a black partner, which can be incredibly difficult for a first-generation black person, because by and large, we don't feel beholden to this logic. Similarly, there is a stereotype within the black community that black people with partners from other races – particularly white partners – prefer them and would forgo a good black partner as a result.

In Chapter Six, I referred to an episode of *Master of None*, where

---

*   The behaviour of some of the fans over the past couple of years has forced me to question this statement.
†   Which he most definitely won't pay for.
‡   Better than being shipped to the motherland, I suppose.

a black parent is explaining to minority children that they will have to work twice as hard. In that episode, the same black parent is appalled not only at the idea that her daughter is a lesbian, but at the prospect that she might bring home a white girl: 'Oh lord. Oh lord! Well, I just hope she don't bring home no white girl, because I don't wanna see no Jennifer Anistons up in here!' This prevailing notion is the reason why I use the football analogy in the context of this stereotype. It's because it touches on the idea of loyalty.

By supporting Chelsea (a team which is believed to have a high number of racist and intolerant supporters), I was being disloyal. The expectation was that since Arsenal had been loyal to the black community by signing black players, I had to be loyal to Arsenal by supporting them. This is similarly the kind of thinking that some (particularly within the previous generation) hold when it comes to interracial dating. To be clear, this chapter is not based on the racist idea that black people should not date white people, or vice versa; but rather examining why some black people believe there should be an allegiance to one's own race or ethnicity. So let's examine this, is it so wrong to prefer this?

Loyalty to one's own is the very nature of evolution. The pack mentality of Homo Sapiens that enabled us not only to survive, but become the most dominant species on earth, still exists today. We seek out the comfort and feeling of belonging to a group where the members are like us.

Research by Inga D. Neumann, Professor for Neurobiology and Animal Physiology at the University of Regensburg, explains that when we are engaged in social activities with a similar group, we release a hormone called oxytocin, which contributes to relaxation, trust, and social stability. In fact, it is commonly known within the scientific community as the 'love molecule'. It is a key component in ensuring the bond between a mother and her new-born: oxytocin is also responsible for helping women get through labour by stimulating contractions, is shared during breast feeding, and helps establish intimacy and trust with the baby.

Additionally, there is research from Cornell University and the University of Indianapolis, which shows that people who met their significant other through family or community had 'stronger ties' compared to couples who met at a bar or online – seeming to suggest that there is some value in dating someone who looks like and is from the same place as you are.

But there is a difference between loyalty and stubbornly holding on to old-fashioned ideas of dating and relationships. Strictly adhering to the notion that black people should only date black people, or that black people in interracial relationship prefer partners of other races over black, is detrimental to the community at large. Not only does it belittle the happy relationships of our brothers and sisters, but it also serves to denigrate the attractiveness of black people, if we continue to perpetuate this stereotype that we are unattractive to our own people.

Also, it is hard enough to fight racism and bigotry on a daily basis without having to watch our backs and face animosity from our own people. Earlier, I discussed how difficult it can be for black people to make it in entertainment, now couple that struggle with the abuse they get for being in interracial relationships once they have made it. We have seen examples of online abuse and sarcastic comments addressed at famous people in interracial relationships:

- On Twitter following the release of the trailer for the movie, *US*, by Jordan Peele, who is married to Chelsea Peretti: *Jordan Peele getting y'all excited using a dark-skinned cast then going home to his Caucasian wife.*

- Comments about actor, Omari Hardwick's white wife: *She is ugly, she sho' is ugly, and unh-unh, she is still ugly! With all these beautiful Black women, and he would get a white woman and an ugly one at that. What a white-minded, uncle tom, cotton-picking negro he is.*

- Some Instagram comments on Serena Williams' page, where she shared a picture of herself, her (white) husband, and their baby: *Serena is a disgrace to her parents, grandparents, our African ancestors because she married and mated with a European, knowing that his ancestors owned Africans as SLAVES, raped our African sistaz, killed our African men.*

- *Why you trying to be white? I used to be a big fan now I'm so ashamed smh. I'm far from hating and will never be a hater but this just isn't right at all . . . have some pride . . . I bet your father feels the exact same way . . . just a true wannabe you even wear your makeup and hair weave to look like these devils just pathetic.*

- *Y black women usually so self-conscious they need to have white babies it's always the really dark girls too, lol.*

- *How Serena Williams goin to consider herself a strong black woman and can't even handle being with a black man???*

While it is important to note that because their avatars, or pictures, are of black people, it does not necessarily mean that these people are black, but it does show the kind of abuse that interracial couples face for nothing other than falling in love with someone who looks different from them.

A HISTORY LESSON ON INTERRACIAL DATING

Unsurprisingly, given the slave trade and lack of civil rights for minorities, interracial coupling was essentially taboo till the late 1980s. One of the most infamous instances of the hatred towards interracial coupling (or even attraction) was the murder of Emmett Till. He was a fourteen-year-old, African-American teenager in Mississippi, who was murdered in 1955 for allegedly flirting with a white woman. The woman's husband, Roy Bryant, and his brother, J.W. Milam, kidnapped

Emmett, beat him and gouged out one of his eyes, before shooting him in the head and throwing his body into the Tallahatchie River.

The brothers were acquitted at trial by an all-white jury after just a little over an hour of deliberation. According to research by Stephen J. Whitfield, Max Richter Professor of American Civilization, one juror had said, 'If we hadn't stopped to drink pop, it wouldn't have taken that long.'

After the brothers were acquitted and protected against double jeopardy (a law preventing citizens from being prosecuted for the same crime more than once), they publicly admitted in an interview with *Look* magazine that they killed Till. Milam was quoted as saying, 'I like niggers in their place – I know how to work 'em . . . And when a nigger gets close to mentioning sex with a white woman, he's tired o' livin'. I'm likely to kill him.' As a result of the murder and confession, there was such a huge uprising in the black community that Till's murder is often credited as being crucial in kick-starting the African-American Civil Rights Movement.

Another major instance where interracial coupling came into the public eye was the marriage between the Rat Pack member, Sammy Davis Jr, and Swedish actress May Britt in 1960. At that time, interracial marriages were forbidden by law in thirty-one US states. In fact, reservations against the relationship were so strong that John F. Kennedy's father asked Sammy (who was friends with JFK) to postpone the wedding till after the election, so it wouldn't hurt his son's chances of being president – to which Davis Jr agreed, although he was still excluded from the inaugural festivities once Kennedy won. The fact that interracial coupling was so taboo that a presidential candidate's father had to intervene, gives a sense of the ramifications of interracial dating.

More recently, in October 2009, Keith Bardwell, a justice of the peace in Robert, Louisiana, refused to officiate the civil wedding of an interracial couple, because of his personal disapproval of the union. He claimed that children of biracial unions are not fully accepted by either black or white society and said he 'didn't want to put children in a situation they didn't bring on themselves. In my heart, I feel the children will later suffer.' Furthermore, he revealed that he had refused applications to four couples over a period of two and a half years before this came to light. Naturally, he was asked to resign his office, which he did.

It appears that the issues with interracial marriage were stronger in the United States than in England. For instance, interracial marriage was only decriminalised in most states in 1967 (although Alabama didn't officially legalise it until 2000, and even then, forty-one per cent of voters were against it). One of the most famous cases that over-turned most of the outdated state laws prohibiting interracial marriage was that of Richard and Mildred Loving.* Richard and Mildred were from Virginia and met when he was seventeen years old and she was eleven. As they grew older, their friendship blossomed into romance. Mildred became pregnant at eighteen and the couple travelled to Washington, DC to be married.

Five weeks after their wedding, they were awakened at 2 a.m. by police and arrested for interracial marriage. They were offered a choice: one year in jail or leave Virginia. They left Virginia for DC, where they campaigned for nine years for their case to be heard before the US Supreme Court. In 1967, the Supreme Court decided unanimously in their favour. Richard later said, 'For the first time, I could put my arm around Mildred and publicly call her my wife.†

And 52 years later, the state of Virginia keeps trying to pull the same shit. A federal judge ruled that a Virginia law requiring couples to reveal their race in applying for a marriage license is unconstitutional. Three couples had to file a lawsuit against the Virginia State Registrar claiming they were denied marriage licenses in the state after they refused to check a box disclosing their race on their applications.

---

* Their honest to God surname.
† There is an annual celebration of the couple called Loving Day and is held on 12 June, the anniversary of the 1967 United States Supreme Court decision.

MY OWN SELF-EXAMINATION

Given these examples are significantly in the past, shouldn't we have moved on to more enlightened thinking? Why is there so much stigma to interracial dating? Even though my family have no problem who I date, they would much prefer me to be with a black woman. Preferably Nigerian. And Yoruba. And Christian. And Pentecostal. And under the age of thirty*. And they haven't stopped introducing me to black women ever since.

> **Some random aunty**: 'Hey, so my daughter just got out of Med School.'
> **Me**: 'Ayo graduated? That's amazing news. Congratulations!'
> **Aunty**: 'You should come round for some food. Ayo's a great cook.'
> **Me**: 'Erm . . . sure. It would be good to see you all.'
> **Aunty**: 'Seriously, her food is so delicious. It's very impressive.'
> **Me**: 'Yes, well . . . so is graduating Med School.'
> **Aunty**: 'Yes, that's true, I think you'll both get on. You'll really like her.'
> **Me**: 'I already like her.'
> **Aunty**: 'Yes, but I mean in a relationship way.'
> **Me**: 'I'm actually in a relationship already. Remember the nice lady I told you about? She's my girlfriend.'
> **Aunty**: 'Well, yes, but you're not going to marry her.'
> **Me**: 'Why not?'
> **Aunty**: 'Because you'd want to be with someone of your own culture. Someone that your family knows.'
> **Me**: 'Someone like Ayo?'
> **Aunty**: 'Yes!'
> **Me**: 'But she's my cousin!'
> **Aunty**: 'Well, not really. I'm not actually your mother's sister, am I?'

* And spins straw into gold. Let's not forget the basics.

Me: 'Well, that's news to me,' but in any case, I don't know her. I literally haven't seen her since she was fifteen.'

Aunty: 'You know she's a good girl from a good family. What more do you need to know?'

Me: 'If we're related would be a good start. But it doesn't matter, because I have a girlfriend.'

Aunty: 'Well, yes, but you're not going to marry her.'

Me: 'Why not?'

Aunty: 'Because you want to be with someone of your own culture. Someone that your family knows.'

And over and over the conversation went. I think I was hoodwinked into actually getting betrothed by the end of the conversation.

A question that I get asked regularly is: 'Why do you also date white girls?' This absolutely astounds me, because it's not a question I would ever consider asking anyone, as I have absolutely no qualms about dating any woman of any race. I have often come across people who say, 'I don't date [insert race here] women.' And I understand that this does not always come from a place of racism or prejudice, it's merely personal preference. However, how does one go about dismissing a whole race? It's as ridiculous as someone saying, 'I don't date blondes,' as if it is a rational conclusion to exclude all blonde women out of their lives.

The fact is, there's not enough distinction between the races, which we have established are nothing more than a social construct, to warrant preferring one over the other when it comes to choosing a partner. People like partners who are smart, funny, intelligent, and sexually adventurous – and these traits are not more prevalent in one race than in others.

Despite knowing the science behind attraction, I couldn't help but question myself, as I have dated women outside of my race. Is there

---

* Africans call any adult who is the same age as their parents, aunty and uncle. It can be terribly confusing as to who is actually related to you. This is why I don't try to pick up anyone at a Nigerian wedding.

any truth to the stereotype, and am I a classic example of it? This worried me greatly, because at the time I was already dealing with the insecurity of not being a stereotypical black person. I was practically heartbroken following a conversation that I had with a black woman at my old job. We had seen each other around and exchanged pleasantries, but the first time we spoke, we spoke of everything Africa – food, music, films, culture, and so on. It was an amazing conversation, but then she ended it by saying, 'Wow, I didn't know you were down like that.' In other words, I didn't get this innate blackness from you by seeing you around.

I genuinely had to take the time to examine not only where this perception came from, but also where my insecurities about not being 'black enough' originated. Upon examination, I was incredibly grateful and relieved to realise that my personality was simply the result of my environment and the circumstances in which I grew up. Even though I was born in London, I moved to Nigeria when I was about five years old and I lived there until I was about fifteen, when I moved back to London.

Those were some of my most formative years, and one of the things that hit me about my time there was that I didn't have to 'act black'. In fact, I wasn't even seen as a black man, because pretty much everyone else was black. It is only outside of Africa and the Caribbean that black people have to identify as black. In the West, the extent to my blackness is arguably judged by how different I am to white, Middle-Eastern, or Asian people. In Nigeria, I wasn't black, I was just . . . Elijah Oluwatosin Lawal. My blackness wasn't determined by how I dressed, how I spoke, who I dated, what kind of music I listened to, or who I was friends with – for my blackness was innate.

So, growing up in an environment where I wasn't distinguished, discriminated against, or determined by my skin colour meant that I didn't have to adhere to some of the stereotypes or expectations of blackness that we get here in the West. Additionally, I spent most of my childhood and part of my teenage years surrounded by black people, so I was completely fascinated by other cultures and religions. For example, the first time I remember seeing a Chinese person in real life was when I was fifteen!

For someone who lives in London, a cultural and diverse melting pot, that sounds absolutely insane, but for someone who spent most of their life living in Nigeria before they were a teenager, that is not an unusual experience. Having moved to London and living in Streatham, which has a huge BAME population, the first time that I actually found myself with a wide diversity of friends was at university. In my university house, I lived with a Ghanaian-British boy, two Indian girls, a Chinese-British girl, and another Brit with Sierra Leonean heritage.

As for dating, I felt a huge amount of guilt, because I felt like I had dated more women outside my race than I had black women. This led to me actively seeking out black women to date, which of course didn't work. I look back at this time with shame, because you can't force yourself to like someone, whether you have the same skin colour or not. And trying to date someone because of the colour of their skin isn't fair; I certainly don't appreciate women who are only interested in me because of my skin colour. When any woman who isn't black whispers to me, 'I've never been with a black man before,'* it just makes me cringe and I feel like an object of fetishisation.

In the end, I realised that I had simply dated women who I liked, asked out, and they had said yes.† Also, the very notion of me at that age – with my bad acne, low self-esteem, and zero game with the ladies – actually being in a position to be picky about who was willing to go out with me is side-splittingly hilarious. Through this process of exam-ination, I realised something that should be obvious but is also very important: I love black women, but I'm not obligated to exclusively date them, any more than I think black women should have to date me. I'm certainly not entitled to a black woman . . . or any woman for that matter.

---

* Guess what, neither have I.
† Essentially, my process for choosing a woman to date is this: is she nice to me and does she like pancakes?

STATISTICAL DATING PREFERENCES OF BLACK MEN

Still, I would be remiss if I didn't at least consider the fact that there might be black men who do indeed prefer women of other races – particularly white women. After all, research from the 2001 UK census shows that black British males are fifty-per-cent more likely than black females to marry outside of their race. There is no hard data on why this might be the case, but we can theorise looking at the research on attractiveness.

A study by Michael B. Lewis, from the School of Psychology at Cardiff University, titled 'Who is the fairest of them all? Race, attractiveness and skin colour sexual dimorphism', showed that white participants displayed a preference for darker male complexions when considering attractiveness. There is nothing more powerful than male ego – it stands to reason that if black men are more actively preferred by white women, then they are more likely to respond in kind, because there is already a pre-existing interest.

Another angle to examine black males' interest in white women is looking at the perceptions of beauty today. When we look at every aspect of our culture, tall, skinny, white women are predominantly depicted as the ultimate essence of beauty – as discussed in Chapter Four. When you look at the current demographic of models, actresses and TV personalities, white women are more widespread than black women, or any other race. Let's take the models in the New York Fashion Week for fall/winter 2017 as an indication of beauty standards. Across the 116 major New York shows and 2,700 runway appearances, more than sixty-eight per cent of castings were white, and thirty-one per cent were non-white (but not exclusively black).

As of 2018, if you look at *People* magazine's Most Beautiful People list, there have only been three women of colour who have ever topped the list – Lupita Nyong'o, Beyoncé, and Halle Berry. This is compared to Julia Roberts, who has won it five times. That is not to say that Julia Roberts is not as good looking or less good looking than Lupita, but it does show that the typical standards of beauty are biased in favour of white women. Given that the current standards of beauty are mostly represented by white women on TV, in movies and in magazines, is it so unreasonable to assume that black men would be just as or more interested in white women – if they are presented as the pinnacle of beauty?

But looking at this from a black woman's perspective, they have the added disadvantage of wondering if a man (of any race) dates black women; considering they are not recognised as society's version of beauty. Run an online search for 'attractive woman' and see how many of the image results are black women, or women of colour.

There is also the well-known stereotype that black men prefer women with big butts, which would be contrary to the opinion that a lot of black men are dating white women, as black women are perceived to have bigger behinds. Interestingly, in an experiment conducted in the States, titled 'Do men hold African-American and Caucasian women to different standards of beauty?', both African American and Caucasian men chose slimmer builds as their preference for ideal women appearance.

The authors of the study understood that it deviated from previous research, which said that African and African-American men preferred bigger women (with bigger butts) and concluded that a possible reason for this was that African-American men were responding to more recent media images depicting smaller, thinner women, and that appears to support the theory in the previous paragraph. This is further supported by research from The Body Project, which found that the desire for 'thinnes' was commonplace in twenty-six countries, across ten world regions.

The unfortunate thing is that there are black men who prefer women from other races for no other reason than some outdated, racist view that black women aren't as attractive. They go out of their way to explain that black women are loud, don't have good hair, or are always angry – you know, the worst things that other races think about us. Which raises the question with me of why these black men who have an interest in women of other races justify their actions by insulting black women. It's almost as if they need to bring black women down unnecessarily, in order for them to feel superior. And it is these types of men that help perpetuate the stereotype that black men with women of other races have a problem with black women. A quick look on Twitter reveals the extent to their racism and misogyny:

@iFuckWhiteGirls: *Dear black women, when will y'all understand that I don't hate y'all a lot of y'all just ugly as shit compared to white girls.*

@1FLYMEXICAN: *BLACC FEMALES R A DISRACE TO BLACC CULTURE* ☺ ☺ ☺

THE PLIGHT OF THE STRONG BLACK WOMAN

Unfortunately, it's an increasingly common situation that black women come off as worse in these stereotypes. This is supported by research from different books on interracial dating (see *Crossing the Line* by McNamara, Tempenis, and Walton and *Multiracial Couples: Black & White Voices* by Rosenblatt, Karis, and Powell), where they argue that in some cases, black women see a black man with a white woman as an indication of his specific preference and (at an extreme) that he has a problem with women of his own race.

Grammy-winning artist and writer, Jill Scott, says in a column for *Essence* magazine that when she found out her friend was with a white partner, she felt her spirit 'wince'. She notes: 'One could easily dispel the wince as racist or separatist, but that's not how I was brought up . . . That feeling is betrayed . . . It's frustrating and it hurts!' A lot of this resentment is aimed at white women, as illustrated in Spike Lee's movie, *Jungle Fever*, which revolves around a black man's intermarital affair with his white secretary. In one scene, his black wife and her friends discuss the affair, noting that 'if it wasn't for the 29,000 white bitches . . . who give up the pussy and are stealing all the black men', they would have men to themselves.

Erica Chito Childs, Associate Professor of Sociology at Hunter College conducted research into the stereotypes of the 'Angry Black Woman', which looked into black women's opinions on interracial dating and found there was a significant number of black women who found it problematic. Here are some statements from the research alluding to this; however, it is worth noting that these are not the conclusive list of responses, only a sample that supports the point about interracial dating being problematic for black women:

'Blacks just like to see other Blacks, especially Black men who are successful, to stay Black, be with a Black woman . . . It's just about respecting and applauding those who don't go inter-racial. Definitely a problem in the Black community, because it takes away from us, and we're already struggling to succeed as a people.'

'My family raised me to [be] very proud of who I am, a Black woman, and they instilled in me the belief that I would never want to be with anyone but a strong Black man.'

'The perception of sell out for Blacks that date interracially comes from Black guys who act white do tend to date white girls.'

From a (black) male perspective, I certainly empathise with some of the opinions from the study and understand the sadness that stems from not seeing a 'good black man' end up with a 'good black woman'.

Research from UC Berkeley into racial preferences in dating found that a possible reason for black men dating white women is they are 'interested in moving up in the power structure, and one way you do that is through intermarriage with the dominant group', thereby integrating into a society (white), where we never would have been accepted if not for the relationship. Similarly, research from OK Cupid shows that on its dating site, black men write to black women far less often than they should. Black women reply the most, yet get by far the fewest replies, and unfortunately, this isn't just from black men; essentially every race is more reluctant to reply to black women.

It has been suggested that for members of the black community who find this problematic, the solution might lie in broadening their dating preference. Black Stanford law professor, Ralph Richard Banks, addresses this in his book, *Is Marriage for White People?*, noting that: 'Black women confront the worst relationship market of any group, because of economic and cultural forces that are not of their own making; and they have needlessly worsened their situation by limiting themselves to just black men.'

Despite this research, I would argue that black women don't have to do anything they don't want to – if they are happy dating only black men and are willing to wait for a good black man to come along, then it's one hundred per cent their choice.

There is a perpetual historical and patriarchal notion that black women should not only end up with black men, but should be supportive of black men, no matter what their flaws. Thus the idea of the 'ride or die chick' and the girl that 'holds a brother down'. To understand the extent of this notion, here's a nursery rhyme that is prevalent in some areas of the American South, sung by young black girls:

> *I like coffee,*
> *I like tea,*
> *I like the coloured boy and he likes me,*
> *So step back white boy, you don't shine,*
> *Cause I'll get the coloured boy to beat yo behind . . .*

There is something profoundly disturbing about the idea that a black woman's worth can only be determined by being with a black man – or any man for that matter.

Because I'm examining this research and indeed this stereotype from the lens of a black man, it is important to note that the level of scrutiny faced by a black man within the community for dating a white woman is nothing compared to the scrutiny that a black woman would face for dating a white man. A lot of black families are still very patriarchal, and women do not enjoy the same freedoms and liberties that men do. In addition, as I've pointed out above, black men can be incredibly harsh and unbelievably critical of black women who are seen as 'selling out' by dating a man from another race – particularly a white man.

It is no surprise then that research showed that black women who are in interracial relationships also expressed hesitancy in the initial stages of the relationship and were not always confident in their decision to date outside their own race, but eventually they were resolute in their choice of partners. Here are some of the quotes from the previous study:

'I had said I would never date someone who's white. Never, ever, and I thought that to do that, it was betraying your race . . . that [I] could never love someone who was from a different racial background because they wouldn't understand me, my culture . . .'

'I thought for a long time that I was selling out. It was also that you didn't see people of your own race as being attractive and desirable and worth being involved with. I don't think that anymore. I don't think all of us sell out; I think that those of us who are married to whites who are actively involved in the African-American community feel we must do it and more likely throw ourselves into it. We might be trying to prove ourselves a bit too much, but there are Black males who fit the stereotype that will never date a Black woman. I think they are insecure and do anything they can to distance themselves from Black, does whatever he can to lighten up his gene pool.'

'I've been called a sell out by Black men, but it doesn't make me feel bad because whites don't owe me anything, so I can't imagine what I'm selling out to.'

'I am a strong Black woman on my own; it's about the man, not the colour.'

WHITE AS A TEMPLATE OF BEAUTY

In the section above, I touched on the idea that we have conventional ideas of what beauty is; and as it is (mostly) based on a stereotypical white, skinny woman, we are seeing the harmful effects in the black community, such as skin bleaching to become lighter. According to a World Health Organization report on mercury in skin-lightening products, over seventy-seven per cent of women in Nigeria use skin-lightening products and Global Industry Analysts believe that global spending on skin lightening is projected to triple to $31.2bn (£24bn) by 2024.

In their book, *Post Colonialism and Mental Health*, Hickling and Hutchinson note that the attainment of whiteness is a symbol of social acceptance, and the evidence of this is the popularity of skin-bleaching creams among black women. It's all kind of gloomy really – that both genders within the black community are seeking acceptance through social standing. Although if you think skin bleaching is a pretty drastic thing to do in order to be or feel attractive, you should remember that white people sit in the blistering sun all day or spend hours in tanning booths to absorb dangerous ultraviolet rays, in order to be tanned. Fortunately, African countries are taking action against skin bleaching. In January 2019, Rwanda followed the Ivory Coast and Ghana to become the third African nation to ban skin bleaching ingredients.

Different races and peoples take extreme measures to meet varying standards of beauty. For instance, it's been theorised that women of the Kayan Lahwi tribe in Myanmar stretch their necks by wearing thick and heavy brass rings around their neck to improve their attractiveness. And some Asian women nowadays undergo eyelid surgery to make their eyes appear rounder and more Western.

This preference for a particular race to the point of excluding all others is not limited to heterosexual partners; it is also prevalent in the gay community. According to LGBT lifestyle magazine, *Attitude*, eighty per cent of black men, seventy-nine per cent of Asian men and seventy-five per cent of south Asian men have experienced racism on the gay scene. This either manifests as pre-emptive rejections based on ethnicity – many dating apps and profiles allow users to specify exclusions such as 'No blacks or Asians' – or fetishising certain ethnic groups, for instance black men for perceived well-endowed penises (as we discussed in Chapter Four). Fortunately, the gay dating app, Grindr, has launched an anti-discrimination campaign – #KindrGrindr – that aims to stamp out blatant racist preferences like 'No blacks, no Asians, no Hispanics', and aims to promote inclusiveness.

INTERRACIAL DATING TODAY

It's comforting to say that in the twenty-first century, attitudes towards interracial marriage are significantly more relaxed. According to the latest census data, the number of people in England and Wales living with, or married to, someone from another ethnic group jumped thirty-five per cent to 2.3 million since the previous census. Overall, almost one in ten people living in Britain is married to, or living with, someone from outside their own ethnic group, as the analysis from the Office for National Statistics shows. And polling shows that concern about mixed-race relationships has fallen from fifty per cent in the 1980s to just fifteen per cent in 2012, with only one in twenty aged eighteen to twenty-four thinking it's now an issue.

Overall attitudes towards interracial dating in the US have also changed. US census data reveals that more than 5.3 million marriages in the US are between husbands and wives of different races or ethnicities. It also shows that they make up one in ten marriages between opposite-sex couples, marking a twenty-eight-per-cent increase since 2000. A Gallup report reveals that around eighty-seven per cent of Americans have no issue with interracial relationships. In fact, according to Gallup, it is one of the 'largest shifts of public opinion in Gallup history'.

Online dating apps have played a huge part in the positive perception of interracial dating. A study by Tinder found that when online dating, sixty-three per cent of twenty-four- to twenty-five-year-olds in the US, UK, Australia, and France felt more comfortable dating outside of their ethnicity or race, with almost eighty per cent of respondents who used Tinder saying they'd been on a date with someone of a different race or ethnicity. Additionally, research from InterracialDating.com, a website dedicated to 'bringing individuals together who believe in choosing character above colour', shows that of the twenty US states with the most people seeking interracial partners, ten of them were states that 'historically voted Republican over the past five presidential elections', i.e. Red States.

Alabama ranked fifteenth for interracial dating on the site (even though interracial marriage wasn't decriminalised till 2000) and other states in the South with chequered racial histories and typically conservative reputations, such as Texas, Georgia, Virginia and North Carolina, are in the top ten, with Texas placing second in the rankings.

All this is a very interesting way to understand the social and cultural implications of who we date, but as I mentioned before, skin colour really should not play a part in the decision to date someone. For as long as we have recognised the romantic urge to date, we have also understood the challenges involved in meeting the 'right person'. And yes, race matters, but it shouldn't be used as a political statement in dating. And you should never assume that someone has no interest in dating someone from their own race – especially if you don't know the dating history of the person.

What's also interesting is that from a scientific perspective, the decision about who we are attracted to isn't up to us – or at least the conscious part of us.

A study published in the *Edmonton Journal* demonstrated that humans are able to gauge beauty at a subliminal level, when shown pictures for a mere one-hundredth of a second. Now that is not nearly enough time to make a conscious decision. It is instinct. So, it turns out that the choice of who to be with is happening on a deeply cellular level, which may register as your decision, but is actually your brain doing its job.

Romantic and sexual relations can begin anywhere and with anyone. And sure, it is often too easy to judge other couples, particularly if you are single and you don't think they are compatible. Yes, there are black men and women dating outside of their race, and we have in this chapter gone through the social and scientific reasons why that might be the case, but maybe the simplest reason is that there are more interracial couples nowadays, simply because it is less taboo. Historically, we weren't allowed to have a mixed-race relationship, but now, nothing* is holding us back from it; it might just be a new and interesting subset of men and women that we might not be used to (particularly if you were raised in a predominantly black community).

I'm fortunate to have parents who have never treated any partner of mine with anything other than acceptance. Perhaps because they fell in love despite being from different towns in Nigeria that weren't on the best of terms culturally – Ijebu-ode and Abeokuta.

Anyone dating in the twenty-first century can agree that it's hard enough finding someone, without further hurting your chances by being exclusive to one race. Warwick University economist Peter Backus, conducted a study using the Drake Equation (a theoretical equation used to estimate the number of active, communicative extra-terrestrial civilisations in the Milky Way galaxy), where he concluded that there were twenty-six women in London with whom he could have a realistically wonderful relationship.

So, on any given night out in London, that's a 0.00034-per-cent chance of meeting the proverbial one. I know that this sounds depressing, but to put it into context, of the twenty-six possible women,

---

* Well, not nothing. Racism is still alive and well, yo.

he needs to meet only one. And those are significantly better odds than finding an alien civilisation that we can communicate with.

It's important that old-fashioned ideas of dating that evolved as a result of racism don't colour our approach to dating today. As comedian and *Daily Show* host, Trevor Noah, notes in his book, *Born a Crime*: 'In any society built on institutionalised racism, race-mixing doesn't merely challenge the system as unjust, it reveals the system as unsustainable and incoherent. Race-mixing proves that races can mix – and in a lot of cases *want* to mix. A mixed person embodies that rebuke to the logic of the system . . .'

Answer to pop quiz: 2.3 million people in England and Wales are living with or married to someone from another ethnic group.

1. **Family:** You are about to be introduced to a shit-ton of family members. At any given time, there are about seven cousins knocking about and at least two uncles and aunties each. And here's the rub, not all of them are actually related to the family; most of them are only family friends or neighbours or (judgemental) community elders. It doesn't matter though – they are all uncles and aunties to you. *Do not* make the mistake of calling anyone who looks like they are as old as your parents by their first name – that is the ultimate rookie mistake.

2. **Language:** At some point when you are in the presence of family

members, the conversations will switch to our ethnic tongue and yes, we are talking about you. My advice: get Duolingo or Google translate and learn a couple of words to find out which family members are throwing shade at you.

3. **Church (a):** You better take your arse to church on Sundays . . . or at least lie that you do. You know, like your parents did to get you into that good Catholic school when you were a kid.

4. **Sex:** If at any point the topic of sex comes up when the parentals are around (and it will, older black people are shameless like that), best pretend it is like a foreign concept to you and you plan on keeping your virginity till after marriage. The last thing you want is the community elder slipping you a condom, or worse, saying they'll pray for your lustful soul.

5. **Church (b):** Never under any circumstances should you accept an invitation to go to black church. Yes, there is amazing singing and dancing and the pastors are hilarious, but it also lasts like fifteen hours. If you absolutely have to go, sit at the back and slip out at hour six.

6. **Words:** We don't find that whole 'I've gone black and I'll never go back' shit cute, so please don't say it.

7. **Hair:** Male or female, we are going to spend a shit-ton of time on our hair, so get used to it. Oh, and don't even think about touching our hair unless you've been made official. And even then, it's on a case-by-case basis.

8. **Lateness:** Yes, we may occasionally be late, but have you seen how fly we look when we eventually roll up?

9. **Motherland:** At some point, you will be expected to visit the motherland with your boo. Strap in.

10. **Wokeness:** The expectations of your wokeness is gonna go through the roof, so you better come correct. Also, if you're white, be prepared for us talking shit about your people but don't worry, we don't mean you.

11. **Future:** From the moment you are obviously boyfriend/

girlfriend, in our families' mind, you are basically husband/ wife. Unrealistic expectations? Sure. But they will also unexpectedly give you gifts and often money, so just enjoy that shit.

12. **Jollof rice:** The golden rule: Love Jollof or get the fuck out.

Based on my family — this is a book about stereotypes after all.

IMMIGRATION
GO BACK TO YOUR OWN COUNTRY/AFRICA

Stereotype/negative narrative: Negative connotations surrounding the word immigrant – that we are lazy, criminals, and a drain on society.

Pop quiz:
The UK believes twenty-four per cent of its population
are immigrants when it's actually . . .

13%

18%

23%

For any minority, labels are a perpetual pain in the arse. In the first chapter, we looked at how difficult it can be to fit into one descriptor and all the baggage that comes with it. But there is another label that follows us around like a wet fart (particularly first-generation minorities) – *immigrant*. For such an innocuous word, it comes with a heavy burden of negativity.

There are two main things that a child of immigrants always has to do. The first is to defend yourself constantly as British, which can be difficult, particularly as you are caught between two worlds: the 'ethnic culture' you experience at home and the 'Western culture' you experience outside the home. It's for this reason that I rarely invited friends back to my house for study dates, or to hang out. How could I claim to be British, when my parents would refer to me by my Nigerian name at home? Or blast Nigerian music regardless of what guest we had in the house? Or eat literally every meal with their hands? It took a long time for me not only to be comfortable accepting that side of my heritage, but to be proud of it.

The other thing that every black first-generation kid has to do is defend the hell out of their immigrant parents, and then by default, every immigrant ever. I would make excuses for my parents' 'ethnic behaviour': 'Oh, they're just old' (my parents are only twenty-five and twenty-eight years older than I am), or 'They just don't know any better; that's how they do things in Nigeria' (my mum was educated in England and my dad in Scotland).

For this chapter, I am going to take slight liberties and address the stereotypes surrounding immigrants, not just from the lens of black people, but using a broad interpretation of immigrants. Because this is not an issue that affects only the black community, but other minorities as a whole, so we need to educate ourselves on how to respond to the negative narrative surrounding immigrants and put it to bed, once and for all.

Defending immigration has become a necessity for children of immigrants. When you think about an immigrant, what's the first image that springs to mind? Don't be ashamed, it's mostly the first thing that springs to my mind, and I imagine that of many others. Maybe you think of a brown or black man, who's unable to speak English/speaks English poorly/speaks English with an accent. Possibly he works in an off-licence, or he's trying to sell you perfume in the toilets of a nightclub after you've taken a whiz and just done a line.* Or maybe you imagine a beefy Polish gentleman, who's come over to fix your plumbing at an unbelievably low rate, or perhaps a Syrian woman, begging on the streets.

Now get out of that frame of mind and think about who you'd consider to be an 'expat'. Probably your white housemate who's spending a couple of years here before she moves back to Australia, or your American colleague who's doing a rotation in 'Europe' for six months. It's easy enough to separate these two groups under the labels of 'expats' and 'immigrants', but the reality is that they are both immigrants – where their stories differ is the reason why, and the methods by which they arrived in this country.

Your American colleague – liberal as he is – probably got a bit frustrated with the increased sense of nationalism in America at the moment, and thought, fuck this, I'm gonna go live in Europe for a while. And so, he builds a business case and presents it to his manager and director, detailing the vast experience he'll get working in Europe and the 'learnings' he'll be able to bring back to his clients in the States after his tenure. The director loves the idea, and so he applies for a visa to the UK, books his flight on his company credit card (premium economy at the least), and *voilà*, he's in the UK.

That's generally acceptable, but the experience for the Syrian woman is a whole different story. Most likely, her husband was captured and tortured by Bashar al-Assad's forces for having the nerve to protest in favour of fundamental human rights. Her eldest son was more likely than not captured, tortured, and killed by Jabhat al-Nusra, because . . . well, that's what terrorists in Syria do – they capture, torture and kill people. So not only has this Syrian woman lost her husband and son,

---

* Definitely the latter if you're a financial trader.

but there is still the real fear that she and her remaining two children will be killed by chemical weapons or barrel bombs, which have become commonplace during Bashar al-Assad's regime.

So, she flees with the children – both under the age of ten – to Turkey or Greece and ends up in a refugee camp. And while life in the camp is shit, at least they are not living under the threat of a tyrant, or the likelihood of a chemical attack. The problem with this scenario, however, is that the millions of people displaced in Syria also have the same idea and so the camps end up being underfunded and over-crowded; not to mention that the economy of Greece is not exactly on the upswing, so she can't just pop out and get a job. But she hears that things are much better in France, Germany and England, so she takes a ridiculously perilous and ill-advised journey across the Mediterranean Sea, risking malnutrition and most likely drowning. The risk of drowning is so prevalent that roughly 1,300 refugees and migrants drown or go missing in a single month.

Somehow, she makes it to the UK – maybe with both her kids, maybe with only one – statistically speaking, the chances are she arrives alone. She was a doctor in Syria, but given she came here 'illegally', and she doesn't speak the language fluently, there is very little oppor-tunity for her here. And given that she risked everything to leave a camp and come here, she doesn't want to live in another one. So, she takes to the streets to beg. To survive. To live. And even though she's left everything she owns behind, will likely never see her home again, has lost her children on the way, and is now a beggar on the street – this life in England is still preferable to her life back in Syria.

And this situation is not exclusive to the Middle East. Several countries in Africa are also facing economic and humanitarian crises. Take Somalia, for example. Hundreds of civilians are killed in indis-criminate attacks by the Islamist armed group, Al-Shabab, and the country is plagued by famine. As a result, around two million Somalis are displaced and those remaining in the country suffer human rights abuses and little to no access to basic services.

In the Democratic Republic of Congo, government officials and security forces repeatedly and systematically ban opposition demonstrations, shut down media outlets, and have arrested more than 300 opposition leaders, journalists, and human rights activists – many of whom are being held without charge or access to legal services.

The story of Haitian nationals fleeing to the US is all too familiar. More than 175,000 individuals remain displaced in the aftermath of October 2016's Hurricane Matthew, and many more have faced food scarcity, due to widespread damage to crops and livestock. As of 2017, there are nearly 38,000 individuals still living in displacement camps since the 2010 earthquake and in addition to this, there is a rapid outbreak of cholera plaguing the nation.

How can anyone have anything but compassion for these individuals who are seeking a better life? How can anyone say that they're here just to take our jobs? How can anyone complain if a doctor, engineer, or architect flees their country under threat of death, only to become a toilet cleaner here? How can anyone ask you to go back to your own country in that circumstance? And if you think that this prejudice against immigrants is only the opinion of a small-minded few, you should know that at a London conference on Somalia in May 2017, partners endorsed a plan that provides financial support for an amnesty programme for former Al-Shabab combatants.

In the case of Syria, the British government withdrew support for search-and-rescue operations that prevented migrants and refugees drowning in the Mediterranean. Then Foreign Office minister, Lady Anelay, claimed the operation simply encouraged more people to attempt the dangerous sea crossing. Of course, one could argue that despite the Syrian woman's existence being horrible, she still made the choice to leave Turkey or Greece and cross the Mediterranean Sea (yes, the choice was driven by necessity, but was a choice nonetheless).

But what about her children; what if she had died on the way to the UK? An estimated 95,000 unaccompanied children come to Europe seeking asylum, so surely there must be a system in place to ensure they survive – after all, it wasn't their choice to come here. Well, there was: in 2016, Lord Dubs sponsored an amendment to the Immigration

Act 2016 to offer unaccompanied refugee children safe passage to Britain amidst the European migrant crisis. But in February 2017, the Home Office abandoned the scheme, after accepting just 350 out of the planned 3,000 child refugees.

So, if it's unconscionable to refuse entry or permission to stay for immigrants, why is there such increasing negative rhetoric and reactions towards immigrants? The answer is simple: it's because they are different. They are not like us. They don't have the same religious doctrines, cultural sensitivities, and we believe they are responsible for bringing terror to our lands. These sentiments are exemplified by three key events in recent times: the Brexit Referendum, the Windrush scandal, and America's current policy on immigration.

THE UNFORTUNATE FATE OF IMMIGRANTS TODAY: BREXIT, WINDRUSH, TRUMP'S AMERICA

On 23 June 2016, nearly fifty-two per cent of the participating UK electorate voted to leave the European Union in the 'Brexit Referendum'. There have been exhaustive articles and opinion papers on why the UK chose to vote the way it did: UK sovereignty, economic stability, 'taking back control of our country', legal independence, and more – so for the purposes of this chapter, we are going to focus on the part that fear of immigration, or fear of 'the other', played in this decision.

A report by Ipsos Mori ahead of the referendum found that immigration was the most important issue for voters (thirty-three per cent) compared to the second most important issue which was the economy (twenty-eight per cent). This was fuelled by the overt propaganda during the campaign that suggested the EU allows for uncontrolled immigration. For example, former UKIP leader Nigel Farage endorsed a poster that showed a queue of mostly non-white migrants and refugees with the slogan, 'Breaking point: the EU has failed us all'. It's no surprise then that the police reported the number of racially or religiously aggravated crimes in England and Wales increased by fifty-seven per cent following the EU referendum. And these weren't just your standard racists insulting anyone who looked different on public transport; a majority of the 134 incidents examined were incidents of racist abuse, including physical assaults, arson attacks, death threats and stabbings. People were targeted for being Muslims, black, Jewish, or just for speaking a foreign language – even children on their way to school were targeted.

Now it would be remiss of me to presume that everyone who voted to leave the EU because of immigration did so because they were racist or held negative perceptions of immigrants. And it's not unreasonable to assume that a significant number were genuinely concerned about overpopulation, loss of jobs and opportunity, foreign terrorists entering the country, and so on. These are perfectly legitimate concerns; however, they were being fuelled by false information.

As I pointed out in the first chapter, British respondents to a survey thought that the Muslim population of the UK was more than three times bigger than it really is, estimating it at fifteen per cent, when it is really less than five per cent. Well, another survey in 2016 found that voters believed, on average, that fifteen per cent of the population were non-UK EU nationals (respondents who intended to vote leave in the referendum estimated an average of twenty per cent), but the official figures from the Office of National Statistics at the time concluded that the number was actually closer to five per cent. In fact, the Home Office had to order an official review of Britain's immigration figures, after exit checks at the borders found that ninety-seven per cent of international students – one of the biggest groups of immigrants – left after finishing their studies.

So, if there are not as many immigrants here as people tend to believe, why is immigration viewed so negatively? Research from the Migration Observatory at the University of Oxford found that negative attitudes towards immigrants are more prevalent among people living in areas of low migration. Which makes sense, if you live near, work with, and interact with people from other countries, you're more likely to see them as nothing more than people; but if you live in a monolithic, non-diverse community, then you are more likely to assume immigrants are members of nefarious communities hell-bent on taking your jobs.

I grew up in Streatham, south London, which was predominantly occupied by BAME (black, Asian, and majority ethnic) nationals. But there was also a healthy number of white people living in my area. I remember that my immediate neighbours were Indian and Guyanese, but the rest of our street was mostly white. And despite that, I didn't experience a shred of racism, or any indication that I didn't belong, until I started attending the Catholic School in Norbury, a couple of miles from my house. There I was witness to people calling me 'African monkey' and making fun of me for my accent, which I had picked up after living in Nigeria for a few years.

For the life of me, I couldn't understand why those white people were any different from the nice white people in my neighbourhood. At first, I assumed there was something fundamentally dislikeable about me* and it wasn't until much later in my life that I realised that these were kids who had grown up with no exposure to anyone that looked different from them.† So, it is easy to see how the immigrant's story gets perverted and for them to be seen as despots, a bunch of chancers and lazy opportunists, who are only in the UK to take advantage of the benefits system. In fact, more than half of Britons (fifty-six per cent) believe our culture is threatened by ethnic minorities living in the UK. A further quarter of Britons think immigrants take jobs away, and a third think they remove more from society than they contribute. It's no surprise that in 2018, immigrants suffered another nationwide assault under the Windrush scandal.

After the Second World War, there was increased immigration of black people into the UK. This was enabled further by the introduction of the British Nationality Act in 1948, which granted British citizenship to those residing in previously Commonwealth nations, which included a lot of West Africa and Caribbean islands/nations. Similarly, a lot of Caribbean nationals who would have previously thought about moving

---

* There isn't. I'm awesome.
† Which, let's face it, is no reason to be an arsehole racist.

to the United States, moved to the UK because of the McCarran-Walter Immigration Act, which limited the number of people who could move to the US from Caribbean nations.

These immigrants came to this country to work, to start families, to create a better life for themselves and they did this willingly, knowing they would face all manner of animosity, hardship, and discrimination. These individuals were known as the 'Windrush generation' (see Chapter One). In 1971, the Windrush generation were given permission to stay in Britain permanently, but the government failed to keep a full record of them and unfortunately, some of them didn't apply for the official paperwork affirming their leave to remain in Britain, because they thought they had automatic right to citizenship. Some of these people also didn't apply for official paperwork like a UK passport.

It is a source of national embarrassment that it wasn't until 2018 that the injustice and discrimination against the Windrush generation was brought to light. They had suffered all manner of humiliation, including wrongful detention, denial of legal rights, and deportation. In fact, there were over sixty cases of wrongful deportation from the UK by the Home Office. Think about how important your passport is to you. It's proof that you are a citizen of (more often than not) the nation that you reside in. Now imagine not having such an important document. How will you get a job, rent a property, buy a car, open a bank account, or get access to any of the benefits afforded to a citizen?

This was the sad fate of the Windrush generation. It is important to know that they weren't illegal immigrants; in fact, they were invited here – many answered adverts to come to Britain where there were lots of different jobs to do. On 21 August 2018, Home Secretary Sajid Javid announced that – after a review of 11,800 cases – eighteen members of the Windrush generation who could have been wrongfully removed or detained would get a formal apology from the government.

This mistreatment of immigrants is not solely a UK/European issue; immigrants in America have their own burden to bear, as a key message in President Trump's election campaign was immigration reform. Trump promised to build a wall along the border with Mexico (and get Mexico to pay for it), to remove all unauthorised immigrants from the United States, and remove or jail unauthorised immigrants with criminal records. But what Trump failed to mention was how he was going to do this exactly – not to mention the impact on the economy.

By the end of 2015 alone, the total number of unauthorised immigrants in the USA was approximately 11.3 million, and about seven million of them had jobs. The Center for American Progress (CAP), a public policy research organisation, estimated that the removal of those seven million workers would immediately reduce the GDP by one and a half per cent, reduce national employment by an amount like that experienced during the Great Recession, and cost the federal government nearly $900 billion in lost revenue over ten years. Now, if you are a hardworking, legal American, you might be thinking, how about we just get rid of the undocumented workers with criminal records? Well, that comes with its own costs. CAP estimated the cost of removal to be over $10,000 per immigrant. This cost includes: arresting the person, detaining them, processing them through the immigration courts and deporting them from the country.

No matter how strongly any American feels about undocumented immigrants, surely there must be exceptions for children who didn't choose to enter the United States of their own volition? Unfortunately, in mid-2018, the Trump administration announced a new immigration policy that separated parents from their children if the family was caught crossing the border illegally. As a result of this policy, the federal government lost – literally lost, as in, could not find – up to 1,500 migrant children they had forcefully taken away from their parents at the border. Even more horrifying are the findings of a report from the ACLU, which found that migrant children under the care of United States Customs and Border Protection were allegedly beaten, threatened with sexual violence, and repeatedly assaulted while in custody.

MOUNTING THE DEFENCE:
DEBUNKING THE OPPOSITION'S ARGUMENTS

As a child of immigrants, you have to know how to debunk the 'devil's advocate' arguments around immigration; you know, those points that always start with, 'Well, to be fair . . .' After all, the opposition can present an emotional argument as well; claiming that immigrants are a drain on society and resources and they are only here to take our jobs. The reality of the situation is that no matter how good your emotional arguments are about the plight of immigrants, you simply cannot get people to vote against their own interests. So, what we must do is debunk the arguments presented by the opponents of immigration.

The UK is tiny. It is literally a tiny island floating on the edge of the Atlantic. It is only the eleventh largest country in Europe, but is the fifth most populous nation. To put that into context, it is smaller than Spain, Finland, Italy, Ukraine and Poland, but has more people than them. So, it is not entirely unreasonable that people in the UK should be worried that accepting more immigrants will lead to over-population.

However, the number of immigrants coming to the UK has actually fallen. The share of immigrants from outside the EU has declined from sixty-three per cent in 2004 to forty-five per cent in 2016. Additionally, the concern of overpopulation doesn't account for emigration, i.e. people leaving the UK. The same report found that there were 60,000 more British citizens moving abroad than those coming to live in the UK – a substantial increase from 2015, when it stood at 40,000. Perception also plays a part in the concern about overpopulation in other countries as well as the UK:

- UK believes twenty-four per cent of its population are immigrants, when it's actually thirteen per cent.
- Americans believe it's thirty-two per cent, but the real figure is thirteen per cent. Also, forty-six per cent of immigrants in

2016 described themselves as white (twenty-seven per cent as Asian, nine per cent as black, and fifteen per cent as some other race).

- Spain believes it's twenty-three per cent, it's twelve per cent.
- Germany believes it's twenty-three per cent, it's thirteen per cent.
- Japan believes it's ten per cent, it's two per cent.
- Poland believes fourteen per cent, it's less than two per cent.
- And Italy believes it's thirty per cent, but it's actually seven per cent.

I guess, when you see a person of colour, it's easy to think of them as an immigrant instead of a citizen.

Another argument that the opposition tends to take is that immigrants come to the UK to take advantage of our benefits. In order to debunk this myth, there is something important that we need to understand. In the wake of the Syrian crisis, natural disasters such as the earthquake in Haiti, and atrocities committed by dictators around the world, a large number of immigrants are refugees – *and refugees don't decide where they want to go*. Refugees go to the nearest, most convenient place where they won't face the atrocities, human rights violations or natural disasters they faced in their homeland. And this is something that privileged people don't understand – refugees get resettled wherever will have them.

So, there is no forward planning to try and live off the UK government's benefit scheme. There is simply no evidence for this notion; in fact, immigrants are less likely than native citizens to claim benefits: between 1998 and 2011 as many as thirty-seven per cent of native citizens were receiving some kind of state benefit or tax credit; European immigrants were nearly eight percentage points less likely to collect them and three per cent less likely to live in social housing than Britons.

Between 2001 and 2011, the net fiscal contribution of recent arrivals from the eastern European countries that have joined the EU since 2004 has amounted to almost £5 billion. Even during the worst years of the financial crisis, in 2007–11, immigrants made a net contribution of almost £2 billion to British public finances, with migrants from other European countries contributing £8.6 billion. Now compare this to the fact that the Brexit decision has reportedly cost a dip of over two per cent in economic output and an estimated 23 billion pounds in lost tax revenue. Not to mention the fact that the cost of Brexit to the British economy is running at £40bn a year according to a Bank of England rate-setter.

Research into EU immigration by the LSE summarises this nicely: 'The bottom line, which may surprise many people, is that EU immigration has not harmed the pay, jobs or public services enjoyed by Britons. EU immigrants pay more in taxes than they use in public services and therefore they help to reduce the budget deficit. So, far from being a necessary evil that we pay to get access to the greater trade and foreign investment generated by the EU single market, immigration is at worst neutral and at best, another economic benefit.'

And in case you're wondering what these immigrants are doing with this money, they're sending it home – not to encourage family members to join them, but instead so that they can save up and buy property to return to their home countries, or to support family members who can't come to the UK themselves. A report from the United Nations' education agency revealed that migrant workers in the UK are sending £8bn a year to support families in their home countries. In fact, the UK is in the top ten countries for overseas workers sending back money – with billions of pounds sent to the three biggest recipients: Nigeria, India, and Pakistan.

We see a similar situation in America; while there are reports of a large number of immigrants in America on welfare/benefits, these numbers are conflated, because they drew inaccurate connections, so that if a child of an immigrant was on subsidised lunch at school, then the whole household would be classed as 'on welfare'. Just because a child is on subsidised lunch doesn't mean their whole family is on welfare; it could simply mean that their boujee parents don't have time to make them lunch in the morning.

Studies in the States have also largely shown that immigrants contribute more to society than they take from it. The American Immigration Council estimates that immigrants earn about $240 billion a year, pay about $90 billion a year in taxes, and use only about $5 billion in public benefits. So, immigrants offer so much more than they take – particularly when it comes to economic and scientific innovation; according to *Time* magazine, they create a higher-than-average number of patents in many countries, start businesses more frequently than native citizens, and have founded forty per cent of the Fortune 500 firms.

And much like the migrants in the UK, immigrants in the States are also sending money home. And this money that they send home – called remittances — is significantly larger than the Foreign Aid budget. For example, immigrants in America officially sent $51 billion in remittances home in 2012, compared to the US government's foreign aid budget of $39 billion that year. Over $24 billion in remittances was sent from the United Kingdom to other countries in 2015 – with over $3 billion going to Nigeria.* Experts estimate that if rich nations around the world were to admit enough migrants to expand their labour force by just three per cent, the world would be $356 billion richer; not only because of the productivity gains in the rich countries, but because migrants send so much money back home.

So, immigrants working in the West actually relieve the burden on the foreign aid budget, which ironically was one of the complaints of the Brexit Leave Campaign – complaining that we were spending too much money subsidising other countries.

And perhaps most significant to counter Trump's narrative around immigrants is the fact that the unauthorised immigrant population is actually declining. A new study from the Center for Migration Studies of New York found that half a million US undocumented residents from Mexico left the undocumented population in 2016 – more than three times the number that arrived that year, leading to an overall decrease of nearly 400,000 undocumented residents from Mexico from

* Represent!

2016 to 2017. Essentially, from 2010 to 2017, the undocumented population from Mexico fell by a remarkable 1.3 million.

IMMIGRANTS AS A SECURITY RISK

One of the prevailing vocal arguments of anti-immigration groups is that allowing immigrants into the country increases the security risk – because to them, immigrants are criminals and pose a significant threat to the citizens of the countries where they are planning to move. We've seen evidence of this in Donald Trump's election campaign rhetoric, calling Mexicans 'criminals' and 'rapists', and calling certain African, Central American and Caribbean countries 'shitholes'; as well as Nigel Farage's commentary around the Brexit referendum. Equally, the increasing number of terror attacks in 2016–17 being committed by Muslims, or people with dark or brown skin, has been considered as evidence that this rhetoric is true.

This is unwittingly a source of huge embarrassment and shame for the first-generation immigrant. The very first thought that goes through our minds when a heinous crime has been committed (after hoping that the victims all survive, of course) is, please God, don't let the perpetrator be black/Muslim/Asian. The reason being that whenever these crimes or terror attacks happen, the pure bile on social media networks, where people lump all members of an ethnic or religious group together under the banner of terrorist, is very hurtful. In the wake of the terror attack on Westminster, all Muslims were considered terrorists to the Twitterati. This allegation is like kryptonite to the first-generation immigrant – how can we continue to defend our ethnicity/religion in the face of surmounting evidence showing that most of the perpetrators of these crimes and terror attacks are minorities?

Well, firstly, we don't have to. It's absolutely ridiculous to believe that because certain crimes and (most of what are generally considered as) terror attacks are committed by people of colour, immigrants or descendants of immigrants, it means that there is something inherently criminal about us. Least of all because any crimes with huge casualties that are committed by Muslims are automatically deemed acts of terror, whereas shootings committed by white Americans are considered as just that – mass shootings. For example, the Las Vegas mass shooting on 1 October 2017, in which fifty-eight people were killed and over 500 people left injured, was not referred to as a terror attack: the gunman, Stephen Paddock, was a white American.

Secondly, research contradicts the notion that immigrants bring crime to communities – in fact, it suggests otherwise. In the United States, studies consistently show that immigrants commit significantly less crime than native-born Americans; what's more, they suggest that immigrants may actually contribute to a decline in crime in the areas where they live. In a study published in the *Journal of Ethnicity in Criminal Justice*, researchers found a reduction of almost five violent crimes per 100,000 residents for every one-per-cent increase in the foreign-born population. Further analyses of cities such as New York, Chicago, Miami and El Paso have similarly found that violent crime rates – homicide rates in particular – are lower in areas with more immigrants. This might help explain how violent crime dropped forty-eight per cent over the same period that the undocumented population grew from 3.5 million to 11.2 million.

A report from the Immigration Policy Center concluded that, 'While lawmakers repeatedly justify their crackdown on immigrants as a means of fighting crime, the reality is that crime in the United States is not caused or even aggravated by immigrants, regardless of their legal status. This is hardly surprising, since immigrants come to the United States to pursue economic and educational opportunities not available in their home countries, and to build better lives for themselves and their families. As a result, they have little to gain and much to lose by breaking the law.'

Finally, the notion that Islam or people seeking refuge from Islamic countries are more of a terror risk is false. As I mentioned earlier, refugees don't get to decide where to go. But in addition to that, refugees undergo the most amount of security screening than any other immigrant. For instance, for a refugee (particularly one from an Islamic country) to enter the United States, database information on the individual is shared with the FBI, the National Counterterrorism Center, the Department of Defense, the UN, the United Nations High Commissioner for Refugees, the Department of Homeland Security, and the goddamn CIA! How can a terrorist possibly manage to fool and evade all of these organisations? Not to mention that roughly only two per cent of refugees are able-bodied men. Most refugees are vulnerable cases comprising of widowed women and children, who, let's face it, are statistically less likely than men to commit acts of terror.

So, it stands to reason that if these 'terrorists' can't get into the country, then immigrants aren't the problem – citizens are. And there is evidence to support this. According to a report by New America Foundation, as of 2017, 'the large majority of jihadist terrorists in the United States have been American citizens or legal residents. Moreover . . . every jihadist who conducted a lethal attack inside the United States since 9/11 was a citizen or legal resident.' The FBI has revealed that the San Bernardino shooter, Syed Rizwan Farook, was a first-generation Pakistani immigrant born in Chicago.

French investigators also believe that the mastermind of the Paris attacks was a Belgian national. Both of the Charlie Hebdo attackers were born in Paris, and three of the attackers in the 2005 London Bombings were British-born Pakistanis. The Manchester Arena bombing in 2017 was the deadliest terrorist attack in the UK and the first suicide bombing in Britain since the July 2005 London bombings – and the attacker, Salman Ramadan Abedi was British. Abedi was born in Manchester, lived in the local suburb, Fallowfield, and attended the Manchester College. So again, it is the perception around immigrants that is harmful, not immigrants themselves.

A point further proved by the executive order issued by President Donald Trump in early 2017, banning entry to citizens from seven majority Islamic countries (Iran, Iraq, Syria, Sudan, Libya, Yemen, and Somalia) over national security concerns. In addition, Republican nominee for the Presidency in the 2016 election, Ted Cruz, voted for a Senate amendment banning immigration from Muslim countries, and Jeb Bush (also then a candidate for the Presidency) called for Christian refugees from Syria to get preferential treatment because of their religion.

What was interesting about Cruz's antagonism towards Muslims was his notion that, 'There is no meaningful risk of Christians committing acts of terror.' Someone really should inform him that the KKK was founded on Protestant Christian ideology and that the Colorado Springs Planned Parenthood shooting was carried out by a Christian, who claimed that attacks on abortion clinics were 'God's work'. In reality, none of the deadly attackers since 9/11 emigrated, or came from a family that emigrated, from one of those countries in the 'Muslim Ban', nor were any of the 9/11 attackers from the listed countries. In fact, eight of the lethal attackers were born American citizens.

This is not unique to America alone, a study in the UK by Hannah Stuart, looking at Islamist terror offences in the UK, revealed that 'more than two out of three "Islamism-inspired" terrorist offenses were carried out by individuals who were either born or raised in the UK.' It's easy for British citizens to look at the terrorist attacks in the UK over the past decade and conclude that they are a result of immigration – after all, most of the attackers tend to be first-generation British citizens, with their parents migrating from other countries. But that is a huge misconception: these terrorists aren't carrying out these attacks because they are immigrants; they are carrying them out because they are fundamentalists.

According to the Cato Institute, the odds of being killed by a foreign-born terrorist in the USA are ridiculously small – one in 3.6 million. That's a 0.00003-per-cent chance; incredibly low, especially when compared to the 12,834 people killed yearly on average by guns in the US. In fact, white supremacists and far-right movements are responsible for far more murders than domestic Islamic extremists; of the thirty-four people killed by extremists in 2017, twenty (fifty-nine per cent) were killed by right-wing extremists and members of the anti-government militia movement. And of the twenty right-wing extremists, eighteen were white supremacists, marking an increase from the seven people killed by white supremacists in 2016. This is in comparison to nine people who were killed by domestic Islamic extremists, eight of whom died in a single attack in New York.

White men overall were responsible for seventy-one per cent of extremist-related deaths in America over the last ten years, according to the Anti-Defamation League. In fact, according to the Home Office, the number of white suspected terrorists being arrested in the UK has overtaken those of Asian appearance for the first time in more than a decade. The Home Office believes this is due to the increase of people holding far-right ideologies, who statistically tend to be white people rather than people of colour.

REAL LIFE IMPACT OF THE NEGATIVE PERCEPTIONS: OPERATION NEXUS

While this negative perception towards immigrants when it comes to classifying perpetrators of acts of terror is emotionally upsetting, it also has some real life, dangerous implications when interpreted by the police. And this is no more evident than in Operation Nexus in the UK. Operation Nexus is a collaboration between the Metropolitan Police Service and the Home Office, which seeks to increase the number of foreign nationals deported from the United Kingdom, on the basis that their deportation is said to be 'conducive to the public good'. So essentially, the police are working with the Home Office to deport people they simply don't like.

I say this without being facetious, because all the Home Office needs to deport these immigrants is a claim that they are not conducive to the common good on the balance of probabilities – they do not even need to have been convicted of an offence by a criminal court. Not only that, but the immigrants are not able to appeal the decision, challenge the allegations made against them, or have the possibility of them or their legal representatives cross-examine any witnesses. Just think about that and its implications for a second. In the UK, a person is presumed innocent until proven guilty. But in the case of immigrants, the police can simply choose not to bother referring the case to the Crown Prosecution Service, and instead refer it to the Home Office for them to be deported. And again, it's important to remember that the police can do this *even if the individual has not committed a criminal offence*.

This is shameful prejudice at least, and at most, a contravention of Article 6 of the European Convention on Human Rights, which gives individuals a right to a fair trial. Having the duties of the police (preventing crime) merged with that of immigration officers raises a most serious issue: it lowers the status of an immigrant to that of a criminal. It's no wonder that the relationship between the police and minority communities is frayed; surely this behaviour is indicative of how minorities are treated in such a horrible way and how this leads to further mistrust.

If that's not enough to put the fear of the Police State into you, you should also know that thanks to a Freedom of Information request from Politics.co.uk, the Met Police have admitted to passing on immigration details to the Home Office – not only of people they've arrested, but the witnesses and even the victims. So, if an 'illegal' migrant is robbed, assaulted, or God forbid, raped – and they report the incident to the police – in addition to the harm they've suffered, not only could they be deported, but even the witnesses who come forward to help the police with their investigation too.

And if all this is still not cause for concern; it's not just the police that the Home Office are relying on to help with deportations, they've roped in our beloved NHS to do their dirty work. The confidential patient records of more than 8,000 people have been handed over by the NHS to the Home Office in one year alone, as part of its drive to track down immigration offenders. And it gets worse still, the Department for Education has agreed to share the details of up to 1,500 pupils a month to the Home Office to help trace potential immigration offenders. At this point, you've probably reached your limit, but I'm afraid there's more. Even homeless charities, organisations dedicated to caring for those among us with the least, are being tapped to help with deportations.

A non-profit organisation, Corporate Watch, has claimed that several homeless charities are working together with local councils in helping the Home Office deport vulnerable foreigners. In its report, it claimed that several outreach teams from homeless charities conducted over a hundred 'joint visits' with the Immigration Enforcement officers, sometimes as often as every fortnight, which led to 133 people who sleep on the streets being detained, while 127 people were deported in under a year in Westminster alone.

If you think it can't possibly get worse, it turns out that elected officials are also sharing information with immigration enforcers. In 2017, the immigration enforcement hotline was called sixty-eight times by MPs or their staff. This essentially cuts off people with unconfirmed immigration status from the democratic process of communicating with their MP, for fear of being deported.

OPEN BORDERS – A CRAZY, BOLD SOLUTION?

It's becoming increasingly clear that issues around immigration are personal perceptions. But this country was built with the help of immigrants (as well as most countries); they are ingrained in the very foundation of our nation and can be no more ignored than 'traditional Brits'. Can you imagine the impact on our economy, healthcare, entertainment, service and financial systems if we decided to get even tougher on immigration? Think of the impact on the NHS alone. On average, eight per cent of the entire workforce of the NHS are migrant workers, and close to a quarter of doctors are migrant workers. I spent a little over a week in the hospital with pneumonia last year and literally everyone who looked after me from the porters, to the doctors, to the X-ray specialist belonged to ethnic minority groups, or were clearly immigrants.

In February 2017, the Davis Museum at Wellesley College in Massachusetts decided to remove all art created by immigrants to demonstrate the impact of immigrants in the world of art – and the exhibitions looked mighty empty. Similarly, a supermarket in Hamburg removed all foreign-made food from its shelves for a day to protest against xenophobia in Germany. The Edeka store tweeted empty shelves with the slogans, 'This is how empty a shelf is without foreigners' and 'This shelf is pretty boring without diversity'. Their tweet was shared over 8,000 times and received 20,000 likes.

Given that there is empirical proof that immigration is good for economies, then instead of restricting immigration, should we be actively encouraging it? Some brave economists such as Bryan Caplan dare to ask this question. He compares immigration to a social right; asking, why is it any less wrong for an immigrant to need the government's permission to enter a country and get a job than it is a citizen's? Caplan proposes open borders, where people can move and work freely as the solution. He notes (correctly) that any restrictions on immigration trap millions of individuals in Third World misery, but cites estimates showing that open borders would roughly double world GDP, enough to virtually eliminate global poverty.

Undoubtedly this notion that we allow any worker free movement to any country to work raises eyebrows and leads nationalists to proclaim blasphemy, but Caplan uses another analogy in an interview with Vox, where he asks us to 'think about what happened in the 1960s and '70s as more and more women joined the workforce. Was the result mass unemployment for men, as women took all their jobs? Of course not, the economy adjusted, and we're all better off for it.'

Although drastic, Caplan's proposal is not entirely without merit – Argentina is a good example of a form of open borders in action. Argentina's current law treats immigration as a human right; with government agencies tasked to help immigrants to obtain residency. It allows free access to healthcare and education, while immigrants are also granted a right to legal counsel, and all residents of neighbouring countries are eligible for residency, regardless of whether or not they have a job. And yet, Argentina still stands. Its economy is booming (it has the third largest GDP in Latin America, behind Brazil and Mexico) and it is significantly richer than some of its neighbours, while being only the fourth most populous country.

What is so encouraging to see with Argentina (compared to the UK with Project Nexus) is that its immigration law mandates that deporting an illegal migrant requires a court hearing, and generally may only be executed if the government offers the migrant a chance to regularise their status and the migrant refuses this offer. In addition, while the court is reviewing the deportation order, the migrant is not even detained; in fact, they are offered legal aid for their case.

Sadly, this may not be a reality in Argentina for much longer. In parallels to the United States, in 2017, Argentinian President Mauricio Macri (also a former real estate tycoon-turned-president) signed an executive order to stop some foreign migrants entering his country and to deport foreign residents with criminal records, claiming: 'Peruvian and Paraguayan citizens come here and end up killing each other for control of the drug trade.'

While advocating for global open borders is a huge ask; surely a bit more compassion when it comes to caring for the least among us isn't? The Syrian Refugee crisis is one of the most troubling of our time and the conditions faced by the migrants and refugees are horrendous. In response, some countries have demonstrated their compassion: in 2015, German Chancellor Angela Merkel enacted a law allowing Syrian refugees (who normally would be deported back to wherever they first entered the EU), to stay and apply for asylum. Thousands of Syrians who would have otherwise faced uncertainty in Europe can now begin the process of rebuilding their lives in Germany. And while Germany still stands, Merkel has suffered politically for this law. But we need more of this compassion; for nothing else than the fact that countries in the West are in part responsible for the reasons why refugees are fleeing their countries.

It's all well and good saying immigrants should go back home, but they have no home to go back to, because we are the ones bombing the hell out of their homes. Take Syria for example: RAF air strikes in the Isil-held cities of Mosul and Ramadi may have killed thirty-two civilians in December 2015 alone. One of the worst civilian tolls was from a US strike on 1 May 2015 near Aleppo, where more than sixty civilians were said to have been killed, perhaps more than half of them children – with nothing more than an 'oops, my bad' from coalition forces. So, you see, the immigrants and refugees can't go home: they have no home to go to.

If you think accepting immigrants and refugees into the country is going to be a drain on society, then think of how much it costs to go and bomb their country. The UK has been bombing Islamic State targets in Iraq since 2014 and in Syria since 2015. While there are no concrete figures to show how much this has cost, according to the Royal United Service Institute, the seven-month bombing campaign by Britain in Libya cost £390 million. So, think about it: each six-hour Tornado bombing mission costs around £210,000, add to that the cost of four bombs at £22,000 each and two Brimstone missiles at £105,000 each. If all weapons are fired on an average mission, the cost of each Tornado mission is therefore £508,000. In April 2017, around 216 bombs and missiles were dropped by the Royal Air Force. This means that from January to April 2017 alone, the taxpayer shelled out over £2.2 million pounds to bomb these countries – and then we complain that their citizens are leaving the region and should go back to the country that we've just bombed.

But all hope is not lost. According to projections by the University of Leeds, ethnic minorities will make up a fifth of Britain's population by 2051, suggesting that the UK will become far less segregated as ethnic groups disperse throughout the country. Researchers attribute this growth to be driven by immigration. So, immigration and the children of immigrants will make us more diverse and as people start to move into other regions of the country, more spatially integrated.

There is undoubtedly a connection between exposure to immigrants and opinions about them; instead of being ashamed, I should have embraced and been proud of my Nigerian heritage and invited friends to learn more about it. People who live in areas that have high concentrations of immigrants are less likely to see them as a burden to society and a threat to traditional customs.

As I pointed out in the first chapter, because of the migration post-Roman Empire, the reality is that we are all descendants of immigrants – no matter which country we are citizens of. We are all capable of committing horrific acts of violence and uplifting acts of great kindness. We all rely on the state for some sort of support or the other and we are all emotionally invested in the countries that we reside in. As long as we can remember these things when thinking about immigrants, we shift ever so slightly to being on the right side of the discussion. So, here's to a beautiful and diverse future.

Answer to pop quiz: The UK believes twenty-four per cent of its population are immigrants, when it's actually only thirteen per cent.

LANGUAGE

WELL, HOW COME YOU GET TO SAY IT?

Stereotype/negative narrative: We are just too PC and overly sensitive when we don't want people of other races saying 'nigga' in songs.

Pop quiz:

What percentage of white Americans believe that discrimination against them is on par with that faced by black people and other minorities?

33%

18%

52%

I was fifteen the first time I was called a 'nigger'.* I know that seems a little late in life compared to most black people, but there's a reason to explain it. From the ages of four to around fifteen, I lived in Nigeria, so there really wasn't cause for anyone to racially insult me, because everyone I knew was of the same race. When I moved back to England, I faced a lot of abuse and taunts at my school because I was black and had a Nigerian accent. Monkey-boy, African boo-boo,† Golliwog – you know the score.

I had lived blissfully untainted by that word until one fateful evening when as I was walking back from a friend's house, a car with three white boys sped by and one of them shouted: 'Go back to Africa, Nigga!' What I did next will probably surprise you. It still surprises me to this day. I turned around to see who they were referring to. Not for one second did it occur to me that I was the nigger. Me, with my perfect grades at school? Me, who had never gotten in trouble with the police? Me, who didn't even know the lyrics to any rap song. Me, a nigger? I'm sorry, sir. You must be mistaken.

After looking round frantically to try and console the poor, unfortunate soul who had just been called a nigger, it finally dawned on me that they were referring to me – I was the nigger. Well, shit! The floodgates of realisation opened for fifteen-year-old me, who in that moment realised that yes, to them I will always be the nigger. That no matter what I achieve in life, no matter my contributions to society, that no matter what, I will always be seen as a nigger.

There's a similarly perfect scene in Neil Gaiman's TV adaption of his book, *American Gods*. In episode two of the first season, there's a flashback to the slavery era with a bunch of slaves on a ship bound for America. The slaves pray to their god, Anansi, for deliverance and when he appears (played to perfection by Orlando Jones), he delivers a powerful monologue telling the slaves what their fate and lives will be in America.

---

* For the purposes of clarity, I'll be using nigga and nigger interchangeably.
† Does anyone know what a boo-boo is? Genuinely want to know.

'Once upon a time, a man got fucked. Now, how is that for a story? 'Cause that's the story of black people in America!' At this point, the slaves look at him quizzically, and then he realises it's confusion at the word 'black'. 'Shit! You all don't know you black yet. You think you just people. Let me be the first to tell you that you are all black. The moment these Dutch motherfuckers set foot here and decided that they white, you all get to be black – and that's just the nice name they call you.'

And like the slaves back then didn't realise they were black, I didn't realise I was a nigger. And not just me – my parents. My sister. My aunts and uncles, and cousins and nephews and nieces. My friends. All niggers. For generations past and for generations to come – we will be niggers. And much like the reaction of the slaves in that episode of *American Gods*, I got angry. So angry that I wished the car would crash into a tree and kill all three of them. Well, not all three of them. I had wished that the one who called me nigger would survive long enough for me to walk over to his barely alive body and the last thing he would see would be me leaning down to whisper in his ear: 'I'm not your nigger.'

At this point, I was a devout Christian, in fact, at that age, my dream occupation was to be a pastor. Imagine that. Picture a word so heinous and hateful and hurtful that would make an innocent young fifteen-year-old not only wish a painful death on another kid, but would want to prolong their suffering just long enough for him to gloat in the face of their death. Imagine what it would take for someone so religious to ignore Christ's teaching to 'turn the other cheek' and to love one's neighbour as much as they loved themselves. For as long as I live, I will never forgive or forget those boys, because they woke me up to something I hadn't realised yet – that how I saw myself was not how others saw me.

I had dismissed the taunts of 'golliwog' as mere childhood banter. After all, we made fun of the ginger kid* in class and called the boy

---

* Till this day, I genuinely still don't understand why people make fun of ginger people.

who had wispy grey hair at fifteen, the pigeon. But nigger wasn't something I thought people still called each other. I thought it was an offensive relic from slavery that rappers sometimes used, or American TV characters would utter to show they were from the hood. I didn't think people actually said it – in England no less.

That, ladies and gentlemen, is how I got what comedian Paul Mooney refers to as my 'nigger wake-up call' – an acknowledgement that this is all I will be to some people and that this word will follow me around for the rest of my life. For months after that incident, whenever I met a white person, I couldn't help wondering if all I was to them was a nigger. It's a word that I still carry around with me, from that moment to today. I am under no illusions that I would have gone through life, blissfully unaware of how people who look like me are perceived. I know now that I would have been called a nigger eventually, but I wanted more time with my ignorance.

Ironically, despite its power to hurt, nigger is arguably used most prevalently within the black community. It is present in our music, our TV shows, and our culture. It appears that its use is more prevalent among African Americans than black communities in the UK and other parts of the world where there are large numbers of black people. For starters, I doubt the stiff upper-lip and self-effacing Brits would have readily adopted this into our lexicon, and as I alluded to earlier, black people in Africa and the Caribbean are not (by and large) referring to themselves as nigger, because we are the majority.

As Anansi suggests in *American Gods*, it's only when the slavers decided that they got to be white that we were designated as black. In Africa and the Caribbean, we just are. In truth, a lot of African-American culture and colloquialisms permeate to black communities around the world. For example, words like woke, ratchet, bae, on-fleek, lit, turnt, and others. The use of nigger in the black community is such an example. Black people use 'nigga' in a variety of ways – to another black person: 'What's up my nigga?' – in reference to a thing: 'Man, did you see that car? That nigga's the shit'– or even a white person: 'Did you hear what Donald Trump just said? Man, that nigga's buggin'.'

Basically, it is a grammatical anomaly that from a black person could refer to a noun, adjective, pronoun, conjunction word, or even a determiner. But more than that, it can also convey comradery and brotherhood. Much like 'the nod' (see Chapter One), it is a recognition of someone with the same heritage as you. Someone who faces the same discrimination. And someone who soldiers on despite that discrimination. It is also an acknowledgement of a role reversal, because even though the word was born from the most horrific of circumstances, the fact that we don the word like a cape and use it to recognise each other is powerful. It's like a language that only we can speak to each other.

American academic and TV personality, Marc Lamont Hill, captured this sentiment perfectly referring to the rapper Trinidad James in a CNN interview, where he said, 'I might see Trinidad James on the street and call him my nigga. You know why? Because he is my nigga. And the difference between Trinidad James and you [referring to white conservative commentator, Ben Ferguson], is that Trinidad James has to deal with the same oppressive situations. He was born into a world where anti-black racism prevails. He lives in a world where police might shoot him on the street no matter how much money he has. We share a collective condition known as nigga. White people don't.'

And so, for this chapter, instead of focusing on racists who use the word to hurt black people, I want to concentrate on the issue of why white people, or people of any other race for that matter, who want to be able to say nigger in certain circumstances when they are not using it to offend or as a slur, shouldn't do it.

WHY YOU DON'T GET TO SAY IT

Words are interesting. At their very basic core, they are a vocalised form of communication by making sounds with our mouths. Hell, even parrots can speak, and they have literally . . . bird brains. So, what is it about the word 'nigger' that even though it is a racial slur, I can use and embrace it with other black people, but the moment a white person says it, even harmlessly and not intending to cause offence, it debases me and hurts to my very core? How can one single word have so much power over me when it comes out of the mouth of a white person?

When I was younger, there was a saying that was very popular to prove that you were being honest and truthful: 'I swear on my mum's life.' The idea being that what you were saying was so true that you would be willing to stake your own mother's life on it. But I never subscribed to that. I lied and got away with things all the time, even though I invoked the saying. In my mind, they were just stupid words; no harm was going to befall my mother because I lied or cheated at games. And I was right: to this day, my mother is hale and healthy.*

So, it seems that rational thought would dictate that the word 'nigger' should not offend me as much as it does, and given it is only a word, should be used by white people in the same way they would use any other word. Particularly given there are countless rap songs that have the word nigger in the title, not to mention the lyrics, as well as some memorable lines from TV or live comedians involving the use of the word – see Chris Rock's famous 'Black People vs. Niggers' set on his album, *Bring the Pain*. It gets even more complicated when you realise it is a legitimate word in its own right. Nigger comes from a bastardisation of the Latin adjective for black – 'niger'.

I've spent a long time thinking about this and reading up on the word from countless sources and this is how I can articulate the feelings of the black community as best I can. Yes, nigger is just a word – and one that we use excessively. But coming from a white person, no matter the circumstances, it serves as a reminder that we used to be slaves – that this one word summed up our entire miserable existence.

It is a reminder that we are treated as less that nothing in the countries that our ancestors slaved and died to build. It is a reminder that even though it has been over four hundred years since slavery, black people are still not free. It's a reminder that we are different,

---

* Although, sorry mum for playing fast and loose with your life.

that we have always been regarded as inferior. And most of all, it is a reminder of white people's power over black people that they feel that even after over two hundred years of slavery, they feel entitled to be able to say that word.

Whenever people of any other race – white people, in particular – say that word, there is always an initial gut reaction from us: what's the intention? Is it racism? Is it ignorance? Is it insensitivity? No matter the circumstance, we always feel like we need to examine the intent, because from the times of slavery to the Jim Crow era, and till today, we've been reduced to offensive words, ridiculous caricatures, and baseless stereotypes such as Jim Crow (black crows dressed in waistcoats – see Disney's *Dumbo* movie), the Coon (white people in blackface in the minstrel shows), Aunt Jemima or Mammy (an overweight black woman with big breasts who is loud and sassy – see *Tom and Jerry*), or Golliwogs (a doll used to perpetuate blackface).

Another example is the gross perversion of 'Uncle Tom' (written originally as an anti-slavery hero by slavery abolitionist writer, Harriet Beecher Stowe. Uncle Tom was a slave who was beaten to death for refusing to reveal the whereabouts of runaway slaves, but the story was rewritten by white people and presented at minstrel shows portraying Uncle Tom as a supporter of slavery and a lover of white people – see Samuel L. Jackson's character in *Django Unchained*).

So, no; white people can't say nigger. Just as we bear the scars and long-term effects of slavery as a community today, so must white people bear the consequences of their forefathers' complicity in slavery. And before the argument is put forward that not all white people are descended from slave owners, consider the fact that not all black people were slaves or descended from slaves, but we all still bear the brunt of its effects today. Today's systemic racist organisations don't discriminate between black people – they treat us all the same. When we are denied management positions or mortgages, when our neighbourhoods are left in disrepair, when our brothers and sisters are unfairly treated by the police, there is no demarcation in the community: we are all just niggers. So, if we are still feeling the effects today, why should the consequences of these actions be any different for white people today?

As for why black people can use this word, and do so frequently, I've never heard it more eloquently explained than by the famous author on African-American culture and *Atlantic* correspondent, Ta-Nehisi Coates, at an event at Evanston Township High School in Illinois – available on YouTube. He explains that black people being able to say nigger and white people not is a cultural norm that people within a group with a certain relationship can use terms to identify each other, and strangers to the group cannot.

He uses his relationship with his family as an example: his wife calls him honey, but it would not be acceptable for a woman he had just met to call him honey. Likewise, his dad's friends call him Billy (his father's name is William), but it would not be acceptable for him to call his own father, Billy. 'That's because the relationship between myself and my dad is not the same as the relationship between my dad and his mother and his sisters, who he grew up with. And we understand that.'

He explains further, 'My wife, with her girlfriends, will use the word "bitch". I do not join in. And perhaps more importantly, I don't have a desire to do it. The question one must ask is: why so many white people have difficulty extending things that are basic laws of how human beings interact to black people.'

One of the most common scenarios where white people would use nigger (without intending to cause offence) is singing hip hop songs. Black people experience a mixture of emotions when Kanye West's 'Gold Digger' comes on in the club.* On the one hand, it's a bad ass tune and guaranteed to get things jumping on the dancefloor. On the other hand, it gives white people the chance to say nigger quite openly and frequently. What is a black person to do? Obviously, you don't want the fact that white people are saying nigger with such reckless abandon to ruin your vibe, but at the same time,

---

* Actually, we experience a mixture of emotions about Kanye in general.

there is something very unsettling about being surrounded by white people yelling nigger.

The TV show, *Dear White People*, depicts an example of how these scenarios tend to play out. In episode six of season one, a black character, Reggie, attends a frat party with mostly white students. He is singing and dancing along to hip hop when his white friend, Addison, says nigger while singing along to the song. Reggie asks him not to say it and Addison explains that he doesn't really use the word, but is just singing along – claiming, 'It's not like I'm a racist.' Reggie explains by saying, 'Just don't say "nigga". Like, you didn't have to say it just then . . . I mean, how would you feel if I started rapping songs that say "honky" and "cracker"?'

Addison replies that he would care. To which Reggie further explains, 'Exactly. That's the difference. Like, that you don't care. And I do. Like, you get it?' Addison takes it personally and goes as far as to say that he has been good to Reggie by allowing him to party in his house and now, political correctness has meant that 'we* can't have fun anymore'. A fight then breaks out and the police get called in to break it up. And guess who ends up with a gun in his face out of all the attendees? Reggie, of course.

There are a couple of things to unpack in this scene. First is: why white people can't say nigger when it is clearly part of the song? If it's so controversial and offensive, then why did the (black) artist put in the lyrics? Surely it is unrealistic and downright ridiculous to expect that the song will only be enjoyed and sung out loud by black people? And the answer is: the (black) artist does not care about you. They are speaking their truth. They are reflecting their language. They are expressing their culture. They are not going to censor themselves for you so that you don't have to make the choice of whether to say nigger, or so you don't have to feel guilty saying the word nigger in the presence of black people. They simply don't care about you.

---

* I assume he means white people, because minorities have not been having fun with this shit since . . . the beginning of time.

For a lot of black musicians, this genre of music is their only avenue to success, the only way they can enter the entertainment world. And more to the point, how many white people get the nuance of the culture and the stories that are reflected in the use of the word nigger in the songs?

At Jay Z and Kanye West's *Niggas in Paris* tour, they took a picture with Gwyneth Paltrow, which she then tweeted with the caption, 'Ni**as in Paris for real'. Given that both Kanye and Jay Z were friends of hers and she used the asterisks to refrain from using the word, she is still effectively calling Jay Z and Kanye, niggers. Comedian Louis CK makes a similar point in his act, *Chewed Up*, noting: 'You say "the n-word" and I go, oh, she means "nigger". You're making me say it in my head!' Also, I wonder if Paltrow, while singing along and saying nigger, understands the meaning behind the lyrics:

Ball so hard, this shit weird, we ain't even 'pose to be here. Ball so hard, got a broke clock, Rollies that don't tick tock. Audemars that's losing time, hidden behind all these big rocks. These lyrics are a recognition that Kanye and Jay had made it from the ghetto to the big leagues and are now welcome in the upper echelons of society and wealth, in this case, Paris.

Ball so hard, I'm shocked too, I'm supposed to be locked up too. You escaped what I've escaped, you'd be in Paris getting fucked up too. In this line, Jay Z is referencing his past as a cocaine dealer and noting that by all rights, he should have been arrested. But he escaped that life and made something of himself and is now enjoying his new life in Paris.

(Ball so hard) act like you'll ever be around motherfuckas like this again. This line speaks to the fact that they have to live it all for today, because there is no guarantee that they'd get to enjoy being on the same level as the same rich people who order fish fillet forever.

Now, of course, there's no way that I can know for certain that Gwyneth Paltrow doesn't get these nuances to the song, but I do know that compared to growing up in the ghetto and having to sell drugs to survive, Paltrow's father was a movie producer and her mother, an actress. She grew up in Santa Monica and did an exchange programme in Talavera de la Reina, Spain. So, I very much doubt she will ever get what it means to be a nigger in Paris.

Another point to take from this example is a sense of common decency. Reggie was clearly explaining to a friend that he finds him saying nigger offensive, and Addison should have respected him by understanding that. And that's something I truly don't understand. If I know that a word is offensive – and offensive to my friend at that – why would I justify the need to have to say that word?

I like Eminem's early songs, I think they are a pinnacle of 1990s rap music, but he uses that slur, 'faggot', in a lot of those songs. I would never dream about saying that word, let alone in front of any of my gay friends, nor would I argue that I should be able to because it was in the lyrics of the song. I don't even say it when I am alone in my house, nor do I have the inclination to want to say it at all. When I'm out in a bar or club with my female friends and Chris Brown's 'Loyal' comes on – with lyrics like, 'Why give a bitch your heart, when she rather have a purse? These hoes ain't loyal,' I don't sing along to calling women hoes, I go and get a drink.* Because I know that the lyrics are offensive to the company I'm with. Instead, what the character Addison did was make it about him and blame political correctness.

Whenever anyone complains that we are too PC these days, or we have been forced to be PC, I always ask, 'What is it you could say before that you really can't live without saying now in our "enforced PC world"?' In this example, Addison complains that he can't say nigger because of political correctness. But the word nigger has always been offensive – it's not a new requirement of the alleged PC era. Jon

---

* For any Chris Brown song actually. He is an abusive twat who is officially cancelled.

Stewart of the *Daily Show* fame pointed out something very interesting about the hypocrisy of political correctness at the live taping of *The Axe Files* – available on YouTube.

He uses Donald Trump (one of the biggest proponents against political correctness) as an example, noting: 'So, the whole idea of political correctness is everybody's so sensitive, just get over it, you know, why should African Americans be so sensitive about police shootings? Why do they have to be so sensitive about years of systemic racism creating economic disparity? Come on. I'm not a slave owner. Donald Trump couldn't handle us making a joke about him. *Vanity Fair*, Graydon Carter, did a joke about Donald Trump's hands twenty-five years ago. He's still not fucking over it . . . But the idea being that Muslims, hey man, all he's saying is they're evil and shouldn't be allowed in this country. He's just telling it like it is, but God forbid you say, "Happy Holidays" in December, then it's fucking war. So, who is it who's exactly sensitive here?'

Therein lies the discrepancy – I wouldn't be able to tell a Newcastle United football fan to simply get over it if I had mistakenly referred to him as a 'Mackem' instead of a 'Geordie', so why should white people get to say nigger? Addison also mentions that he wouldn't care if Reggie had sung along to a song that said 'cracker' or 'honky'. Yes, I'm sure he wouldn't, because cracker and honky are ridiculous terms that some idiot made up to try and insult white people. It is as ridiculous as the word 'boo-boo'. Unlike nigger, it is not a weapon that has been used to destroy and systematically undermine an entire people.

You don't hear black people complaining about being called 'bastard' or 'arsehole'; sure, they are bad words, but don't have the same connotation as nigger. Calling a white person 'cracker' or 'honky' is offensive, but it doesn't come with the connotation of being subjected to unfair stop-and-search laws, and it doesn't prelude law enforcement creating a drug policy and sentencing guidelines specifically to incarcerate you. It doesn't mean that you will pay the same taxes as your black friends and yet statistically earn less than them. And for damn sure the word wasn't created in an era where your family were raped, lynched, and enslaved.

I have sung along to rap songs with white people when they've used nigger, without saying a word; in some instances, I've spoken up and asked them not to; and in other instances, I've simply left the dance floor because there were way too many white people to confront about it.* So, I can't offer any advice as to what black people should do when white people say nigger along with the lyrics of a song. I can only tell white people reading this that we'd very much prefer that you didn't. The reality is, no black person would ever thank a white person for saying nigger – under any circumstances. Even if the black person doesn't say anything, I promise they're hurting. It is just not something you should say. Not unless you are prepared to go through everything black people have gone and still go through: if you want to be able to say nigger, then get ready to be treated like one.

Ta-Nehisi Coates, in his lecture at Evanston High School, actually uses the fact that white people shouldn't say nigger in hip hop songs as a lesson to understanding what it means to be black: 'The experience of being a hip-hop fan and not being able to use the word "nigger" is actually very, very insightful. It will give you just a little peek into the world of what it means to be black. Because to be black is to walk through the world and watch people doing things that you cannot do, that you can't join in and do. So, I think there's actually a lot to be learned from refraining.'

THE CURIOUS CASE OF QUENTIN TARANTINO

It is not only in music lyrics that white people have argued for being able to say nigger; it is also a point of view with regards to movies. The notion that it is just a word – and one that is used prevalently in the African-American and black community – is commonly used by the director Quentin Tarantino to justify his use of the word frequently and in several

---

* That's what you get for going out in Shoreditch.

of his movies. In an interview with *The Vibe* magazine, he claims that he wants to defuse the word's power, noting: 'My feeling is the word nigger is probably the most volatile word in the English language. The minute any word has that much power, as far as I'm concerned, everyone on the planet should scream it. No word deserves that much power. I'm not afraid of it. That's the only way I know how to explain it.'

You would be forgiven if you were confused as to why Tarantino felt that he's entitled to 'defuse' the power of nigger and urge people to scream it out. I personally am not surprised that Tarantino is not afraid of the word nigger. That's because no one has ever shouted it at him in a derogatory way. No one denies him a job because he is a nigger. People of other races didn't go to his ancestral home to rape, enslave, and eventually kill his people, just because they were nothing more than a nigger to their captors. Also, it's important to recognise that there isn't going to be a utopian future where nigger will no longer be an offensive word, with the power all sapped out of it. To forget the meaning of nigger and the context in which it has been used is to forget the atrocities that accompanied it, which is a fucking stupid and insulting idea.

For better or worse, the word nigger is a testament to the brutality that black people faced at the hands of white people and recognising its negative significance of that era is not something to be eroded. But in the spirit of objectivity, let's take him at his word and see his use of the word nigger through two of his movies that featured gratuitous use of the word nigger.

In his (brilliant) movie, *Pulp Fiction*, Tarantino has a cameo in which he berates Samuel L. Jackson and John Travolta's characters for wanting to store a dead black man in his house. He says, 'Did you notice a sign out in front of my house that says "Dead Nigger Storage"? . . . it ain't there, 'cause storing dead niggers ain't my fucking business, that's why!' Tarantino justified this scene by explaining that's the way that character would talk, and he doesn't censor his characters. Fair enough. And I believe there is worth in separating the artist from the art. But in this case, the argument simply doesn't wash.

If it was essential to the scene that the character use the word nigger, fine. But did it have to be Tarantino to fill that role? After all, he is not an actor. He is a director. So, he inserted himself into that role (and there were many other roles that he could have played in that movie) and for what? For the opportunity to say nigger while hiding within the context of his art? We may never know for sure, of course, but it is certainly plausible. And let's not forget that this is the same movie in which a black man (Marsellus Wallace, played by Ving Rhames) is raped by a white racist – in a scene that adds nothing more to the plot other than to shock and give the character a reason for revenge afterwards.

If you look at the spate of interviews that Tarantino has done, he prides himself on reflecting the truth; he tries to be authentic in his movies and reflect how people would act in any given situation. In *The Hateful Eight*, rather unsurprisingly given the movie features characters in the South during the American civil war, nigger is said approximately sixty-five times. So, it becomes logical (and indeed authentic) that this Tarantino movie should feature frequent use of the word nigger – and it could be argued that it would be hypocritical to berate Tarantino for using the word nigger in this movie simply because he's white.

In real life at that time, I'm certain that white people would have said nigger even more than sixty-five times in the hours within the timeline of the movie. But let's compare *The Hateful Eight* to another movie, *12 Years a Slave*, which was literally set over the course of twelve years. You'll find that nigger was only said approximately fifty-four times (excluding the lyrics of the song, 'Run, Nigger, Run'), which is less than in the couple of hours that *The Hateful Eight* was set. And even if you did include the lyrics to the song, then nigger was said approximately eighty-six times over the course of twelve years, compared to Tarantino's sixty-five in only a few hours.

Tarantino's claim to want to focus on authenticity falls apart once you take a closer look at his movies – take *Kill Bill*, for example, which features a woman who singlehandedly (after being in a coma for years) defeats a whole theatre-full of sword-wielding Yakuza members. And I get it, with movies, we have to suspend our belief in order to move the narrative along and fully enjoy the movie. After all, a movie about her physiotherapy after the coma and then training to fight the Yakuza would not be fun.

So, instead let's look at a subtle example that doesn't require us to suspend belief. In his movie *Inglorious Basterds*, Brad Pitt's character, Aldo Raine, is meant to be of Native-American heritage and is scripted to scalp Nazis because of his heritage as an 'injun'. Well, this is not authentic, because it's an incorrect stereotype that scalping was a Native-American custom; in actual fact, Europeans used to scalp Native-Americans and their scalps were used as a payment and a demoralisation tactic. Not very authentic, Mr Tarantino.*

To be clear, I don't think that Tarantino is racist. Tarantino's movies are always over the top and exaggerated, so he believes the use of the word nigger should be, too. What I do think is that he feels he's entitled. I think he's an artist who believes that as long as it is going into the art, it's okay. That as long as it is entertaining, cultural heritage and appropriateness be damned. And it is this sense of entitlement that allows him to use this racial slur so flippantly to his advantage, under the misguided notion that he is dissolving the power of the word. He has waded into a conversation about race and taken a position that is not his to take. And how do I know this, because he's pretty much said so himself.

In an interview on *Django Unchained*, a movie where nigger was said over a hundred times, Gawker reports that he said: '[*Django Unchained*] is creating a nice debate . . . I am responsible for people talking about slavery in America in a way that they have not in thirty years. Violence on slaves hasn't been dealt with to the extent that I've dealt with it.' Forget about the killings of black men at the hands of the police. Or the fact that some of the policies following slavery are the main reasons why black people are at a disadvantage today. But Quentin Tarantino is responsible for people talking about slavery in America.

---

* Also, spoiler alert, the movie concludes with Hitler being shot to death by the Basterds. I don't remember that as an authentic ending to WW2 from my history class.

WHAT WE MEAN WHEN WE SAY WHITE PRIVILEGE

The 36th President of the United States, Lyndon B. Johnson, reportedly referred to the Civil Rights Act of 1957 as the 'nigger bill' and upon appointing African-American judge Thurgood Marshall to the Supreme Court, reportedly said, 'Son, when I appoint a nigger to the court, I want everyone to know he's a nigger.'

Ronald Kessler in his book, *Inside the White House: The Hidden Lives of the Modern Presidents and the Secrets of the World's Most Powerful Institution*, reveals that Johnson also said, while explaining why the Civil Rights Bill was important to him, 'I'll have them niggers voting Democratic for two hundred years.' Additionally, according to Johnson's biographer Robert Caro and reported in Snopes.com, Johnson is alleged to have told his black chauffeur (who had asked to be called by his name instead of nigger): 'As long as you are black, and you're gonna be black till the day you die, no one's gonna call you by your goddamn name. So, no matter what you are called, nigger, you just let it roll off your back like water, and you'll make it.'

That's not all. In his 2001 book, *Nigger: The Strange Career of a Troublesome Word*, author Randall Kennedy notes that President Harry S. Truman called Congressman Adam Clayton Powell 'that damned nigger preacher', while President Richard Nixon was caught on his own White House tapes referring to black people as 'niggers' and 'jigaboos'.*

The reason I bring these examples up is in comparison to the first time that the only black President of the United States said nigger publicly. He was on the comedian Marc Maron's 'WTF' podcast, where he noted (referring to the racially motivated murders in a Charleston church): 'Racism, we are not cured of it. And it's not just a matter of it not being polite to say nigger in public.' So, Barack Obama, as well as being the first black president, was also the first president to say nigger in front of other people and not mean it in a derogatory way. However, there were media articles (not to mention social media

---

* First boo-boo, now jigaboo. Seriously, what do these things mean. Is this white people's version of jive talking?

backlash) explaining why the President of the United States shouldn't use that word — despite other presidents using it liberally. And this wasn't reserved to American politicians, former prime minister and arguably one of the most liberal PMs the UK has had, Lloyd George reportedly once said, 'We must reserve the right to bomb niggers.' Not to mention that as early as 2017, the Conservative party's chief whip Anne Marie Morris, the MP for Newton Abbot in Devon, said nigger in a discussion about Brexit: 'Now I'm sure there will be many people who'll challenge that, but my response and my request is look at the detail, it isn't all doom and gloom. Now we get to the real nigger in the woodpile, which is, in two years what happens if there is no deal?'

The idea of white privilege when it comes to the word nigger is based around a lesson that is important for white people to learn. A lot of the black experience is centred around being denied things and having to work twice as hard simply to be allowed to participate; while a lot of the white experience is based on (nearly) complete access. Proportional to any other race, white people dominate politics, are economically more well-off, own media companies, and hold leadership positions in business. I use the word 'proportional', because there are a handful of minorities who do hold these positions, but institutional privilege is not measured individually, it's systemic.

So, white people wanting to be able to say nigger is attempting to take advantage of the privilege that they already have. In his lecture, Coates explains further: 'When you're white in this country, you're taught that everything belongs to you. You think you have a right to everything . . . the laws and the culture tell you this. You have a right to go where you want to go, do what you want to do, be however — and people just got to accommodate themselves to you. So here comes this word that you feel like you invented, and now somebody will tell you how to use the word that you invented. "Why can't I use it? Everyone else gets to use it. You know what? That's racism that I don't get to use it. You know, that's racist against me. You know, I have to inconvenience myself and hear this song and I can't sing along. How come I can't sing along?"'

White people haven't had to bear the trauma of the word nigger, nor do they have its comparative like in the English language. And because they have largely been free to do and say whatever they want from a cultural perspective, the notion that they can't say nigger seems unfathomable.

Despite the obvious disparity between the fates of white people and black (as well as other minorities), some white people simply cannot accept their privilege, and honestly, that is not an entirely blameless situation to be in. After all, who wants to admit that they benefit from racism?

In a *Vice* article, Erikka Knuti, a political strategist, observes: 'Part of white privilege has been the ability to not know that your privilege exists. If you benefit from racism, do you really want to know that? They must be honest with themselves and their co-citizens and admit that white privilege shapes a lot of life in this country. They must understand that the truly pernicious, life-defining sort of racism is not interpersonal, it's institutional. The systems that shape who lives where, who gets educated, who gets jobs, who gets arrested, and so on, these things shape lives, and they are all heavily weighted in white people's favour.'

If this seems like an unfair categorisation about white people, let's examine a couple of stats. According to a survey by NPR, fifty-five per cent of white Americans believe there is discrimination against white people in America today. Another survey, by the Public Religion Research Institute has revealed that fifty-two per cent of white Americans said that they believe discrimination against them is on par with discrimination faced by black people and other minorities.

That's almost laughable, because as Eduardo Bonilla-Silva notes in his book, *Racism without Racists*, black people lag behind white people in virtually every area of social life: we are three times more likely to be poorer, we earn on average forty-per-cent less, and we have an eighth of the net worth compared to white people. We receive inferior education, our houses are valued at thirty-five-per-cent less, and we are primarily targeted by law enforcement, resulting in a high percentage of us being arrested, prosecuted, incarcerated and executed.

How is it possible to have this much racial inequality in a country where the majority claim there is equal discrimination? This is so rooted in the belief of white Americans that in Chicago, two white students sued their school for $1 million because they were expelled for sending racist texts.

Anthony Morgan, a civil rights and human rights lawyer, explains in a *Vice* article why this colour-blindness to white privilege exists: 'When you're so deeply invested in your privilege, and in this case white privilege, racial equality feels like oppression. Racism is based on a couple of things – historical, systemic oppression and power. And as far as history goes, white people have never been persecuted for the colour of their skin, so there's no point comparing their experiences to those of black, brown, and indigenous folks. It's slavery, colonialism, theft, all kinds of violations on systemic proportions . . . versus feelings being hurt.'

And I get it. I get that life can be just as hard for some white people as it can be for black.* I get that not every white person benefits from the privilege of whiteness. And I certainly get why a white person who has struggled all his life and not received any help from their government would see unfair discrimination when he sees a person of colour benefitting because of anti-discrimination policies or affirmative action. And I get that white people can also be unfairly stopped by the police. But it is also important for white people to understand that black people face these challenges, all the while being socially and systemically handicapped because of the simple virtue of them being black.

White privilege doesn't mean a white person's life hasn't been hard; it means that your skin colour isn't one of the things making it harder. And if you still don't understand white privilege, consider being in the minority at a rap concert and still getting away with saying nigger. Consider a black person going to a heavy metal concert and using a derogatory word for white people – who are we kidding, there is no comparison of nigger for white people.†

---

* *Hillbilly Elegy* by J.D. Vance is an excellent book if you want to understand the plight of poor white people from middle-America.

† Also, no sensible black person would be caught dead at a heavy metal concert.

It's important to understand that when we say white privilege, it's not an insult. It's not a bad thing that you specifically have done. It simply means that society treats you better than people of colour because of systematic advantages resulting from a racist past. I think about this a lot when I consider my own privileges. I am a man who is well educated and decidedly middle class. It's important for me to accept that even though I've worked hard in life to accomplish what I have, the systemic sexism that allows men to succeed over women has contributed to that success – and I would be ignorant (and wrong) not to accept this notion. Even though I am not sexist, I benefit from a system that was built and is still maintained by sexism. As such, I feel a responsibility to support women and be an ally to their cause wherever I can. The examination of one's privilege is very important, because at some stage, we can all point to something that we have or are that makes us better off than others in society, in other words, there is always someone else who is worse off.

I talked about white privilege in a previous paragraph, but it doesn't mean that because you are white, you are not a member of a minority, or do not suffer from any systemic injustices. Even though I'm a black man, I still enjoy the privileges of being a man, so if a woman tells me to check my privilege, that is not for me to start reading into a discussion of who has it worse in the workplace: a black man or a white woman. Instead, it is an opportunity to examine what privileges we each benefit from, and a chance to do what we can to improve things for both of us – after all, a rising tide carries all boats.

RACISM VS. RACIST

I suppose one of the difficulties in white people not understanding why 'that word' is off limits for them is because the majority of them are not racist. In their heart, they don't bear any ill will towards black people. They are simply fans of rap music, or hip hop, and want to enjoy it as it was intended. As such, it's important to draw the distinction between racism and racists. This is something I had come across and struggled with before I started writing this book. I was with a group of friends in a pub, talking about the traits we most find attractive in a partner. One of the people present admitted that he didn't find black women attractive and, of course, I had to go the fuck off.

'That is incredibly racist,' I said. 'How could you possibly say such a thing out loud?' He explained very firmly that it wasn't that he thought black women were unattractive, or that black people were somehow different from white people, or that he had any problem with black people, but it was that he hadn't found any attractive. 'Not even Kerry Washington or Halle Berry?' I asked. And he said no.

As someone who doesn't prefer any specific race when it comes to dating,* it was hard for me to understand why this wasn't a racist opinion to have. It wasn't until I started to do research for the chapter on interracial dating that I came to understand that he wasn't racist; he was simply prejudiced. Probably by the negative perceptions with regard to black women mostly depicted in modern media – as we've discussed in Chapter Ten. I couldn't reconcile how someone can dismiss an entire group of people and claim not to be racist. But as I explained in previous chapters, we all have implicit biases and it is important to recognise them.

So, it is important to draw the line between an action that constitutes racism – saying nigger, and a person who is racist – someone who hates black people as a race. Eduardo Bonilla-Silva notes in *Racism without Racists* that: 'The more we assume that the problem of racism is limited to the Klan, the birthers, the tea party or to the Republican Party, the less we understand that racial domination is a collective process and we are all in this game.'

Anytime someone begins a sentence with the phrase, 'I'm not racist but . . .' or 'I have a lot of black friends,' it's a pretty certain bet they are going to say something racist. Anytime someone attempts to explain police brutality by using 'black on black crime' as an excuse, or someone tries to take a seemingly liberal view by saying, 'I don't even see

---

* And is more than slightly in love with Kerry Washington.

colour,' or 'All lives matter,' then you can be sure that what they are saying is racist.

More likely than not, it could well be that they have nothing against black people, or people of colour; it is more that they have embraced a point of view that is inherently racist. While it might seem noble to proclaim that you do not 'see race' and you want to treat everyone equally, what you are actually saying is that you fail to see or acknowledge the plight of minorities, and how they have suffered and continued to do so today. You are essentially equating minorities with white people who were not enslaved, or Jews who were in concentration camps in Germany, with a racial group who weren't. Aside from that, you'd also be lying.

Howard J. Ross, author of *Everyday Bias*, reveals in his book that we start to see race from a very young age: as early as three months old, children prefer to be around people of their own race. Ross notes: 'Human beings are consistently, routinely and profoundly biased.' This is supported by a study from the department of Economics at Cornell University, which showed that white NBA referees call more fouls on black players, and black referees call more fouls on white players.

An experiment reported in *Everyday Bias* showed people a photograph of two white men fighting, one unarmed and another holding a knife. Then they showed another photo, this time of a white man with a knife fighting an unarmed black man. When people were asked who was armed in the first picture, most people picked the right one. Yet, when they were asked the same question about the second photo, most people (black and white) incorrectly said the black man had the knife.

Ross explains in a CNN article that: 'The overwhelming number of people will actually experience the black man as having the knife because we're more open to the notion of the black man having a knife than a white man. This is one of the most insidious things about bias. People may absorb these things without knowing them.' Thus, the distinction between racism and racist is important – if for nothing else than you could unintentionally say a racist statement, apologise and be forgiven, but once you are branded a racist, that's the ball game.

The word nigger and the discussions around who is allowed to say it will always be controversial. Especially now that the legislative system in the States is allowing people to profit from slurs. In a judgment by the Supreme Court (that I am confident is to allow the football team to continue to be called by the highly offensive name, Washington Redskins), racial slurs and derogatory symbols can now be trademarked. A forward-thinking black man from Mississippi, Curtis Bordenave, rushed to file an application with the US Patent and Trademark Office for the word 'nigga'. Well, at least black people are finding more ways to make money off that word other than through rap music.

Interestingly, the NAACP didn't feel the same way about nigger, and decided to put that word to rest . . . literally. It held a public burial for the word nigger during its annual convention in 2007 – complete with a pine box adorned with a bouquet of fake black roses and a black ribbon printed with a derivation of the word. The coffin is placed at the historically black Detroit Memorial Park Cemetery and even has a headstone. Detroit Mayor Kwame Kilpatrick said at the funeral, 'Die N-word, and we don't want to see you 'round here no more.'

So, there you have it, if even the NAACP is against the word nigger, then surely white people shouldn't be so keen about saying it either. And if you absolutely have to get your Kanye on – please, for the love of God, don't use it around us.

Answer to pop quiz: Fifty-two per cent of white Americans believe discrimination against them is on par with discrimination faced by black people and other minorities.

CONCLUSION
EQUAL RIGHTS FOR OTHERS DOES NOT MEAN FEWER RIGHTS FOR YOU. IT'S NOT PIE.

I love being black. If I believed in reincarnation, I would come back black every time – sign me up, Jesus. I feel tremendous pride in what we have accomplished as a people, the love we have for each other and our community, and what we continue to strive to accomplish. My pride is given life from big things such as sharing my culture with people of other races, to little things, such as choosing a black skin for my emojis. I always use a black emoji when I give a 'thumbs up', or a wave, and every black person I know does the same. For me, being black is as much a part of who I am as my name. And while I have to acknowledge that race is nothing more than a social concept, we'd be blind to ignore its significance in our society.

For people of colour, our race or the colour of our skin is always a factor – as early as a very young age. Research in Social Psychology and Personality Science reveals that for minority children, 'race is central to their identities, a source of psychological well-being, and a lens through which others perceive them.' For us, colour has always been a blessing and a burden, but it can often be a huge shock when white people are forced to take the colour of their skin into account: a white friend of mine who volunteered in Tanzania told me of her experience there, explaining it was very unnerving for her to be in the minority for the first time.

As much as I can understand how that scenario can be very unnerving, it was not actually the first time she had been in a minority. We had been in meetings where she was the only woman, we had watched football games together with a larger group of friends where she was the only female, she had attended a few Afro-Caribbean gatherings at work, and we had been to gay clubs together, where we were in the minority there. What white people unknowingly experience when they go to a country where their colour of skin is in the minority is the absence of the comfort that comes with the societal dominance of their white skin.

All of a sudden, you become 'the other'. People come and touch your blonde hair. People want to take pictures with you, as if you are an alien from outer space. People look at you suspiciously, thinking, what is she doing here? People ask you where you are from . . . originally. And when you attempt to speak the language, people condescendingly tell you, 'Your [insert language] is quite good.' Welcome to our world – the big difference here is that you get this when you go to another country. We get this in the country of our birth.

This is why it is often so hard to talk about race. Hell, it's hard just being black. For something as inconsequential as the colour of our skin, it sure does cause a lot of problems. You're always aware of it: when you go to work and fail to see other people who look like you. When you go to the supermarket and the security guard follows you around. When you are walking on the street with your white partner. Being black is a full-time job – and it wears on you.

In an article in *Psychology Today*, titled 'Can Racism Cause PTSD?' by Dr Williams, associate professor at the University of Connecticut, who conducts PTSD research and treats PTSD cross-culturally, she notes that while 'much research has been conducted on the social, economic and political effects of racism, little research recognises the psychological effects of racism on people of colour.' Williams now studies the link between racism and PTSD, known as race-based traumatic stress injury. She notes that race-based stress reactions can even be triggered by events that are experienced through a third party – like social media or national news events. As someone who cried for the first time in six years over the continued death of young men who looked like me in a country 3,459 miles away, I have to say that I most certainly agree.

Here are just a couple of examples from the States in the past few years alone showing how black people are discriminated against:

- An employee called the police on a black student who was sitting in a common room at Smith College. The employee said to the police that she seemed 'out of place'. In truth, the student was working at the private women's liberal arts school and was just reading and eating lunch.

- A lemonade business owner in San Francisco was questioned by police outside his own store on suspicion of burgling it, after someone had called the police.

- A white student called campus police on a black graduate student at Yale, for napping in her own common room. The white student had reported it as an 'unauthorised person in the common room'.

- The police were also called on three black men in a Starbucks in Philadelphia, who were doing nothing more than waiting for their friend.

- A white man killed a black teenager in Arizona because he reportedly claimed he felt unsafe because the teen was listening to rap music – noting that people who listen to rap music are a threat to him and the community.

- And the cherry on this terrible sundae is when a white woman called the police on a couple of black people enjoying some pool time, because they wait for it . . . refused to talk to her. Apparently, she was depressed and was offended when they didn't want to talk to her!

There is this prevailing idea that there is something black people could do, to ensure that we don't become victims of racism. If only we didn't talk in slang, or wear hoodies, or give our children black names; if only we'd act right and be more respectable, then white people would be equally accommodating. Bill Cosby's infamous 'Pound Cake' speech, given during an NAACP awards ceremony in Washington, DC, seems to suggest that.

In his speech, he berated activists who accused the criminal justice system of racism, saying, 'These are people going around stealing Coca-Cola. People getting shot in the back of the head over a piece of pound cake. Then we all run out and are outraged: "The cops shouldn't have shot him!" What the hell was he doing with the pound cake in his hand? I wanted a piece of pound cake just as bad as anybody else. And I looked at it and I had no money. And something called parenting said, "If you get caught with it, you're going to embarrass your mother."'

He also attacked black naming traditions: 'Ladies and gentlemen, listen to these people. They are showing you what's wrong . . . What part of Africa did this come from? We are not Africans. Those people are not Africans. They don't know a damned thing about Africa – with names like Shaniqua, Shaligua, Mohammed, and all that crap, and all of them are in jail.'

Someone should have pointed out to Cosby that regardless of how wrong and illegal it is, the penalty for stealing pound cake is not execution; and that Shaniqua means God is gracious, while Mohammed means praiseworthy, and is the name of the founder of Islam – a religion practised by over twenty-four per cent of the world's population. Cosby's speech was based on a ridiculous notion; good behaviour and the right clothing does not prevent racism.

Discrimination does not come with a code of conduct. We don't need to conform to other cultures or what other races consider to be acceptable in order to be accepted. Racism should be eradicated, because it is an illogical idea. Discriminating against someone for the colour of their skin is as ludicrous as doing it because of the colour of their hair. So, we don't need to conform; we need to celebrate and revel in our blackness.

MEDIA PORTRAYAL OF BLACK PEOPLE

As I mentioned in Chapters Six and Ten, the media portrayal of black people has a huge impact on our stereotypes –white as a template of beauty, and the portrayal of black people in movies. It is undeniable that the media impacts our beliefs, assumptions, personal experiences and public ideology; what we see on our screens and in our papers influences how we see the world, and black people are disproportionately depicted in a negative light. Again, this has its origins in racism and white nationalism.

In the early days of media consumption, black people were historically played by white people with wearing black face. This helped send a symbolic message that black people were not good or talented enough to represent themselves, so their roles had to be filled by white people. So began the perpetuation of black stereotypes in media – if white people were playing black people on stage and on screens, what the audience were seeing was nothing more than a white person's assumption or bias of what a black person is, or acts like.

Eventually, this had a roll-on effect, as black people continued to face hindrances in representing their own stories, beliefs, opinions, and identities. During the 1970s, there was a glimmer of hope in that black people began starring in 'blaxploitation' movies (which in itself is self-defining – they were movies to exploit the attention of black people), to show the world that black people (particularly African Americans) could be a protagonist. Unfortunately, those movies were not embraced by the then majority white audience and so were dropped by companies such as Columbia Pictures and the Motion Picture Association of America.

Over time, black people became more prevalent in movies and television shows and we saw positive black families in shows such as *Desmond's*, *The Cosby Show*, *Fresh Prince of Bel Air* and *Girlfriends*. But whereas black people had suffered from a lack of representation in the entertainment sector, in the news and reporting media sector, we faced an overrepresentation of negative associations – and this is still ongoing today. If you look at how the deaths of the African-American men I referenced in Chapter Seven were reported, you can see how they could reinforce stereotypes about the black community, and black men in particular:

The big, strong, animalistic black man

- *New York Times* about Eric Garner: *The 350-pound man, about to be arrested on charges of illegally selling cigarettes, was arguing with the police.*
- *New American* about Michael Brown: *Brown certainly was a giant, as surveillance footage seems to prove, showing his 6'4", nearly 300-pound self, towering over a petrified convenience-store employee.*
- Officer Darren Wilson's description of Brown in a media interview given in November 2014: *When I grabbed him, the only way I can describe it is I felt like a five-year-old holding onto Hulk Hogan . . . and then after he did that, he looked up at me and had the most intense aggressive face. The only way I can describe it, it looks like a demon, that's how angry he looked.*

  It's worth noting that officer Wilson and Michael Brown were both 6'4" at the time of his death.

Drugs, alcohol and hip hop

- *New York Times* about Michael Brown: *He lived in a community that had rough patches, and he dabbled in drugs and alcohol. He had taken to rapping in recent months, producing lyrics that were by turns contemplative and vulgar.*

How necessary is it to know how much the victims weighed, or what music they were listening to? What does that serve other than to provide some sort of weak rationale for why they were shot by the police, or to reinforce existing negatives that will be unconsciously and unjustifiably attached to these individuals. What is worse is that because this potential triggering is done in the immediacy following their deaths, when all information is novel, the perception created is very difficult to alter, even in the face of more sound, debunking information.

We see this overly negative representation again with black athletes – an area, don't forget, in which black people are supposedly meant to excel. Just look at how the media, particularly the *Sun*, has treated Black-British, England footballer, Raheem Sterling. He has been unfairly criticised in the media for the most normal of things, ranging from buying a house for his mother, proposing to his girlfriend, flying through easyJet, then for hiring a private jet, buying clothes at Primark, for getting a personal tattoo of a gun to remember his father, who was shot and killed when Raheem was only two, to buying batteries!

It's a similar story with tennis pro Serena Williams. Time and time again, she has been portrayed as 'powerful', 'beast', 'heavy' and 'angry'. It culminated in 2018 with a racist cartoon in the *Herald Sun* newspaper by the Australian cartoonist, Mark Knight – showing Williams with big sambo lips and nappy hair jumping above a broken racket next to a baby's dummy, while at the same time, depicting her Haitian-Japanese opponent as white.

The stereotypical coverage of the black community needs to end, and journalists need to understand the power of stereotypical and racialised language and imagery. These things help shape emotional opinions, not informed ones, and we rely too heavily on the media for information for them to be so complacent. The media needs to report facts, not embellish stereotypical notions that may been based on what they think will be a more interesting story.

As Stephan Lewandowsky, a psychologist at the University of Bristol and co-author of *The Debunking Handbook* explains: 'There's evidence that when people stick with wrong facts, it isn't just stubbornness – but actually some sort of brain glitch . . . what people remember is the information, but not the fact that it's false. Now, one of the ways to get around that is to tell people not just that something is false, but tell them what's true.'

WHY WE CAN'T AFFORD TO STOP TALKING ABOUT RACE

So often I'll hear someone complain that we are 'too PC' these days or overly sensitive. And we have certainly seen and heard a lot of this commentary in the media and online. This is a distraction – nothing more, nothing less. It is a recognised ploy by antagonists in the majority, whenever a disadvantaged community strives for equality; because these antagonists have no legitimate reason why we can't all be equal, they seek to distract by playing the victims, or positioning the equality movements as unnecessary. We've seen this numerous times across different movements: in the civil rights movements, black people were not asking for 'better' rights than white people, only 'civil' and 'equal' rights. They wanted to be able to go to good schools, vote, use clean toilets – exactly the same as white people are able to do. But white nationalists positioned them as enemies of the state and communists.

We saw a similar thing during the women's suffrage movement. All women wanted to do was be able to vote – not get more votes than men – just vote. We still see that today when women demand equal pay for equal work, and men position them as wanting to take jobs from men. Same thing with the LGBTQ+ movement; all they want to do is have the same rights as heterosexuals – to be able to have jobs, get married, and have a family – but ignorant straight people position them as immoral and overly sexualised.

We see this with literally every equality movement. All it takes is one diversity programme in the workplace for white people to claim that they are being discriminated against. All it takes is a celebration of International Women's Day for men to complain that there should also be an International Men's Day – which there actually is, for some reason.*

It's the same with stereotypes: 'Yes, I accept that the origins of black stereotypes are from slavery, but that was ages ago. So what, we can't make jokes two hundred years later? Slavery was so long ago!' Yes, slavery was so long ago, but the systems that allowed it to happen are still in place today. Also, how can people not understand that we don't want to relive the indignities of slavery hundreds of years after we are supposedly free? How can anyone complain that we are being too PC when we don't want to be referred to as 'coloured people', like we were during the Jim Crow era? How can anyone deny racism still exists when the NSPCC has found that children are whitening their skin with make-up to avoid being bullied or racially abused at school?

I once had someone complain to me that they could no longer use the word 'Oriental' to describe Asian people, because of political correctness. Really? I had to explain ever so calmly that firstly, Asian is a lot easier to say, because it is only two syllables compared to Oriental's four. And secondly, using Oriental to refer to an Asian person is not just offensive but factually wrong. The word Oriental is a colonial expression, which means 'furthest point east', and at the time it was coined, the Ottoman Empire was the furthest point east the colonials had gone. So, unless you are referring to a Turkish person as Oriental, it doesn't make sense. How can America as a country still refer to Native Americans or the First People as Indians? Americans knew since literally 1492 that what is now America was not India, and yet people still refer to them as Indians. All minorities and disadvan-

---

* The most redundant day in the history of the human calendar. Given the benefits we enjoy, every day is International Men's Day.

taged people want is respect, equality, and more often than not, to be left alone to live their lives happily. It is not political correctness to want this. It is our basic human right.

A question I am commonly asked is whether we can realistically get rid of racism. As hopeful as I am, I still harbour a healthy dose of scepticism. The reason being that racists (and xenophobes, homophobes, misogynists, and the rest) get their power from the societal hierarchy that refuses to change, or changes too slowly. Racial structures remain in place for the same reasons other structures do – they benefit the majority and those at the top. Since the systemic racial disparity of society caused by colonisation and slavery has white people as the dominant race, thus enjoying the benefits of that position, what incentive do they have to let go of that privilege? So, what can we do?

Now is as important as ever to keep having these conversations about race. We need to speak our truth. We need to take to the streets and proclaim that we have as much right to enjoy the freedoms that our ancestors fought for, and that we helped bring to our countries. Not only do we need to educate, but we need to bolster speaking truth to power with facts and action – making these arguments based solely on emotion and a strong narrative simply won't cut it.

Most of the negative stereotypes and narratives about black people come from a place of ignorance, habit or fear, and people tend to accept information that is consistent with their beliefs. As such, defining the problem of the negative narratives and explaining why they are incorrect with facts is crucial in solving the problem. And hopefully, bit by bit, that will make things better for the generation that comes after us.

This is needed now more than ever, as we see an increasing rise in right-wing nationalists and their power in government. As of late 2018:

In Austria, the right-winged Freedom Party gained twenty-six per cent of the vote in the 2017 legislative election and entered government as junior partner of chancellor.

In Cyprus, far-right party ELAM entered parliament for the first time in its May 2016 elections.

In Denmark, the Danish People's Party (DPP), received twenty-one per cent of the vote in the 2015 general election, becoming the second largest party in Denmark for the first time. Worryingly, this is the party in government that has given its police the authority to seize valuables worth more than 10,000 kroner (£1,045; $1,514) from refugees to cover housing and food costs, has cut migrant benefits overall, and put adverts in Lebanese newspapers warning against migration to Denmark.

France's National Front party received 4,712,461 votes in the 2014 European Parliament election, finishing first with almost twenty-five per cent of the vote and twenty-four of France's seventy-four seats. This is the party whose leader, Marine Le Pen, infamously compared Muslims praying in the street to the Nazi occupation of France, and whose founder (and Marine's father), Jean-Marie Le Pen, had been convicted numerous times for inciting racial hatred and holocaust denial. Fortunately, Le Pen was defeated by Emmanuel Macron for the presidency in May 2017.

The AfD in Germany (Alternative for Germany/Alternative für Deutschland) secured representation in fourteen of the sixteen German state parliaments by October 2017 and became the third largest party in Germany after the federal election, claiming ninety-four seats in the Bundestag (this was the first time the AfD had won any seats in the Bundestag). In 2018, the AfD introduced an online scheme to get schoolchildren to inform on teachers who are politically partial.

In Hungary, far-right Jobbik is the third largest party in the National Assembly, winning nearly twenty-one per cent of the vote in the 2014 general election. This party has organised patrols by a uniformed 'Hungarian Guard' in Roma neighbourhoods. In 2018, Hungary's

Prime Minister, Viktor Orban, secured a third term in office with a landslide victory. The party polled 1,092,806 votes in the parliamentary election (19.06% of the total), making them Hungary's second largest party in the National Assembly. One of the key issues in the election was immigration – Orban said that the victory gave Hungarians 'the opportunity to defend themselves and to defend Hungary [from immigrants]' and had previously warned against the threat of 'a Europe with a mixed population and no sense of identity'.

Italy's two populist parties – the anti-establishment Five Star Movement and right-wing League – formed a coalition government with the stance of mass deportations for undocumented migrants, with Italy's interior minister and League leader Matteo Salvini noting that Italy must stop being 'the refugee camp of Europe'.

In the Netherlands, Geert Wilders and his party, Party for Freedom, won twenty seats in the 2017 election, making it the second largest party in the House of Representatives. Wilders campaigns include stopping the 'Islamisation of the Netherlands', comparing the Quran to Mein Kampf, asking for the Quran to be banned in the Netherlands, advocating for ending immigration from Muslim countries, and banning the construction of new mosques.

The anti-immigration Sweden Democrats exceeded the four per cent threshold for parliamentary representation for the first time in the 2010 general election, gaining twenty seats in the Riksdag. In the 2014 Swedish general election, it secured forty-nine seats in parliament, becoming the third largest party in Sweden.

In the UK, UKIP has three representatives in the House of Lords and twenty MEPs, making it the joint largest UK party in the European Parliament. As well as opposing the 'Islamisation' of Britain, they are also staunchly anti-immigration. And according to a study by political action group, Hope Not Hate, five of the world's top ten far-right activists on the internet are British: Milo Yiannopoulos, Paul Joseph Watson, Stephen Yaxley-Lennon aka Tommy Robinson, Katie Hopkins, and Carl Benjamin aka Sargon of Akkad. And our current Prime Minister, Boris Johnson has referred to black people as 'piccaninnies', a racist colonial term and well as referring to African people as having 'watermelon smiles'.

In the United States, President Donald Trump has directly and indirectly shown support for the far-right by: appointing Steve Bannon, founder of Breitbart News, a far-right website, as one of his senior counsellors; refusing to denounce David Duke, Grand Wizard of the KKK, and the KKK itself;* said in reference to a march by white nationalists, with people giving the Nazi salute and chanting Nazi slogans including 'Sieg heil', that there were, 'Some very fine people on both sides'; retweeted a handful of anti-Muslim videos posted by the deputy leader of a British far-right group, Britain First; called Haiti and African nations: 'shithole countries, told four minority Democratic congresswomen, all of whom are American citizens and three of whom were born in the United States, to "go back to the totally broken and crime infested places from which they came" and the list goes on.

SO, WHAT CAN WHITE PEOPLE DO TO HELP?

Despite my scepticism, all is not lost. We can not only stem the tide of racism and far-right nationalism, but we can also turn it around. Research shows that by having these positive and empathetic conversations, we can successfully address bigotry and bias. As an example, David Broockman at Stanford University and Joshua Kalla at the University of California Berkeley looked at how simple conversations can help combat anti-transgender attitudes.

The research asked participants simply to put themselves in the shoes of trans people and to understand their problems through a

---

* Come on, Donald. KKK always = bad.

ten-minute, non-confrontational conversation, in the hope that it would lead them to re-evaluate their biases. And it worked! The study found that not only did the anti-trans attitudes decline, but that they remained lower as long as three months later, and better than that, it also increased support for a non-discrimination law, even after exposing voters to counterarguments.

Although it goes without saying, it's worth pointing out that there is a huge number of non-people of colour who stand up for the rights of BAME people and are culturally aware of racial sensitivity. There is also a healthy number of white people who may want to learn/do more for race relations. If you are such a person, the first thing to understand is that it is not going to be easy; in most cases, you'll have to unlearn everything you know about race relations. Arguably the most difficult part will be accepting criticism and the discomfort that comes with being white in a conversation about race relations. Even though all of the examples being brought up may not relate to you directly, you'll have to accept that this reflects common beliefs and attitudes among white people.

You'll also have to accept that when it comes to race relations, minority issues are more deserving of time and attention – Black Lives Matter is not a justification for starting White Lives Matter or All Lives Matter. White people need to recognise why there is a disparity between races in the first place. And on that note, don't attack black people or minorities when they need a safe space to talk openly about their issues.

There is no need for a White History Month or a Caucasian Society, because all of modern history has been dictated by white people, and that's all we have been taught. In the same way that you wouldn't barge into an AA meeting demanding a Sober People Anonymous meeting, don't criticise black people for needing a space to talk about their challenges. Because there are oh so many challenges. And while, sure, an individual black person can oftentimes be at the top of an institution, but the overwhelming majority of decision-makers will still be white; white people can also have problems and face barriers, but systemic racism won't be one of them. This distinction – between individual prejudice and systemic racism – is important to recognise.

This is a long and difficult road to take to become fully 'woke', but never give up. You cannot imagine the breadth of appreciation that a black person or person of colour has when someone of another race just gets it and is ready to jump in and block bullshit from an All Lives Matter arsehole. But if for nothing else, let me leave you with some advice. You're never going to go wrong keeping to these simple rules:

Where are you from . . . originally?

As discussed in the first chapter, some black people (particularly those who are first-generation) identify as being British – if that's how they've chosen to respond, take them at their word. Remember, we don't have to reveal our history just to satisfy your curiosity. First generation or biracial people don't owe you an answer. Our identities are not curiosities, small talk, or conversation starters. You don't know what our backgrounds mean to us, nor do you have the right to know.

You're not like other black people I know/I'm blacker than you

Cut that shit out. There isn't a prescribed way all black people should act. I know you probably mean it as a compliment – probably insinu- ating that the black person in question doesn't fit the negative stereotypes that you associate with other black people. But no, it's not a compliment; your delineated stereotypes of the black community are wrong. Imagine how insulting it would be to say to an intelligent woman who happens to be blonde: 'You're not like other blondes.' Also, do not joke about being blacker than your black friend, because you engage in more stereotypical aesthetics. Your characterisation of what black means is based on something you saw on TV and not by knowing anything about black people.

You're so well spoken

Er, yeah. I'm an educated adult. At first sight, this doesn't seem to be an offensive comment, but in my entire life, I've never heard that comment addressed to a white person. Everyone always talks about how Barack Obama is well spoken; no one ever compliments Joe Biden or Hillary Clinton on being well spoken. Again, it stems from the expectation that we're all supposed to speak like a character from *The Wire*. For God's sake, Obama is a constitutional rights lawyer – of course he's well spoken.

Touching our hair

Yes, black hair might be a source of curiosity and wonder to you, but you don't get to touch it because it's unfamiliar. It's not a race thing; it just bad manners.

Black don't crack

Thanks for the compliment but leave the saying to us.

Brother/sister/fist bumps

I cannot begin to fathom the metaphor that will describe appropriately how frustrating it is to be called brother by someone outside the black community; particularly when they have been referring to other people as 'mate' or 'sir'. I feel a sense of community when another black person calls me brother, but I feel patronised when other people do it and then refer to white people differently. Also fist bumps aren't a secret black people handshake; we are perfectly capable of and appreciate a nice firm handshake. It's especially embarrassing when someone tries to do it in a business meeting – you look stupid.

I've been told I have a black girl's arse

Yeah, by another white girl. Congratulations on having a nice voluptuous behind, but black people's arses differ as much as white people. When you try to compare your figure to a black person's, you just sound ignorant.

Is Brexit going to affect you?

Mate, Brexit going to affect us all. Also, thanks, but I was born here.

(To an interracial couple) Oh wow, your kids are going to be so beautiful

Hey, stop fetishising our non-existent kids; it's fucking creepy. This is how you get weirdos like the crazy prison officer who tried to smuggle a black inmate's sperm out of jail, because she 'wanted a chocolate baby'. Besides we've only been dating for three months so thanks for the additional pressure on the relationship, arsehole.

Blackface for Halloween

No. Just, no.

Making fun of a characteristically black or Afro-Caribbean name

Most African and Caribbean names have meaning in their native languages. Don't make fun because it sounds unusual to you.

Try to talk to us about how woke you are . . . especially on a night out

We get it, you're woke. Nice one. So, let's just chill and have a good time together. Believe it or not, black people don't want to spend their entire time talking about racism. We certainly don't want to talk about it on a night out. This is supposed to be our time off. Can we please talk about something else? What about the theory of quantum entanglement? I'm interested in that, let's talk about that. Or at the very least, let's laugh about whatever crazy shit Kanye did this week. I appreciate you're woke, but remember this: *You don't get points for not being racist.*

I'm not racist, I have black friends

Standard rule of thumb: If you ever find yourself having to prove you're not racist, chances are you said or did something racist. Also having black friends does not excuse you being racist – in the same way that having a police officer as a friend doesn't excuse you dealing meth.

I don't even see race

It's great that you are enlightened enough that race is not a factor for you, but remember not everyone feels this way, so when you say you 'don't see race', you're ignoring racism, not helping fight against it.

ACKNOWLEDGEMENTS

Writing a book is hard, lonely, and often boring. So firstly, I have to thank the person who has been with me throughout the entire process and hopefully, my future best friend – Solange Knowles. I can't even count how often I listened to and drew inspiration from your album A Seat at the Table, while writing this book. It kept me sane, and more importantly, motivated. Thank you! Let's do Nando's soon.

To my wonderful agent, Niki Chang. Thank you so much for believing in me and this book. You saw the potential in my crazy ramblings and odd sense of humour, and helped turn this into a book that I will forever be proud of. You are a superstar, destined to do great things in the publishing world, and I'm honoured to call you my agent.

I'm proud to have signed with The Good Literary Agency; a literary agency dedicated to not only representing but developing and supporting writers who are BAME, working class, disabled, and LGBTQ+. Julia Kingsford, Nikesh Shukla (the unofficial 'uncle' to underrepresented writers in the UK), Niki Chang, Arzu Tahsin, Abi Fellows, and Salma Begum, I'm in awe of what you've accomplished so far and have no doubt in my mind that you'll revolutionise the publishing industry for the better.

Huge thanks to the entire team at Hodder & Stoughton for helping to make this dream of mine a reality. My amazing editor, Huw Armstrong who believed in this book from the start and read it in record time. Thank you so much for embarking on this journey with me and for championing the book. Cameron Myers and Barry Johnston, thank you for your help editing this book and apologies for my atrocious spelling and over-use of exclamation points!!!! My publicist, Rebecca Mundy and marketeer, Caitriona Horne, thank you for getting people interested in this book. You're both *absolutely fabulous* (ba dum tss). Jeanelle, thanks for all the hype on Twitter. You're jokes.

Thank you to Penguin Random House for their WriteNow programme, which I was a recipient of. There is so much work to be done in ensuring diverse voices in books and WriteNow is crucial to bringing us closer to true representation in publishing.

I owe a debt of gratitude to my fellow writers who have been there for me throughout the gruelling and frankly, heart-attack inducing process of getting published. Real life Tormund Giantsbane, Dave Rudden; Prince of Satire, Nels Abbey; Sarah Davis Goff, the mansplainer slayer; and the scourge of Twitter trolls, Amna Saleem. Your support means everything to me and I'm so proud of you all. I wish you all the success in the world in your future endeavours.

I have the most amazing group of friends and I certainly would not be who I am today without them. Aysha, my best friend. Ricardo and Vijiyan, my childhood friends and brothers – I guess the joke is not so cruel after all. To my friends of the Lost Generation: Gareth (my Sal Paradise), Stuart, Siobhan, Mark, Molly, and Samantha. The

Womanses: Lara, Eleanor, and Sonia – you make my heart soar. Bionic Becky with the titanium back. We're rarely ever in the same country but our friendship is international baby! Nataleigh, thank you for seeing the very best in me. My mentors turned dear friends: Alison, Lucian and Jen. Sarah, we're big-time now but you'll always be my loser friend and I'll always be your smelly one. And to so many others, countless to mention, thank you and I love you all. And of course, to Allie, my wholesome Midwestern darling, and El Toro Taqueria where we had our first date.

To my family: Thank you mum for everything. I love you so much I can't find the words, which is ironic because you know . . . writer. Sorry I'm no longer a lawyer but I promise, this Google gig is working out pretty well. Dad, I wish you could have been here to see me get published. I miss you every day. Sis, I love you – sorry you look so much like me. And a very special thank you to the John family (Uncle Harry and Aunt Thrisse) for letting your home be my refuge when I had nowhere else to go and to the Lapis (Uncle John, Aunt Mini, and Susana) for making me a part of your family every Christmas. Words cannot express how much that meant to me.

And last but by no means least: to Stan Lee, for showing a young Elijah that superheroes can be black. Rest in Peace.

Introduction

1. YouGov Survey, July 2014. The British Empire is 'something to be proud of'.

Chapter One – Where are you from . . . originally?

1. CNN online, 27 January 2018. Here's Chimamanda Adichie's epic clapback when asked if Nigeria has bookshops.
2. Buzzfeed online, 8 July 2017. This Woman Always Thought She Was British. Now, After 30 Years, The Home Office Says She's Not.
3. Barbara J. Fields, March 2001. Presentation given by historian Barbara J. Fields at a School for the Producers of RACE.
4. The Telegraph online, 1 July 2014. Nazi 'perfect Aryan' poster child was Jewish.
5. James Silk Buckingham, 28 January 2013. The Eastern and Western States of America: In Three Volumes.

6. Plessy v. Ferguson, 163 US 537 (1896).

7. Pew Research Center, 11 June 2015. Multiracial in America: Proud, Diverse and Growing in Numbers.

8. O DIA online, 2 February 2016. Médico se declara negro e passa em 1º lugar em concurso (Translation: Doctor declares himself black and comes 1st in competition).

9. The Washington Post online, 25 September 2018. A DNA test said a man was 4% black. Now he wants to qualify as a minority business owner.

10. CNN/ORC International Poll, 4–8 September 2015. Interviews with 1,012 adult Americans conducted by telephone by ORC International.

11. 2016 American National Election Study (ANES) pilot survey.

12. Gallup Poll, 4 June 2001. Public Overestimates U.S. Black and Hispanic Populations.

13. Buzzfeed online, 14 December 2016. 9 Things British People Get Wrong About Their Own Country.

14. Matthew Winkle, *The Bloomberg Way: A Guide for Reporters and Editors* (John Wiley & Son, 2014)

15. Erika V. Halla, Katherine W. Phillips, Sarah S.M. Townsend (January 2015). *Journal of Experimental Social Psychology*. 'A rose by any other name?': The consequences of subtyping "African-Americans" from "Blacks"'. Volume 56, Pages 183-190.

16. Sirius XM blog, 20 December 2016. Denzel Washington on why 'Fences' needed a black director: 'It's not color, it's culture'.

17. BBC News online, 23 November 2015. DNA study finds London was ethnically diverse from start.

18. The Guardian online, 10 November 2016. Black and British: A Forgotten History review – this is what it means to share a heritage.

19. Miranda Kaufmann (Oneworld Publications. Oct. 2017). *Black Tudors: The Untold Story.*

20. Channel 4, 18 February 2018. First Brit: Secrets of the 10,000 Year Old Man.

21. Book of Judges, chapter 12, verses 1–6.

22. BBC Online, 4 May 2015. What happened when an anti-Semite found he was Jewish?

23. Katarzyna Bryc, Eric Y. Durand, J. Michael Macpherson, David Reich, Joanna L. Mountain. 18 December 2014. *American Journal of Human Genetics:* 'The Genetic Ancestry of African Americans, Latinos, and European Americans across the United States.'

24. PBS, 23 March 2015. Little White Lie by Lacey Schwartz.

25. The Guardian online, 24 September 2011. Different but the same: a story of black and white twins.

26. BBC online, 27 September 2016. First 'three person baby' born using new method.

27. BBC online, 8 April 2002. Couple 'choose' to have deaf baby.

28. New York Times online, 7 March 2017. Activist Who Identified Herself as Black Takes an African Name.

29. New York Times online, 22 August 2000. Do Races Differ? Not Really, DNA Shows.

30. The Sloan Digital Sky Survey, 5 January 2017. The Elements of Life Mapped Across the Milky Way by SDSS/APOGEE.

Chapter Two – But . . . black guys can't swim

1. R. Irwin, J. Drayer, C. Irwin, T. Ryan and R. Southall, Memphis, TN: University of Memphis. Constraints Impacting Minority Swimming Participation.

2. Julie Gilchrist, MD and Erin M. Parker, PhD (16 May 2014). Center for Disease Control and Prevention – Racial/Ethnic Disparities in Fatal Unintentional Drowning Among Persons Aged <29 Years – United States, 1999–2010.

3. The Daily Beast online, 7 August 2010. The Louisiana Drowning: Why Many Blacks Can't Swim.

4. Gregson v Gilbert (1783) 3 Doug KB 232, 99 ER 629 (KB).

5. Emory News Center online, 27 June 2014. The anatomy of fear: Understanding the biological underpinnings of anxiety, phobias and PTSD. Martha McKenzie.

6. Tablet magazine online, 11 December 2014. Do Jews carry trauma in our Genes? A conversation with Rachel Yehuda.

7. R.L. Allen and David L. Nickel (1969). *The Journal of Negro Education*, 'The Negro and Learning to Swim: The Buoyancy Problem Related to Reported Biological Differences.' Vol. 38, No. 4.

8. D. Booth and J. Nauright (2003). Journal of the African Diaspora, Embodied identities: sport and race in South Africa.

9. Matthew W. Hughey and Devon R. Goss. 10 August 2015. A Level Playing Field? Media Constructions of Athletics, Genetics, and Race.

10. Swimmingwithoutstress.co.uk, 16 May 2014. Black Men Can't Swim?: Why can so few black people swim compared to the UK population as a whole?

11. A.V. Rawlings 2006. *International Journal of Cosmetic Science*, 'Ethnic skin types: are there differences in skin structure and function?'

12. Osmond, Gary and Phillips, Murray G. (2004). *The Journal of Pacific History*, '"The bloke with a stroke" – Alick Wickham, the "crawl" and social memory.'

13. Theodorus B.M. 27 February, 1879. The preservation of life at sea: a paper read before the American Geographical Society.

14. K. Dawson (2006). *The Journal of American History*, 'Enslaved swimmers and divers in the Atlantic World.'

15. J. A. Simoneau and C. Bouchard (1995). 'Genetic determinism of fiber type proportion in human skeletal muscle'.

16. Dean Cromwell (McGraw-Hill Book Company, 1941). *Championship technique in track and field: A book for athletes, coaches, and spectators.*

17. Christopher McDougall (Profile Books, 2010). *Born to Run: The Hidden Tribe, the Ultra-Runners, and the Greatest Race the World Has Never Seen.*

18. Yuval Noah Harari (Vintage Books. 2015). *Sapiens: A Brief History of Humankind.*

Chapter Three – Is it cuz I'm black? Part 1

1. The Guardian online, 21 September 2016. Stop and search still targets black people, police watchdog says.

2. Stopwatch Coalition, 14 October 2018. The Colour of Injustice: 'Race', drugs and law enforcement in England and Wales.

3. The Guardian online, 27 October 2016. Police satisfied with stop and search reform despite racial inequality.

4. Ministry of Justice – The Lammy Review, 1 September 2017. Exploratory analysis of the youth secure estate by BAME groups.

5. The Guardian online, 17 March 2016. Mass stop and search by police doesn't reduce crime, says study.

6. New York Daily News, 3 April 2013. NYPD stop-and-frisk policy yielded 4.4 million detentions but few results: study.

7. Institute of Race Relations, 5 January 2012. 96 murders since Stephen Lawrence's.

8. The Independent online, 13 January 2014. Race hate – a crime the police will not solve.

9. BBC News online, 4 September 2016. Hate crimes prosecutions fall despite rise in reporting.

10. Home Affairs Committee Publications, Session 2006–07. Second Report.

11. Fullfacts online, 6 September 2017. What do we know about the ethnicity of people involved in sexual offences against children?

12. Pew Research Center online, 27 June 2016. On Views of Race and Inequality, Blacks and Whites Are Worlds Apart.

Chapter Four – Is it true what they say about black guys? You know . . . down there?

1. Richard Lynn, University of Ulster (2012). An examination of Rushton's theory of differences in penis length and circumference and r-K life history theory in 113 populations.

2. David Veale, Sarah Miles, Sally Bramley, Gordon Muir, John Hodsoll. 2 March 2015. 'Am I normal? A systematic review and construction of nomograms for flaccid and erect penis length and circumference.' *British Journal of Urology.*

3. Capital News online, 16 September 2011. Chinese condoms too small for South Africans.

4. BBC News online, 8 December 2006. Condoms 'too big' for Indian men.

5. XO Jane online, 18 December 2014. Representation in Porn, Or A Lack Thereof, And Why It Matters.

6. Elizabeth F. Loftus, James A. Goan, Jacqueline E. Pickrell (1996). *Manufacturing false memories using bits of reality. Implicit memory and metacognition.*

7. Kevan R. Wylie and Ian Eardley. 12 March 2007. 'Penile size and the "small penis syndrome"'. *British Journal of Urology.*

8. N.K. Ruppen-Greef, D.M. Weber, R. Gobat and M. R. Landolt, August 2015. 'What is a Good Looking Penis? How Women Rate the Penile Appearance of Men with Surgically Corrected Hypospadias.' *Journal of Sexual Medicine* 12(8).

9. New York Times online, 24 January 2015. Searching for Sex – Seth Stephens-Davidowitz.

10. Herbert Samuels (Garland Publishing 1994). *Race, Sex, and Myths: Images of African American men and women.*

11. Philip Dray (Modern Library; Reprint edition. Jan. 2003). At the Hands of Persons Unknown: The Lynching of Black America.

12. B. Holden-Smith (1996). 'Lynching, federalism, and the intersection of race and gender in the Progressive era.' *Yale Journal of Law and Feminism.*

13. William Lee Howard (1903), *The Negro as a Distinct Ethnic Factor in Civilization.*

14. Gail Dines and Jean M. Humez (2003), *Gender, Race, and Class in Media.*

15. Huffington Post online, 8 January 2016. Paul LePage Makes Racist Claim About Drug Dealers Named D-Money Getting White Girls Pregnant.

16. New York Times online, 9 December 2016. Jurors Hear Dylann Roof Explain Shooting in Video: 'I Had to Do It'.

17. BBC News online, 7 January 2016. The significance of Sarah Baartman.

18. Caren M. Holmes (2016), *The Colonial Roots of the Racial Fetishization of Black Women*.

19. Mic.com, 24 February 2015. Disney Star's Response to Criticism of Her Dreadlocks Deserves a Standing Ovation.

Chapter Five – All black people love chicken and watermelon

1. OkayAfrica YouTube channel, 'Jollof Wars: Ghana vs Nigeria, The Official Taste Test'.

2. The Spruce online, 21 September 2017. What Defines Authentic Soul Food?

3. NPR online, 22 May 2013. Where Did That Fried Chicken Stereotype Come From?

4. Nigger Love a Watermelon Ha! Ha! Ha! – Performed by Harry C. Browne – Recorded March 1916 with Columbia Records.

5. NPR online, 11 May 2014. Recall That Ice Cream Truck Song? We Have Unpleasant News for You.

6. St. Clair Bourne (The Black Scholar Vol. 21 1990). The African American Image in American Cinema.

7. Oneabjure YouTube channel, Insanely Ridiculous Korean Fried Chicken Commercial.

8. The Golf Channel online, 22 May 2013. Garcia's 'fried chicken' remark shows disdain for Woods.

9. CNN online, 1 October 2014. Boston Herald apologizes for Obama cartoon after backlash.

10. Talking Points Memo online, 6 February 2014. School Apologizes for Serving Fried Chicken, Watermelon at Lunch on Black History Month.

11. AP News online, 2 January 2017. Lawsuit: Dude ranch owner asked chef for 'black people food'.

12. Providence Journal online, 27 June 2017. Providence firefighter fired over racist remark.

13. BBC Newsbeat online, 31 October 2016. That black British feeling ... and stereotypes. 'Is it true all black people like chicken'.

14. Blavity online, 1 February 2018. Michigan Bar Owner and Staff Under Fire for Giving Biracial Employee a Watermelon On MLK Day.

15. Yuval Noah Harari (Vintage Books 2015). *Sapiens: A Brief History of Humankind*.

16. MotherJones online, 2 September 2013. Has the World Reached Peak Chicken?

17. Huffington Post online, 4 December 2013. African Americans and the Watermelon Stereotype.

18. The Atlantic online, 16 May 2016. The Complex Psychology of Why People Like Things.

19. Brian Wansink and Jeffery Sobal. January 2007. Environment and Behavior, 39:1, Mindless Eating: The 200 Daily Food Decisions We Overlook.

20. The Guardian online, 18 February 2011. Britain's fried-chicken boom.

21. The Provisioner online, 24 October 2016. State of chicken: Consumption at all-time high.

22. Business Insider UK online, 29 January 2017. Forget burgers and fries – fried chicken is taking over the fast-food industry.

23. Bill Gates' blog – Gates notes, 7 June 2016. Why I would raise chickens.

24. Medium online, 7 June 2016. The Small Animal That's Making a Big Difference for Women in the Developing World.

Chapter Six – But I worked my way up from nothing; why can't you?

1. New American Economy, January 2018. Power of the Purse: How Sub-Saharan Africans Contribute to the U.S. Economy.

2. Department of Work and Pensions report online, 13 April 2016. BME employment reaches record high.

3. Economic Policy Institute online, 14 May 2014. Resilience of Black Labor Force Participation.

4. USA Today online, 12 October 2014. Tech jobs: Minorities have degrees, but don't get hired.

5. Kenneth D. Gibbs Jr., John McGready, Jessica C. Bennett, Kimberly Griffin, 10 December 2014. Career Interest Patterns by Race/Ethnicity and Gender. National Institute of General Medical Science.

6. Sonia K. Kang, Katherine A. DeCelles, András Tilcsik, 17 March 2016. 'Whitened Résumés: Race and Self-Presentation in the Labor Market'. University of Toronto Mississauga. Administrative Science Quarterly, (3).

7. Marianne Bertrand and Sendhil Mullainathan (2004). Are Emily and Greg More Employable Than Lakisha and Jamal? A Field Experiment on Labor Market Discrimination. University of Chicago and MIT.

8. The Guardian, 17 January 2019. Minority ethnic Britons face 'shocking' job discrimination.

9. BBC News online, 12 March 2015. Are race discrimination laws still needed in the workplace?

10. RHR International (2017), Journey to the Top: Developing African American Executives.

11. Devah Pager (University of Chicago Press; April 2009), *Marked: Race, Crime and Finding Work in an Era of Mass Incarceration*.

12. Daniel Cox, Ph.D., Juhem Navarro-Rivera, Robert P. Jones, Ph.D. August 2016. Race, Religion, and Political Affiliation of Americans' Core Social Networks. Public Religion Research Institute.

13. USA Today online, 9 October 2014. High-tech pay gap: Minorities earn less in skilled jobs.

14. Equality and Human Rights Commission, Pay Gaps report. August 2017.

15. Trade Union Congress online, 1 February 2016. Black workers with degrees earn a quarter less than white counterparts, finds TUC.

16. Okay Africa online, 21 January 2017. Because Racism: White South Africans Make 5 Times More Than Black South Africans.

17. National Partnership for Women and Families, 2015 report. Black Women in the United States.

18. Double Jeopardy 2014 report: Gender Bias Against Women of Color in Science. UC Hastings College of Law.

19. EY online, 2 November 2016. A Report into the Ethnic Diversity of UK Boards: 'Beyond One by '21'.

20. Fortune magazine online, 22 January 2016. Why race and culture matter in the c-suite.

21. USA Today online, 29 March 2017. #BlackWomenAtWork outcry isn't just about respect, it's about money.

22. Executive Leadership Council report, 6 February 2017. Despite modest gains, women and minorities see little change in representation on Fortune 500 boards.

23. Higher Education Statistics Agency report, 19 January 2017. Staff at higher education providers in the United Kingdom 2015/16.

24. Royal Historical Society report, October 2018. Race, Ethnicity & Equality in UK History.

25. BBC News Online, 7 December 2018. Ethnic minority academics earn less than white colleagues.

26. McKinsey online, January 2015. Why diversity matters.

27. Judy T. Benjamin, (John Wiley & Sons; June 2006), *A Brief History of Modern Psychology*.

28. Richard J. Herrnstein and Charles Murray (Simon & Schuster Ltd; 1st Free Press; January 1996). *The Bell Curve: Intelligence and Class Structure in American Life.*

29. Yuval Noah Harari (Vintage Books 2015). *Sapiens: A Brief History of Humankind.*

30. The Financial Times online, 28 November 2014. James Watson to sell Nobel Prize medal.

31. New York Times online, 26 October 1994. In America – Throwing a Curve.

32. David G. Sansing (Univ. Press of Mississippi, 1999). *A Sesquicentennial History.* The University of Mississippi.

33. The Salon online, 13 November 2016. Yep, race really did Trump economics: A data dive on his supporters reveals deep racial animosity.

34. Slate online, 7 November 2016. How Do Trump Supporters See Black People?

35. Upjohn Institute for Employment Research, June 2016. Who Believes in Me? The Effect of Student-Teacher Demographic Match on Teacher Expectations.

36. BBC News online, 20 Oct 2017. What it's like being black and working class at Cambridge.

37. The Root online, 30 Jan 2013. The 'Acting White Theory' Doesn't Add Up.

38. Blavity online, April 2017. Statistics Show Drop Out Rates Are Lower When Black Students Have A Black Teacher.

39. Douglas B. Downey and James W. Ainsworth-Darnell (February 2002). *American Sociological Review*, 'The Search for Oppositional Culture among Black Students.' Vol 67, No. 1.

40. American Medical Association, Physician Characteristics and Distribution in the U.S., 2015.

41. NCAA study, April 2018. Estimated probability of competing in professional athletics.

42. NJ.com, 8 September 2015. What are the odds of a high school football player reaching the NFL?

43. The Undefeated online, 26 April 2017. The NFL's racial divide.

44. The Guardian online, 2 March 2015. Football Association welcomes a 70% rise in reporting racist abuse.

45. Daily Express online, 23 Jan 2017. Mario Balotelli tormented with 'monkey' taunts during racist tirade.

46. The Guardian online, 22 December 2018. US high school wrestler made to cut dreadlocks or face forfeit.

47. Billboard magazine online, 12 February 2016. Billboard's 2016 Power 100 List Revealed.

48. The Economist online, 21 January 2016. How racially skewed are the Oscars?

49. Annenberg Center for Communication and Journalism, July 2017. Inequality in 900 popular films: examining portrayals of gender, race/ethnicity, LGBT, and disability from 2007–2016.

50. British Film Institute online, 6 October 2016. New BFI Research Reveals Representation of Black Actors in UK Film over last 10 Years.

51. USC Annenberg School for Communication and Journalism, 31 July 2018. Happy to fire, reluctant to hire: Hollywood inclusion remains unchanged.

52. Nicole Martins and Kristen Harrison, 16 March 201. Racial and Gender Differences in the Relationship Between Children's Television Use and Self-Esteem. Communications Research study.

53. Variety magazine online, 25 November 2014. 'Exodus: Gods and Kings' Director Ridley Scott on Creating His Vision of Moses.

54. Box Office Mojo, 23 July 2017. 'Dunkirk' Delivers $50.5M Debut, 'Girls Trip' Opens with $30M and 'Valerian' Stumbles.

55. CNN Money online, 2 February 2018. 'Black Panther' is outselling every previous superhero film in advance ticket sales.

56. Motion Picture Association of America, Theatrical Market Statistics 2016.

57. Resolution Foundation, Diverse outcomes living standards by ethnicity. August 2017.

58. The Federal Reserve, 27 September 2017. Recent Trends in Wealth-Holding by Race and Ethnicity: Evidence from the Survey of Consumer Finances.

59. Institute of Policy Studies online, 8 August 2016. Report: Ever-Growing Gap Without Change, African-American and Latino Families Won't Match White Wealth for Centuries.

60. Brookings Institution, YouTube channel, Is America Dreaming? Understanding Social Mobility.

61. Forbes richest list online, The World's Billionaires 2017.

62. The Guardian online, 24 Sep 2017. Britain's most powerful elite is 97% white.

63. Ministry of Housing press release, 10 October 2017. Communities and Local Government report, Home ownership.

64. Laura Sullivan, Tatjana Meschede, Lars Dietrich & Thomas Shapiro (21 Jun 2016). The Racial Wealth Gap: Why Policy Matters. Institute of Assets and Social Policy.

65. Department of Justice news release, 12 July 2012. Justice Department Reaches Settlement with Wells Fargo Resulting in More Than $175 Million in Relief for Homeowners to Resolve Fair Lending Claims.

66. Department of Justice news release, 21 December 2011. Department Reaches

$335 Million Settlement to Resolve Allegations of Lending Discrimination by Countrywide Financial Corporation.

67. The Guardian online, 13 January 2017. UK banks have a racial discrimination problem. It's time they admitted it.
68. Save Brixton Arches online campaign: http://savebrixtonarches.com
69. Next City online, 8 April 2013. Separate and Unequal in D.C.

Chapter Seven – Is it cuz I'm black? Part 2

1. The Independent online, 24 May 2018. Met Police four times more likely to use force against black than white people in London, show new figures.
2. The Independent online, 12 Dec 2017. White people more likely to be carrying drugs when stopped and searched, report reveals.
3. ProPublica online, 10 October 2014. Deadly Force, in Black and White.
4. American Psychological Association online, 6 March 2014. Black Boys Viewed as Older, Less Innocent Than Whites, Research Finds.
5. The Guardian online, 1 June 2015. Black Americans killed by police twice as likely to be unarmed as white people.
6. Department of Justice press release, 23 March 2015. U.S. Department of Justice releases report on Philadelphia Police Department's use of deadly force.
7. Free Thought Project, 6 April 2015. American Cops Just Killed More People in March than the UK Did in the Entire 20th Century.
8. Blavity online, January 2018. Former Assistant Police Chief Urged A Recruit To Shoot Black People: 'Fuck The Right Thing, If Black Shoot Them'.
9. The Washington Post, Fatal Force. Police shootings database.
10. The Tampa Bay Times, 4 April 2017. Police are more likely to shoot if you're black.
11. Huffington Post online, 12 November 2018. Former Frat President Accused Of Drugging And Raping Woman Fined $400 And Set Free.
12. Police Reform Organizing Project, Broken Windows Policing: A True Tale of Two Cities.
13. The Guardian online, 21 March 2015. No convictions over 500 black and Asian deaths in custody.
14. The Guardian online, 5 June 2018. Rashan Charles inquest: officer failed to follow safety rules.
15. Fader magazine online, 29 March 2016. We Need To Talk About Police Brutality In The U.K.
16. Copcrisis.com, Cops are indicted in less than 1% of killings.

17. QZ.com, 24 May 2016. Freddie Gray verdict: US police officers who kill rarely get punished, but they might get rich.

18. Reuters, 21 May, 2016. Gun used to kill Trayvon Martin sold for $250,000: TV reports.

19. American Psychological Association, 13 March 2017. People See Black Men as Larger, More Threatening Than Same-Sized White Men.

20. The Independent online, 27 January 2015. US clergy respond to police shooting pictures of black men for target practice: 'Use Me Instead'.

21. Pew Research Center, 27 June 2016. On Views of Race and Inequality, Blacks and Whites Are Worlds Apart.

22. New York Times online, 23 April 2015. Black Mayor Is Voted In and a Small Town's Staff Empties Out.

23. Donald Braman, *Doing Time on the Outside: Incarceration and Family Life in Urban America* (University of Michigan Press 2007).

24. D. Baumrind (Mar 1972). 'An Exploratory Study of Socialization Effects on Black Children: Some Black-White Comparisons', *Society for Research in Child Development*, Vol. 43, No. 1.

25. The Metro online, 14 June 2018. Maps highlight shocking link between poverty and violent crime wave in London.

26. House of Commons Briefing Paper, Knife crime in England and Wales. November 2018.

27. 2011 Census: Cultural diversity in Kent – Kent Population by Ethnic Group.

28. Jill Leovy (Spiegel & Grau. January 2015) *Ghettoside: A True Story of Murder in America.*

29. Vox, 26 August 2016. Americans are supposed to turn to police after a murder. In black communities, they often can't.

30. The Guardian online, 30 December 2015. Oliver Letwin memo borders on criminality, says Darcus Howe.

31. FBI Uniform Report, Murder: Race, Ethnicity, and Sex of Victim by Race, Ethnicity, and Sex of Offender, 2014.

32. US Department of Justice, Race and Hispanic Origin of Victims and Offenders, 2012–15.

33. The Economist online, 23 April 2018. As knife crime rises in England, police look to Glasgow.

34. LA Times online, 10 February 2017. San Diego police body cameras reducing misconduct, aggressive use of force, report says.

35. NPR, 6 May 2015. Chicago Creates Reparations Fund For Victims Of Police Torture.

36. Huffington Post online, 18 May 2017. Cops In This City Haven't Killed Anyone Since 2015. Here's One Reason Why.
37. Lorie A. Fridell (Springer Criminology. August 2016). *Producing Bias-Free Policing: A Science-Based Approach.*

Chapter Eight – You know where to get weed, right?

1. Ronald Siegel (Press US; New Ed edition Mar 2005). *Intoxication: The Universal Drive for Mind-Altering Substances.*
2. Li H. L. and Lin H. 'An archaeological and historical account of cannabis in China. Econ Bot. 1974; 28(4)
3. Li H. L. 'Hallucinogenic plants in Chinese herbals.' *J Psychodelic Drugs.* 1978, 10(1) 17–26.
4. M. Touwn 'The religious and medicinal uses of Cannabis in China, India and Tibet.' *J Psychoactive Drugs.* 1981, 13(1) 23–34.
5. Barney Warf, 1 October 2014, 'High Points: An Historical Geography of Cannabis', *Geographical Review*, 104(4).
6. John Peter Wild (Shire Publications April 2003). *Textiles in Archaeology.*
7. UK Cannabis Internet Activists, A Cannabis Chronology.
8. Snopes.com, 29 April 2007. Strawberry Quick Methamphetamine Warning: Rumors that drug dealers are selling colored methamphetamine known as 'Strawberry Quick' to children are largely unfounded.
9. Daily Mail online, 8 March 2010. Police reveal 180 pupils at one school off sick after taking legal 'Meow Meow' party drug.
10. BBC News online, 28 May 2010. Teenagers' deaths 'not caused by mephedrone'.
11. Society of Editors online, 23 April 2012. Newspaper's correction over cancer-inducing weed claim.
12. New York Times online, 30 July 2014. The Federal Marijuana Ban Is Rooted in Myth and Xenophobia.
13. Richard J. Bonnie and Charles H. Whitebread, II (Bookworld Services; June 1999). *Marijuana Conviction: A History of Marijuana Prohibition in the United States.*
14. New York Times online, 8 February 1914. Murder and Insanity Increasing Among Lower Class Because They Have Taken to Sniffing Since Being Deprived of Whisky by Prohibition. Edward Huntington Williams, M.D.
15. Salon magazine online, 10 August 2013. 4 biggest myths about crack.
16. The Nation online, 29 January 2014. How the Myth of the 'Negro Cocaine Fiend' Helped Shape American Drug Policy.

17. Harper's Magazine online, April 2016 issue. Legalize it all: How to win the war on drugs, by Dan Baum.

18. Release report, The Numbers in Black And White: Ethnic Disparities In The Policing And Prosecution Of Drug Offences In England And Wales.

19. ACLU report, The war on marijuana in black and white: billions of dollars wasted on racially biased arrests.

20. The Telegraph online, 3 January 2019. Student drug dealers spared jail as judge says he was impressed by the grammar in their text messages.

21. Lammy Review – Published 16 November 2016. Black, Asian and Minority Ethnic disproportionality in the Criminal Justice System in England and Wales.

22. Prison Reform Trust, Home truths: housing for women in the criminal justice system. September 2016.

23. Vox.com, 1 July 2014. Everyone does drugs, but only minorities are punished for it.

24. Institute of Race Relations online, Criminal Justice System Statistics.

25. United States Sentencing Commission, 2012 report to the Congress: Continuing impact of United States V. Booker on federal sentencing. December 2012.

26. Michelle Alexander (The New Press. Jan. 2010). *The New Jim Crow: Mass Incarceration in the Age of Colorblindness.*

27. Vice magazine online, 28 March 2015. Kofi Annan: The War on Drugs Has Failed in West Africa and Around the World.

28. Vice magazine online, 29 March 2016. How Governments Have Used the War on Drugs to Oppress Their Enemies.

29. Obama White House website, Office of National Drug Control Policy: National Drug Control Strategy.

30. WhiteHouse.gov, Office of National Drug Control Policy: Grants & Programs.

31. Associated Press online, 13 May 2010. After 40 years, $1 trillion, US War on Drugs has failed to meet any of its goals.

32. European Monitoring Centre for Drugs and Drug Addiction, EMCDDA report presents latest evidence on heroin-assisted treatment for hard-to-treat opioid users. Lisbon 19.04.2012 (No 1/2012).

33. Scientific Reports – Published online January 2015, Comparative risk assessment of alcohol, tobacco, cannabis and other illicit drugs using the margin of exposure approach. Dirk W. Lachenmeiera and Jürgen Rehm.

34. Vice Magazine online, 13 October 2015. Cannabis Legalization Could Raise Hundreds of Millions for UK Government.

35. The Guardian online, 4 November 2010. Cost of re-offending is around £11bn – prison is a colossal failure.

36. CATO Institute, The budgetary impact of ending drug prohibition.

37. RAND Corporation online, 20 May 2014. Developing Public Health Regulations for Marijuana: Lessons from Alcohol and Tobacco.

38. Buzzfeed online, 17 March 2016. How Black People are Being Shut Out of America's Weed Boom.

39. Drug Policy Alliance online, 4 March 2014. 'It's not enough to end the drug war. We must also repair the harms caused by it.'

40. Center on Juvenile and Criminal Justice, 21 March 2016. Pot legalization hasn't done anything to shrink the racial gap in drug arrests.

41. NPR online, 29 June 2016. As Adults Legally Smoke Pot In Colorado, More Minority Kids Arrested For It.

42. Metropolitan Police tweet: https://twitter.com/metpoliceuk/status/899914758866051072

43. Vice magazine online, 23 August 2017. Here's a List of Festivals That Have More Crime Than Carnival.

44. Transform Drug Policy Foundation, After the War on Drugs: Blueprint for Regulation.

45. BBC News online, 4 April 2016. Cannabis arrests down 46% since 2010 – police figures.

46. Vice magazine, 28 May 2016. Can America's Weed Industry Provide Reparations for the War on Drugs?

47. Assembly Bill No. 1793 Cannabis convictions: resentencing. 2017–2018.

Chapter Nine – You've got that natural rhythm

1. BBC online, 22 October 2013. Why piano-mania grips China's children.

2. Ruth M. Stone (Routledge, 1997). *The Garland Encyclopaedia of World Music: Africa.*

3. Ndlovu Ceaser (South Africa 1991), Transcription of African Music, unpublished paper presented at the African Music conference at the University of Venda.

4. Robert Orsi (Princeton University Press, 2005). *Between Heaven and Earth: The Religious Worlds People Make and the Scholars Who Study Them.*

5. Carla De Sola (The Sharing Company 1986). Spirit Moves a Handbook of Dance and Prayer.

6. Brenda Dixon Gottschild (Praeger Publishers 1998). *Digging the Africanist*

Presence in American Performance: Dance and Other Contexts (Contributions in Afro-American & African Studies).

7. Pew Research Center online, 13 February 2013. The Global Catholic Population.

8. People magazine online, 19 May 1980. You Got Trouble in Elmore City: That's Spelled with a 't', Which Rhymes with 'd' and That Stands for Dancing.

9. PLOS Genetics, online, 30 September 2005. AVPR1a and SLC6A4 Gene Polymorphisms Are Associated with Creative Dance Performance.

10. Science Magazine online, 30 September 1988. Hormonal control of behavior: amines and the biasing of behavioral output in lobsters, Eva Kravitz.

11. Nature magazine, 24 September 2013. Genotyping serotonin transporter polymorphisms 5-HTTLPR and rs25531 in European- and African-American subjects from the National Institute of Mental Health's Collaborative Center for Genomic Studies. Z. Odgerel, A. Talati, S. P. Hamilton, D. F. Levinson & M. M. Weissman.

Chapter Ten – Why do you date those white boys/girls though?

1. BBC News online, 27 February 2002. Soccer violence declining say fans.

2. Inga D. Neumann, 1 June 2008, 'Brain oxytocin: a key regulator of emotional and social behaviours in both females and males', *Journal of Neuroendocrinology.*

3. Sharon Sassler & Amanda Jayne Miller First. 10 March 2014. *Journal of Social and Personal Relationships*, 'The ecology of relationships: Meeting locations and cohabitors' relationship perceptions'.

4. Joseph J. A. Whitfield, (New York Free Press, 1989). *Death in the Delta: The Story of Emmett Till.*

5. Look Magazine, 24 January 1956. The Shocking Story of Approved Killing in Mississippi.

6. Loving v. Virginia, 388 U.S. 1 (1967).

7. Beth A. Auslander, PhD, Frank M. Biro, MD, Paul A. Succop, PhD, Mary B. Short, PhD, and Susan L. Rosenthal, PhD. February 2009. Racial/Ethnic Differences in Patterns of Sexual Behavior and STI Risk Among Sexually Experienced Adolescent Girls. Journal of Pediatric & Adolescent Gynecology.

8. Michael B. Lewis. January 2011. 'Who is the fairest of them all? Race, attractiveness and skin color sexual dimorphism'. *Personality and Individual Differences* Volume 50, Issue 2.

9. The Fashion Spot online, 23 January 2017. Diversity Report: Landmark Gains at New York Fashion Week Fall 2017, but Is It Enough?

10. Rachel E.K. Freedman, Michele Carter, Tracy Sbroccob, and James J. Gray. 'Do men hold African-American and Caucasian women to different standards of beauty?' *Eating Behaviors*, Volume 8, Issue 3.

11. 'The attractive female body weight and female body dissatisfaction in 26 countries across 10 world regions: results of the international body project I.' *Personality and Social Psychology Bulletin*, 2010 Mar; 36(3): 309–25.

12. Essence magazine online, 26 March 2010. Commentary: Jill Scott Talks Interracial Dating.

13. EC Childs. 2005. 'Looking behind the stereotypes of the "angry black woman" an exploration of Black women's responses to interracial relationships. *Gender & Society* 19 (4).

14. Michelle Alexander (The New Press. Jan. 2010). *The New Jim Crow: Mass Incarceration in the Age of Colorblindness*.

15. National Vital Statistics Reports Volume 64, Number 2, Deaths: Final Data for 2013, 16 February 2016.

16. Berkeley News, 11 February 2011. In online dating, blacks more open to romancing whites than vice versa.

17. OK Cupid blog, 30 September 2009. How Your Race Affects The Messages You Get.

18. Ralph Richard Banks (E. P. Dutton & Co Inc. Sept. 2011). *Is Marriage for White People?: How the African American Marriage Decline Affects Everyone*.

19. John Birger (E. P. Dutton & Co Inc. Sept. 2011). *Dateonomics*.

20. World Health Organization online report: MERCURY IN SKIN LIGHTENING PRODUCTS

21. Frederick W. Hickling and Gerrard Hutchinson. 2000. 'Post-colonialism and mental health: Understanding the roast breadfruit.' *Psychiatric Bulletin*.

22. The Glow Up, 14 January 2019. Enough: Rwanda Becomes the 3rd African Nation to Ban Skin-Bleaching Ingredients.

23. Attitude online, 11 June 2015. 80% of gay, black men have experienced racism on the scene.

24. BBC News online, 19 September 2018. #KindrGrindr: Gay dating app launches anti-racism campaign.

25. Office of National Statistics, 2011 Census.

26. Britain Thinks, The Melting Pot Generation: How Britain became more relaxed on race.

27. US Census, 2010. Household and Families: Interracial and Interethnic Coupled Households Appendix Tables.

28. Gallup News online, 25 July 2013. In U.S., 87% Approve of Black-White Marriage, vs. 4% in 1958.

29. Emoji.Tinder.com, Online Dating Apps & Interracial Marriages.

30. Interracialdating.com press release, 11 October 2012. Red States Top List for Online Daters Looking for Interracial Love.

31. S. McKeen 10 February 2006. 'A beauty fix plumps up psyche and overall health.' *The Edmonton Journal.*

32. Psychology Today online, 1 March 1996. The Smell of Love.

33. Michael Stoddart (Cambridge University Press 1991). *The Scented Ape.*

34. Peter Backus. 12 December 2011. Why I Don't Have a Girlfriend: An Application of the Drake Equation to Love in the UK. Warwick University.

35. Trevor Noah (John Murray 2017), *Born a Crime: Stories from a South African Childhood.*

Chapter Eleven – Go back to your own country/Africa

1. UN Refugee Agency, July 2015. The sea route to Europe: The Mediterranean passage in the age of refugees.

2. Human Rights Watch, 2018 Report online – Somalia, DRC, and Haiti.

3. The Guardian online, 27 October 2014. UK axes support for Mediterranean migrant rescue operation.

4. Ipsos MORI online, 9 June 2016. The Perils of Perception and the EU.

5. Office of National Statistics, August 2015. Population by Country of Birth and Nationality Report.

6. The Guardian online, 25 May 2017. Majority of Britons think minorities threaten UK culture, report says.

7. Institute of Race Relations, Racial violence and the Brexit state.

8. The Telegraph online, 23 August 2017. Immigration figures under review as new checks suggest numbers are far lower than thought.

9. The Independent online, 3 July 2018. Windrush generation: Home Office 'set them up to fail', say MPs.

10. Migration Observatory online, 28 November 2016. UK Public Opinion toward Immigration: Overall Attitudes and Level of Concern.

11. Center for American Progress, 20 September 2016. The Economic Impacts of Removing Unauthorized Immigrant Workers.

12. Fast Company online, 23 October 2016. Crunching the Numbers On Trump's Plan To Deport Immigrants.

13. USA Today online, 31 May 2018. The feds lost – yes, lost – 1,475 migrant children.

14. American Civil Liberties Union, 23 May 2018. Neglect & Abuse of Unaccompanied Children by U.S. Customs and Border Protection.

15. Migration Observatory online, 2 June 2017. Long-Term International Migration Flows to and from the UK.

16. Ipsos MORI online, 14 December 2016. Perceptions are not reality: what the world gets wrong.

17. Migration Policy Institute, 8 February 2018. Frequently Requested Statistics on Immigrants and Immigration in the United States.

18. University College London report, 5 November 2013. Recent immigration to the UK: New evidence of the fiscal costs and benefits.

19. The Guardian online, 15 February 2019. Cost of Brexit to UK economy running at £40bn a year'.

20. London School of Economics, Brexit and the Impact of Immigration on the UK.

21. BBC News online, 20 November 2018. Migrant workers send home £8bn to families.

22. The Economist online, 8 November 2014. What have the immigrants ever done for us?

23. Bloomberg online, 22 June 2018. Brexit Has Already Cost the U.K. More than Its EU Budget Payments, Study Shows.

24. CATO Institute, 2 September 2015. Center for Immigration Studies Report Exaggerates Immigrant Welfare Use.

25. American Immigration Council, 14 December 2015. Giving the Facts a Fighting Chance: Addressing Common Questions on Immigration.

26. Time magazine online, 23 November 2015. How Keeping Migrants Out Will Cost America Billions.

27. Pew Research Center, 23 January 2018. Remittance Flows Worldwide in 2016.

28. Center for Migration Studies, 16 January 2019. US Undocumented Population Continued to Fall from 2016 to 2017, and Visa Overstays Significantly Exceeded Illegal Crossings for the Seventh Consecutive Year.

29. Robert Adelman, Lesley Williams Reid, Gail Markle, Saskia Weiss & Charles Jaret (13 July 2015). 'Urban crime rates and the changing face of immigration: Evidence across four decades'. *Journal of Ethnicity in Criminal Justice.*

30. Immigration Policy Center, 2017. Immigrants and crime: are they connected?

31. New American Foundation, Terrorism in America After 9/11.

32. Hannah Stuart, *Islamist Terrorism: Analysis of offences and attacks in the UK* (1998–2015).

33. Anti-Defamation League, Murder and Extremism in the United States in 2017.

34. Anti-Defamation League, White Supremacist Murders More Than Doubled in 2017.

35. The Independent online, 13 September 2018. Number of white people arrested for terror offences outstrip any other single ethnic group, new figures show.

36. CATO Institute, 13 September 2016. Terrorism and Immigration: A Risk Analysis.

37. Politics.co.uk, 5 April 2017. Met police hands victims of crime over to the Home Office for immigration enforcement.

38. The Guardian online, 24 January 2017. NHS hands over patient records to Home Office for immigration crackdown.

39. The Corporate Watch, 7 March 2017. The round-up: Rough sleeper immigration raids and charity collaboration.

40. BBC News online, 12 October 2018. MPs 'informing' on immigration hotline.

41. CNN Online, 20 February 2017. Museum removes every piece of art created by immigrants.

42. BBC News online, 25 August 2017. This supermarket took foreign food off its shelves to protest against racism.

43. Bryan Caplan. 2012, vol. 32, issue. 'Why Should We Restrict Immigration?' *Cato Journal*.

44. Vox.com, 15 December 2014. The case for open borders.

45. The Independent online, 30 April 2016. UK air strikes kill 1,000 Isis fighters in Iraq and Syria but no civilians, officials claim.

46. The Guardian online, 1 December 2015. Syria airstrikes: everything you need to know.

47. True Repblica online, 8 December 2015. Osborne wrong: Britain's bombing of Syria will cost hundreds of millions.

48. ILM Feed, 29 November 2015. How Much Will Each Airstrike Mission in Syria Cost Britain?

49. BBC News online, 15 April 2017. How many bombs has Britain dropped in 2017?

Chapter Twelve – Well, how come YOU get to say it?

1. CNN Tonight online, 17 March 2015. If I use the N-word it could cost me my career.

2. Random House YouTube Channel, Ta-Nehisi Coates on words that don't belong to everyone.

3. Chicago Institute of Politics YouTube Channel, Live Taping of 'The Axe Files' with Jon Stewart, hosted by David Axelrod.

4. Vibe magazine, Dec 1994 – Jan 1995 issue.

5. Gawker online, 21 December 2015. The Complete History of Quentin Tarantino Saying 'Nigger'.

6. Ronald Kessler (Pocket Books, April 1996). *Inside the White House: The Hidden Lives of the Modern Presidents and the Secrets of the World's Most Powerful Institution.*

7. Snopes.com, 7 Jul 2016. I'll Have Those N*****s Voting Democratic for 200 years.

8. Randal Kennedy (Random House USA; Vintage Books; July 2003). *Nigger: The Strange Career of a Troublesome Word.*

9. WTF with Marc Maron Podcast, Episode 613 with Barack Obama.

10. Vice magazine online, 17 Sep 2015. White People Explain Why They Feel Oppressed.

11. NPR online, 24 Oct 2017. Majority of White Americans Say They Believe Whites Face Discrimination.

12. Public Religion Research Institute, 10 June 2014. Americans' Racial Disconnect on Fairness and Discrimination. Joanna Piacenza.

13. Eduardo Bonilla-Silva (Rowman & Littlefield Publishers; January 2010). *Racism without Racists: Color-blind Racism and the Persistence of Racial Inequality in the United States.*

14. Chicago Sun Times online, 6 December 2016. Marist students sue after being expelled for racist text messages.

15. Vice magazine online, 2 Oct 2016. Dear White People, Please Stop Pretending Reverse Racism Is Real.

16. Howard J. Ross (Rowman & Littlefield Publishers; September 2014). *Everyday Bias: Identifying and Navigating Unconscious Judgments in Our Daily Lives.*

17. Cornell University Department of Economics, Racial Discrimination Among NBA Referees. Joseph Price and Justin Wolfers.

18. CNN online, 27 November 2014. The new threat: 'Racism without racists'.

19. Associated Press online, 9 July 2007. NAACP Symbolically Buries N-Word.

20. USA Today online, 27 July 2017. Man wants to trademark a variation of the N-word.

Conclusion

1. Kristin Pauker, Evan P. Apfelbaum, and Brian Spitzer, November 2016. 'When Societal Norms and Social Identity Collide: The Race Talk Dilemma for Racial Minority Children'. *Social Psychological and Personality Science.*

2. Psychology Today online, 20 May 2013. Can Racism Cause PTSD? Implications for DSM-5.

3. Narissa Punyanunt-Carter, 2008, 'The Perceived Realism of African American Portrayals on Television, *Howard Journal of Communications.*

4. Stephan Lewandowsky & John Cook, 23 January 2012. The Debunking Handbook. Global Change Institute, University of Queensland, School of Psychology, University of Western Australia.

5. Hope Not Hate. February 2019. State of Hate 2019, The People vs The Elite.

6. David Broockman and Joshua Kalla. 8 April 2016. Durably reducing transphobia: A field experiment on door-to-door canvassing. Science magazine online.

PICTURE ACKNOWLEDGEMENTS

The author and publisher would like to thank the following
copyright-holders for permission to reproduce images
in this book.

Page 7: © United States Holocaust Memorial Museum, courtesy of
Hessy Levinsons Taft
Page 28: © Bettmann Archive/Getty Images
Page 34: © Uncredited/AP/Shutterstock
Page 66: © Granger/Shutterstock
Page 72: Both images © Granger/Shutterstock
Page 74: Images courtesy of the Jim Crow Museum, Ferris State
University.